CW01213038

Conversational Pressure

Conversational Pressure

Normativity in Speech Exchanges

SANFORD C. GOLDBERG

OXFORD
UNIVERSITY PRESS

OXFORD
UNIVERSITY PRESS

Great Clarendon Street, Oxford, OX2 6DP,
United Kingdom

Oxford University Press is a department of the University of Oxford.
It furthers the University's objective of excellence in research, scholarship,
and education by publishing worldwide. Oxford is a registered trade mark of
Oxford University Press in the UK and in certain other countries

© Sanford C. Goldberg 2020

The moral rights of the author have been asserted

First Edition published in 2020

Impression: 1

All rights reserved. No part of this publication may be reproduced, stored in
a retrieval system, or transmitted, in any form or by any means, without the
prior permission in writing of Oxford University Press, or as expressly permitted
by law, by licence or under terms agreed with the appropriate reprographics
rights organization. Enquiries concerning reproduction outside the scope of the
above should be sent to the Rights Department, Oxford University Press, at the
address above

You must not circulate this work in any other form
and you must impose this same condition on any acquirer

Published in the United States of America by Oxford University Press
198 Madison Avenue, New York, NY 10016, United States of America

British Library Cataloguing in Publication Data

Data available

Library of Congress Control Number: 2020932449

ISBN 978–0–19–885643–6

Printed and bound in Great Britain by
Clays Ltd, Elcograf S.p.A.

Links to third party websites are provided by Oxford in good faith and
for information only. Oxford disclaims any responsibility for the materials
contained in any third party website referenced in this work.

Contents

Acknowledgments — vii

1. The Phenomenon of Conversational Pressure — 1

PART I. THE ACT OF ADDRESS

2. Your Attention Please! — 13

PART II. THE SPEECH ACT: PERFORMANCE AND UPTAKE

3. Conversational Pressures, Interpersonal and Epistemic — 61
4. The Speaker's Expectation of Trust: Some False Starts — 71
5. How to Treat a Testifier — 89
6. Anti-Reductionism and Expected Trust — 102
7. Does Friendship Exert Pressure on Belief? — 124

PART III. UPTAKE OF UPTAKE

8. Conversational Silence — 151
9. Silence Misinterpreted: The Double-Harm of Silencing — 187
10. The Social Epistemology of Public Uptake — 206
11. The Epistemic Costs of Politeness — 230
12. Conclusion — 234

References — 237
Index — 249

Acknowledgments

This book is the result of many conversations over the years. Although I cannot be sure to think of everyone from whom I have benefited, special thanks are owed to many individuals. These include Kristoffer Ahlstromm-Vij, David Alexander, Teresa Allen, Claudio Almeida, Eduardo Alves, Mark Alznauer, Charity Anderson, Janice Anderson, Nomy Arpaly, Murat Aydede, Dorit Bar-On, Heather Battaly, Bert Baumgaertner, James Beebe, Erin Beeghly, Endre Begby, Hugh Benson, Hanoch Ben-Yami, Sven Bernecker, Cristina Bicchieri, Stephen Biggs, Kevin Biolsi, Paul Bloomfield, Paul Boghossian, Cameron Boult, Michael Brady, Fernando Broncano, Jessica Brown, Emma Bullock, Anne Burkhardt, Tyler Burge, Herman Cappelen, Fabrizio Cariani, Carla Carmona, Adam Carter, Matthew Chrisman, Annalisa Coliva, Charles Cote, Lindsay Crawford, Finnur Dellsén, Tom Doherty, Katherine Dormandy, Ranpal Dosanjh, Trent Dougherty, Julian Dutante, Paul Egré, Naomi Eilan, Gretchen Ellefson, Jesús Vega Encabo, Pascal Engel, Kati Farkas, Paul Faulkner, Steven Finlay, Mark Fiocco, Rachel Fraser, Lizzie Fricker, Miranda Fricker, Gregory Gaboardi, Manuel Garcia-Carpintero, Heimir Geirsson, Mikkel Gerken, Adriano Gershom Palma, Margaret Gilbert, Michael Glanzberg, Alvin Goldman, Lee Goldsmith, Jeremy Goodman, Peter Graham, John Greco, Mitch Green, Patrick Greenough, Alex Gregory, Amber Griffoen, Stephen Grimm, Thomas Grundmann, Hanna Gunn, Yu Guodong, Caiying Han, Reza Hadisi, Caiying Han, Katherine Hawley, Sam Heal-Cohen, Jeffrey Helmreich, Barbara Herman, Frank Hoffman, Claire Horisk, Joachim Horvath, Dan Howard-Snyder, Frances Howard-Snyder, Graham Hubbs, Hud Hudson, Michael Hurwitz, Jonathan Ichikawa, Sherri Irvin, Henry Jackman, Christoff Jäger, Aaron James, Carrie Jenkins, Robin Jeshion, Marc Jiménez, Stephen John, Casey Johnson, Jesper Kallestrup, Yuliya Kanygina, Eric Kaplan, Stefan Kaufmann, Chris Kelp, Tim Kenyon, Muhammad Ali Khalidi, Ian Kidd, Dan Korman, Maria Kronfeldner, Quill Kukla, Christos Kyriacou, Jennifer Lackey, Rae Langton, Janet Levin, Feng Li, Hao Liang, Kathryn Lindeman, Clayton Littlejohn, Guy Longworth, Dom Lopes, Bill Lycan, Michael Lynch, Jack Lyons, Adian McGlynn, Mary-Kate McGowan, Conor McHugh, Robin McKenna, Rachel

McKinnon, Colleen Macnamara, Fiona McPherson, Michaela McSweeney, Heidi Maibom, Jon Matheson, Felipe Medeiros, Giacomo Melis, Mari Mikkola, Ivan Milic, David Miller, Garrett Mindt, Lisa Miracchi, Martin Montminy, Richard Moore, Jessie Munton, Jesús Navarro, Thi Nguyen, Catarina Dutilh Novaes, Trevor Nyman, Gloria Origgi, Carry Osbourne, Alex Papulis, Andy Peet, Fabienne Peter, Herman Philipse, Manuel de Pinedo, Fung Ping, Kathryn Pogin, Mihaela Popa, Duncan Pritchard, Quassim Quassam, Aleta Quinn, Gurpreet Rattan, Baron Reed, Steven Reynolds, Mike Ridge, Wayne Riggs, Gina Rini, Sven Rosenkranz, Patrick Rysiew, Daniel Pino Sánchez, Jennifer Saul, Kristin Schaupp, Henry Schiller, Johanna Schnurr, Mark Schroeder, Eric Schwitzgebel, Joe Shieber, Seana Shiffrin, Zhang Shuangli, Mona Simion, Dan Singer, Jurgis Skilters, Paulina Sliwa, Martin Smith, Rob Stainton, Jason Stanley, Isadora Stojanovic, Bart Streumer, Michael Strevens, Alessandra Tanesini, Claudine Tiercelen, Neal Tognazzini, Zev Trachtenberg, Jonathan Tsou, René van Woudenberg, Cullen Padget Walsh, Kate Padget Walsh, Gregory Ward, Gary Watson, Lani Watson, Michael Weisberg, Howie Wettstein, Steve White, Dennis Whitcomb, Daniel Whiting, Tim Williamson, Stephen Wright, Yaxin Wu, Huang Xiang, Yingjin Xu, Guiming Yang, Guiping Yin, Yang Yu, Linda Zagzebski, Yan Zhao, and Aaron Zimmerman for helpful discussions of these and related topics.

I also owe a big debt of gratitude to various audiences at talks I have given. These include audiences at Oxford University, Cambridge University, University of St Andrews, University of Edinburgh, the University of Glasgow, the University of Warwick, UC-Irvine (where I had the good fortune to spend a week in residence giving several of these chapters as talks), the University of California-Santa Barbara, the University of California-Riverside, the University of Connecticut, the University of Idaho, Iowa State University, the University of Utrecht, the University of Groningen, the University of Riga, the University of Cologne, York University, Central European University, the University of Oklahoma, the University of British Columbia, Western Washington University, LOGOS at the University of Barcelona, Fudan University, Shanxi University, the University of Seville, the University of Granada, the Pontifícia Universidade Católica do Rio Grande do Sul, the First Annual Social Epistemology Network Event at the University of Oslo, the Epistemic Significance of Non-epistemic Factors conference at the University of Osnabrück, the Nature of Trust conference at the University of Innsbruck, the Epistemic Norms conference at KU Leuven, the European Summer School in Social Epistemology at the Autonomous University of Madrid, the Nature of Normativity Conference at the University of

Southampton, the Mind and Language Conference in Valparaiso, the Themes in Social Epistemology Conference at Humboldt University, the Ethics and Epistemology group at Fordham University, the Principia Symposium in Florianópolis (Brazil), and the European Epistemology Network annual meeting in Paris; as well as Jennifer Lackey's Spring 2016 graduate seminar at Northwestern, where I presented a chapter of this book.

Thanks too to the Philosophy Departments at the University of Pennsylvania, the University of Southern California, and New York University, where I spent the academic year of 2017–18 on sabbatical, and where I completed a first draft of this book; and to Northwestern University, which gave me the sabbatical and which has been my philosophical home for more than a decade.

Finally, thanks to two anonymous referees from Oxford University Press, who gave me excellent feedback on an earlier draft of this manuscript; to various referees from the various journals where some of this material was first presented in article form; and to Peter Momtchiloff and his colleagues at Oxford University Press, who are invariably helpful and supportive throughout the process of publication.

Some of the chapters in this book are based on previously published work of mine, and I want to express my gratitude to each of the journals that have allowed me to borrow heavily (sometimes in their entirety) from papers I have published. These include *Philosophy and Phenomenological Research*, for allowing me to include (as Chapter 4) parts of my commentary on Richard Moran's book *The Exchange of Words: Speech, Testimony, and Intersubjectivity*, which was first published as part of a critical discussion of his book in *PPR*; *Pacific Philosphical Quarterly*, for allowing me to include (as Chapter 6) a slightly redacted version of a paper published there under the same name; *Philosophical Studies*, for allowing me to include (as Chapter 7) a revised version of 'Against Epistemic Partiality in Friendship: Value-Reflecting Reasons'; *Proceedings of the Aristotelian Society*, for allowing me to include (in Chapter 9) large portions of 'Arrogance, Silencing, and Silence', published in *Proceedings of the Aristotelian Society* 40: pp. 93–112; *Australasian Journal of Philosophy*, for allowing me to include (as Chapter 10) most of 'Can asserting that p improve the speaker's epistemic position (and is that a good thing)?', published in *Australasian Journal of Philosophy* 95: pp. 157–70; and *Think*, for allowing me to include (as Chapter 11) the entirety of my article (co-authored with Guiming Yang) 'The Epistemic Costs of Politeness', first published in *Think* 46:16, pp. 19–23.

I dedicate this book, with love, to Judy. May we forever remain susceptible to the joys (and pressures) of conversation.

1
The Phenomenon of Conversational Pressure

1

In *Wise Choices, Apt Feelings*, Alan Gibbard remarks that 'conversation is full of implicit demands and pressures' (p. 172). The aim of this book is to identify several of the most salient forms of these 'demands and pressures', and to theorize about their types, source, and nature.

It must be conceded at the outset that the forms of conversational pressure are many, and that it is far from clear that they constitute a single cohesive class worthy of an extended investigation. Consider the range of pressures one might feel in the course of a conversation. Focusing just on the kinds of conversations whose primary aim is to exchange information, there is (or can be) felt pressure for example (i) to attend to someone who is addressing one, (ii) to take turns in the course of a conversation (and to avoid taking up too much air time oneself), (iii) to tell others what one knows on a topic at issue, (iv) to respond to another's speech act when it is addressed to one, or (v) to believe what another person tells one. But in addition one can also feel pressure (vi) to keep an enjoyable or fruitful conversation going, (vii) to end an unproductive or unenjoyable conversation, (viii) to raise a topic that we feel should be discussed but hasn't been, (ix) to treat other speakers with respect and courtesy, (x) to include people who have been left out of the conversation, or (xi) to shut down a speaker who is obnoxious or bullying or aggressive. Indeed, this list, which is already motley, is only the tip of the iceberg when it comes to the pressures we can feel in the course of a conversation. And the types of pressures themselves are far from uniform: some of the pressures in (i)–(xi) might be described as ethical, others as social (deriving from the norms of our social practices), and still others as epistemic. It is far from clear that there is any cohesive phenomenon to be investigated here—let alone any cohesive account that can cover all of these cases.

Conversational Pressure: Normativity in Speech Exchanges. Sanford C. Goldberg, Oxford University Press (2020).
© Sanford C. Goldberg.
DOI: 10.1093/oso/9780198856436.001.0001

However, it is possible to demarcate a principled subject matter here by restricting our focus on the sorts of pressures that derive from, or implicate, *the nature of the speech acts that are performed* in the course of a conversation. Thus, there is a difference between the pressure in (i) or (iv), for example, and that in (ix) or (x): it is plausible to suppose that the pressure one feels to respond to speech that is addressed to one is itself generated by the very act of being addressed in speech, whereas the pressure one feels to include others who have been left out of a conversation, like the pressure one feels to be respectful in conversation, is not specific to speech but rather is a generic normative dimension of our interactions with others. Once we recognize this, we are in position to limit our focus to the sorts of conversational pressures that are generated by the performance of speech acts themselves—as opposed to the sorts of pressure that derive from general features of our social life independent of whether the context is one involving a talk exchange. (That we should treat others with respect is not something that is generated by any talk exchange;[1] so too for the sense that we ought to try to include others in our activities when it is feasible.) We might think of pressures that are generated by the performance of speech acts themselves—those that are generated as a result of the nature of such acts, together with the fact that the acts have been performed and observed in the context at hand—as *distinctly* conversational pressure. It is pressure of this sort that will constitute the domain of the present investigation.

While I will occasionally have things to say of various types of speech act—demands, requests, promises, invitations, and so forth—most of my attention will be on the more restricted class of *assertoric* speech acts: statements, assertions, testimonies, avowals, reports, and tellings. This is not because I assume that such acts are central to our understanding of speech acts more generally,[2] nor do I assume that understanding the conversational pressure involved in assertoric acts is central to understanding conversational pressure more generally. Rather, my motivations for this restriction are partly strategic and partly ideological. My strategic motivation for this restriction is twofold: in so restricting my focus I can make this investigation manageable, and in addition doing so enables me to capitalize on my previous research on assertoric speech.[3] My ideological motivation is

---

[1] However, the form that this respect should take can itself be shaped by the nature of the speech acts we perform; more on this in the rest of the book.
[2] Many authors have followed Austin (1975) in calling this into question. See Sbisà (forthcoming, 2002), and Kukla and Lance (2009), among many others.
[3] See especially Goldberg (2015b).

also twofold. First, I think many authors have made errors or else have missed important data points when theorizing about the conversational pressures involved in this class of speech acts, and part of my aim in this book is to offer a better account. But second, a restricted focus on this class of speech acts best enables me to frame a big-picture question that I think has attracted less attention than it deserves: how distinct normative domains bear on one another in the context of speech exchanges. The normative domains I have in mind include the interpersonal (including but not limited to the ethical) and the epistemic. For these reasons I will focus my attention on the members of a narrow class of speech acts within the category of the assertives as this category of speech act, more than others, enables us to highlight questions at the intersection of these two normative domains.

The conversational demands or pressures I will be exploring are, I will be contending, of two fundamental types. One source of such pressure, I contend, is *social* or *interpersonal* in nature. Grice taught us that conversations are governed by various norms in virtue of the fact that they are rational, cooperative activities, and when one performs a speech act (or observes another do so) the expectations that derive from these norms amount to a kind of conversational pressure or demand on participants. A second source of conversational demands or pressures is *rational* or *epistemic* in nature. This sort of pressure obtains in contexts in which a speech act purports to represent how the speaker takes the world to be. It is here, of course, that the focus on assertion yields dividends. Speech is a rule-governed activity, and there are epistemic requirements on speakers who make assertions or statements (or who testify etc.). As a result, insofar as conversations are cooperative endeavours, there is normative pressure on speakers to live up to those epistemic demands when they perform the acts in question, and a corresponding normative pressure on the audience to assess those acts in the epistemic terms imposed by the rules themselves. I will be designating this sort of pressure as 'rational' or 'epistemic' pressure.

As Gibbard's quote suggests, I am not the first person to have theorized about the various forms of conversational pressure.[4] But—as I hinted above—I believe that a good deal of the extant theorizing has been misguided.

Some theorizing has been misguided insofar as it embodies *the pretentions of reduction*, aiming to reduce the various normative pressures in a

---

[4] Others who have done so under this very description—'conversational pressure'—include Ridge (2013) and Swanson (2017).

conversation to one kind of normative pressure—to what we owe, *in that single normative dimension*, to the various conversational participants. Part of the aim of this book is to argue that such a reductive view is untenable: we should not conflate the interpersonal pressures and the epistemic pressures generated by assertions and other testimony-constituting speech acts.

But there are other extant theories that go wrong, not by their reductive pretensions, but by their *reaction* to others' reductive pretensions. Thus I worry that many epistemologists who take up these issues throw out the proverbial baby with the bathwater: in their effort to criticize single-dimension approaches to these matters, they rightly highlight that the epistemic dimension requires its own treatment, but they often fail to take account of the various *other* normative dimensions of speech and conversation. As many others have noted previously, such dimensions are seen in cases involving assertion itself—the speech act whose use is particularly apt for the transmission of knowledge and justified belief. Epistemologists who fail to take account of the other normative dimensions commit a sin of omission that can only encourage those with the reductive pretensions to feel as though their case has not been fully resisted, as the data they sought to account for fail to show up in many more epistemologically oriented accounts.

What is wanted, I think, is an account that accommodates the various forms of conversational pressure, and that does this in as economical and simple a way as possible. Hence the task I set myself in this book: I aim to show, first, that the various types of conversational pressure that have been at the heart of recent discussions are of two fundamental kinds (social/interpersonal and epistemic); second, that, on the assumption that conversation is a cooperative activity, these pressures can be understood using only tools from speech act theory; and third, that doing so will force us to recognize that there is a distinctively epistemic form of conversational pressure—one not reducible to any of the interpersonal forms of conversational pressure.

In bringing these claims out my guiding hypothesis is that, while there are two distinct types of conversational pressure, there is one fundamental mechanism that is responsible for each of these two types: the *normative expectations*[5] that are generated by the acts, including the speech acts, that are performed in the course of initiating and participating in conversation.

---

[5] By 'normative expectation' I understand the attitude through which we hold one another accountable to given standards. The normative expectations to which I will be appealing in my

The main theoretical task I will be setting myself in this book, then, can be framed as an exploration of the generation and subsequent effects of these normative expectations. I will be investigating a range of acts that we perform in the course of initiating or sustaining conversations. My focus will be limited to (i) the act of address wherein we aim to initiate a conversation, (ii) a restricted set of speech acts in the *assertives* family (assertions, statements, testimonies, and the like), and (iii) some of the acts we perform on observing another's speech act. In each case, the goal is to shed light on how the performance of the act in question *generates* a set of normative expectations that speakers and audience members have of one another, and to make clear how the presence of these expectations, once generated, constitutes the various distinct forms of *conversational pressure* on speakers and audiences.

2

The organization of the book reflects what I regard as the three 'loci' or 'moments' of central interest to the normativity of speech exchanges: the act of address itself, the performance of the speech act, and its uptake by an audience. These three components of speech exchanges, I will argue, are normative by nature: under suitable background conditions, the corresponding acts (of address, speech, or uptake) generate mutual normative expectations between participants in the exchange, and these in turn underwrite the normative dimensions of speech exchanges.

The structure of this book reflects this orientation.

Following this introductory chapter I begin, in Chapter 2, by exploring the act of address. I construe the act-type in question as one through which one subject, S, makes it manifest to another subject (or other subjects) that S aims to initiate a conversation or other cooperative venture. In this way addresses can be seen as 'calling' on another (or others) to give the speaker his (their) attention, and my thesis is that when such an act is performed in a manifest effort to initiate or sustain a speech exchange, the act exerts one of the basic forms of conversational pressure. In particular, so long as the speaker's intentions were indeed cooperative and her address was intelligible

---

account reflect not only the mutual expectation of cooperativity in conversation, but also the norm-governed nature of the speech acts we perform in each other's presence.

(to the audience) as the type of act it was intended to be, the audience 'owes it' to the speaker to give her a minimal form of attention.

By engendering the most basic of the normative expectations that frame our conversations, acts of address create the sort of context in which speech acts are performed and observed. Once we are in such a context, additional normative expectations follow suit. Thus the mutual awareness that a speech act has been performed generates additional normative expectations between speaker and audience. I discuss these in the second section of the book, Chapters 3–6. Focusing my attention on the nature of acts of assertoric speech that constitute an ongoing conversation between two or more parties, I aim to characterize how the performance of such acts entitles speaker and audience alike to have certain normative expectations of one another. My thesis is that these expectations underwrite the sort of conversational pressure that is characteristically exerted by of acts of assertion, telling, testifying, and the like. In the course of this discussion I have occasion to discuss and criticize other attempts to locate the conversational pressure exerted by these acts; my claim is that no other account captures this pressure in all of its forms.

Of course, speech acts are not acts one performs alone; they are (typically) intended for public consumption, and it is in this connection—uptake by an audience—that we encounter the final component of conversational pressure I explore in this book. Since the performance of a speech act (I will argue) calls on the audience to respond in certain ways, the normative dimension of what I will call *first-order* uptake is best considered in connection with the speech acts whose performance engenders the normative demands themselves. The relevant speech acts are discussed at length in Chapters 3–6, when I discuss such matters as what audiences owe to speakers whose assertions they have observed, and whether (and if so how) this can be affected by personal relationships such as friendship. In this regard, I am addressing some familiar faces of the norms of uptake.[6]

At the same time, while discussions of the norms of *first-order* uptake are thus familiar, it has long seemed to me that there has been a missing element in discussions of the norms of uptake. In a nutshell, the missing element concerns the norms of *higher-order* uptake: our uptake of another's uptake

---

[6] These familiar faces are seen in the pragmatics literature, in discussions of how the dynamics of context is affected by the type of speech act that is performed; in the epistemology literature, in discussions of the epistemology of testimony; and in the emerging literature at the intersection of ethics and epistemology, in discussions of what audiences owe to speakers who tell them things, or make promises, etc.

(of a speech act). It should be uncontroversial that when we attend to another's speech in contexts involving face-to-face conversations with multiple individuals present, we also typically attend to others' attending to the same speech act(s). My contention is that this—uptake of uptake, or higher-order uptake—is an important yet often overlooked dimension of conversational pressure. This is the topic of Chapters 7-9. To model the conversational pressure involved here, my strategy is to derive further normative expectations in conversation from the fact that the norms of (first-order) uptake are common knowledge among speech participants. I argue that these further normative expectations (associated with our uptake of others' uptake) are implicated in such matters as the potential significance of conversational silence, the harms of silencing, and the tendency of groups to exhibit belief polarization and groupthink.

3

If there is a single take-away point in this book, it is this: while the richness of our conversational practices—the social practices that inform (and explain various patterns we see in) our conversations—generate various kinds of conversational pressure, it is often difficult in practice to distinguish the distinctive types of pressures thereby generated. A failure to do so can result in a distortion of the various normative dimensions of our talk exchanges. I hope this book advances our understanding of these matters.

Doing so, I think, should be to the benefit of (certain parts of) epistemology, social philosophy, and speech act theory.

In epistemology, the benefits will be seen primarily (though not exclusively) in the epistemology of testimony and other parts of social epistemology. Precisely how does someone's telling you that p relate to your coming to know or believe justifiably that p? Various views are popular in the literature. Of special interest to me here are those views which seek to link the epistemology of testimony to the normative dimensions of the act of telling someone something. Scanlon's (1990) account of promising is one model here. He holds, first, that when S promises A that S will F, this speech act manifests to A that S is aware of the moral wrongness that would attach to S's failure to F, and second, that in communicating this to A, S has given A an *epistemic* reason to believe that S will F. Some proponents of the so-called assurance view of testimony regard the act of telling as proceeding in an analogous fashion. According to such views, when S tells A that p, in effect S offers a promise or guarantee to A that S has fulfilled all of the responsibilities A would expect her to have fulfilled (given the act she has performed), and that this generates for A an epistemic reason to believe that S has fulfilled these responsibilities. Since these are responsibilities in connection with S's discerning whether p, in effect this is an epistemic reason for A to believe that p.

I believe that such views go wrong in trying to get epistemic mileage out of what is essentially a point about the normative (in this case, ethical) demands on one who has made a promise. I am not alone in levelling such a charge. But where other critics remain satisfied simply to point out this epistemic shortcoming, I think we need to recognize the normative insight in assurance theories: the speech act of telling or assuring is essentially an interpersonal act of a very specific kind, and without understanding the normative pressures associated with the interpersonal aspect of the exchange we have not understood the nature of the act itself. The challenge is to square these normative pressures, deriving from the interpersonal aspect of these acts, with the normative pressures associated with the epistemology of testimony. While others are right, I think, in their criticisms of the epistemology of the assurance view of testimony, they leave us unsatisfied if they fail to address the normative pressures deriving from the distinctive interpersonal nature of the transaction. Without doing so, these critics leave us with the impression that the act of telling generates conversational pressures not recognized by epistemologists; and while I agree, I worry that if the impression is not addressed, many people will be tempted to draw the wrong conclusion, opting for merely revising assurance views rather than seeing them as committed to a faulty assumption about the nature of the reasons generated by the act of telling someone something. In short, epistemology stands to gain from a full reckoning of the nature of the act of testifying or telling.

In social epistemology, it is widely recognized that other people are a rich source of information in ways that go beyond their serving as informants (that is, as testifiers).[7] In particular, we often rely on others not only as testifiers but also as consumers of testimony in their own right: we often rely on their reactions to others' testimony as we seek to determine what to believe. The unhappy side of this, of course, is seen in such phenomena as echo chambers, belief polarization, and groupthink. But there is a happy side

---

[7] Indeed, I myself have characterized social epistemology as the systematic investigation of the epistemic significance of other minds. See e.g. Goldberg (2011a, 2013, 2015a).

too: insofar as the members of our epistemic communities are knowledgeable, our reliance on their assessment of others' say-so is an epistemically virtuous way of distributing a demanding epistemic task. I believe that this practice emerges in real-time conversations, in both its good forms and its bad forms, and that when it does it reflects the cooperative norms of conversation itself. Social epistemology is thus enriched by attending to how norms of cooperativity in conversation can have an epistemic upshot far beyond what is often recognized in this connection.

In social philosophy, the benefits will be an understanding of how speech act norms combine with social norms to yield normative requirements bearing on our behaviour in contexts of conversation. This will bear on topics such as the normative significance of addressing another (and of being addressed) through speech, the norms of trust (and of inviting another's trust), what we owe one another in conversations aiming at information exchange, the nature (and costs) of politeness as a normative requirement, the conditions on (and limits of) a duty to speak out, and the basis for the injunction of sincerity in speech. Most of these topics have been explored, piecemeal, by others. But even when they have been explored, it is rarely with an eye to understanding speech in *all* of its normative dimensions (epistemic and otherwise).

Finally, in speech act theory, the benefits are largely in application. What has been of interest to me—and what was one of the core contentions of my (2015b)—is the work that can be done when we use the insights of speech act theory to explain various familiar aspects of conversation. Here my hope is to show that (and how) speech act theory can be used to explain many of the core normative features we find in conversations aimed at the exchange of information.

PART I
THE ACT OF ADDRESS

2
Your Attention Please!

1

This book concerns the normative pressure we bring to bear against one another in conversation. It is perhaps fitting, then, that we should begin with the act of address itself, in which a speaker calls for another's (or others') attention. In this chapter I develop the claim that in so doing the speaker puts her target(s) under normative pressure to attend to her, at least for the brief period during which she indicates why she is calling for his/their attention.

Such acts are ubiquitous in our engagements with one another. They are involved in such acts as *your calling out my name*; *my asking you* the time,[1] and *your telling me* that it is 2 o'clock; *Sally's requesting to Frank* that he stop singing; *Mark's directing Ginger* to close the window; *Molly's promising Dolly* that she will be back by 11. They are also involved in such things as *Patricia's casting a meaningful glance at Veronica* (giving Veronica to understand that now is the time to act); *Paul's waving his arms frantically at a passerby* in an attempt to get her attention (thereby trying to flag her down while he is stuck on the side of the road with a flat tyre); *Francesca's engaging Juanita's gaze* while motioning with her index finger that Juanita should join her table; and so forth.

My thesis is that the very act of *addressing of another person* puts normative pressure on the addressee to direct his attention (if sometimes only briefly) to the source herself. By speaking of 'normative' pressure here, I mean to be highlighting the prospect that targets of an address who resist the pressure to attend to the person who is addressing them end up *wronging* that person. The basic phenomenon is easy to appreciate, at least in outline form. Suppose it is manifest to the various people around Paul that he dropped his phone and is having trouble retrieving it. If Francesca, manifestly aiming to offer Paul her help, tries to catch Paul's attention by saying

---

[1] In each case, italics are used to emphasized the core act of address.

'Excuse me' to him several times in a way that is clearly directed at him, and he fails so much as to acknowledge her doing so, he has wronged her (unless there are further relevant conditions).[2] Another case: if Melissa, manifestly looking Sam in the eyes, asks for the time, and Sam refuses so much as to acknowledge that he has been addressed, Sam wrongs Melissa. The wrong that is perpetrated in these cases is not merely that the target does not respond to the act that is addressed to him; it is also that the target fails to acknowledge having been addressed in the first place. To be sure, if circumstances are normal, then the one of whom a request is made owes a response to that request. But in this chapter I am interested in the normative pressure generated by *the act of address itself*.[3] My claim is that being addressed puts one under some pressure to do something—namely, attend to the speech act itself—which, when one does it competently, can have additional downstream effects of putting one under further sorts of normative pressure.

The sort of normative pressure generated by an act of addressing another, I will argue, derives from the nature of cooperation itself, and from the sorts of expectations we, as creatures who are social by nature, are entitled to have of one another in this regard. In particular, I submit that when one person (the speaker) addresses another (the addressee) in speech, where this is a would-be initiation (or is itself a part) of a cooperative exchange, the speaker's doing so generates a reason for the addressee to attend to the speaker.[4] This chapter aims to identify the source, nature, and scope of these address-generated reasons.

2

I begin with a programmatic statement of the account I will be developing and defending in the rest of this chapter.

Human beings are both rational and social by nature. As such, we have a deep and abiding interest in cooperating with one another. The notion of cooperation I have in mind is a very generic one: an activity involving more

---

[2] This description is based on an actual scene I witnessed some time ago.
[3] That is, I am interested in the normative pressure of the address itself, independent of the speech act (in this case, the request) that is addressed to one.
[4] In an attempt to maintain a rough gender equity in the use of pronouns, I will normally use female pronouns when speaking of the speaker, and male pronouns when speaking of the addressed audience. However, I will occasionally vary from this when doing so is unlikely to cause confusion.

than one subject is *cooperative* in the relevant sense when it is structured around a common interest (often, though not always, a jointly accepted aim), such that having this common interest gives each party reasons to act in certain ways and not others at various points throughout the activity itself. Conversation is a cooperative activity in this sense, as it is structured around a common interest in communication (and so in attaining communicative aims). Obviously, conversation is not the only, or even the most basic, of cooperative activities. Other such activities include: making dinner together (something that can be done wordlessly), helping another person to fix a flat tyre, deciding together where we should eat dinner, playing one's role on a team, and playing a competitive game (where the common interest is in playing the game to its proper conclusion, even if one's interests diverge from those of the other party in that one wants one's side to be the winner).

Our abiding interest in cooperation gives us an abiding interest in coordinating with one another as well, as cooperation is a practical impossibility without coordination. But to coordinate, we must be able to initiate—and having initiated, to sustain—various acts of coordination (including planning and other joint actions). Language use is central to these acts of coordination. But coordination (whether through language or in some nonlinguistic way) cannot even get off the ground unless we have some way to capture and sustain one another's attention: we need to do so not only at the point at which we hope to initiate a cooperative activity, but also at crucial points throughout the activity. Attention capture and sustainment is so important to coordination, and hence to potential cooperation, that having a way to accomplish this is not something that can be left to chance and ability. Rather, a tool has evolved whose use enables us, as rational and social subjects, to 'call for' another's attention[5]—to make the giving of one's attention (and of the subsequent paying of attention) something that is *owed* to us. One subject 'calls for' another's attention when she performs an act, manifestly directed at the individual(s) in question, whose salient social significance is to make manifest her intention to capture their attention, and therein to initiate a (possibly very brief) cooperative action with them, where these results are intended to be achieved by way of the target's

---

[5] Lance and Kukla (2013) use the term 'call' to pick out the range of second-personal addresses in such acts as requests, entreaties, and imperatives. They write, '...second-person addresses...[are] speech acts that call upon "you to give uptake to specific normative statuses by acting in some range of ways. We refer to these generically as "calls"' (2013: 457).

recognition of this intention.[6] *To perform an act which one manifestly intends to be taken as having this profile is to address another person.*

If this sort of view is correct, an act must have several features in order to count as an act of address. First, it must be manifestly directed or targeted at another person or persons. Second, it must be manifestly performed with the intention to capture their attention, and therein to initiate a (possibly very brief) cooperative action with them.[7] And third, it must be readily recognizable by the targets as having these features.

I propose to account for the normative dimension of address in terms of these features, as they constitute the basis of the idea that in addressing another one 'calls for' their attention.[8] In light of the manifest rationality of the speaker (the producer of the address) and the mutual (objective) interest all rational social creatures have in cooperation, one who performs an act with this profile is owed respect. Among other things, this respect mandates that her act be acknowledged by the target(s).[9] Proper acknowledgement involves recognizing the act as manifesting the actor's intention to capture the addressee's attention, and therein to attempt to initiate a cooperative action. A speaker who is entitled to expect this acknowledgement thereby generates a reason for her audience to attend (or to continue attending) to the speaker—at least long enough to discern the nature of the would-be cooperative activity that the speaker proposes to engage in. This reason to attend reflects the respect and acknowledgement that are owed to a rational subject who performs an act of this sort. This, I submit, is the basis of the claim that in addressing someone the speaker has a claim on the addressee's attention.

This model will allow us to say several things about the nature of the address-generated claim on the addressee's attention. Insofar as this claim is underwritten by the subject's status as a rational, social being with an

---

[6] Compare Gilbert (1989: 218) and Gilbert (2011: 280). Talking about acts intended to initiate joint mutual recognition (a precondition for indicating joint readiness to act), Gilbert (1989) writes, 'What one needs is some way of attracting the other person's attention, and then, or at the same time, engaging in whatever behavior will communicate willingness jointly to acknowledge co-presence.' She adds—and I agree!—that '[i]t is not obvious that the only means of doing this will depend on social convention.'

[7] Here I have in mind something like what Gilbert (1989: 191-7) called the 'openness*' condition on common knowledge. And among cooperative actions I include what Gilbert (1989) and others call a 'joint' action as a special case.

[8] I borrow both the terminology of a 'call', and the conception of an act as a kind of *calling for* something, from Kukla and Lance (2009).

[9] The point that acknowledgement is owed to one who addresses you is stressed by Darwall (2006) and Kukla and Lance (2009).

abiding interest in cooperation, the claim on the addressee's attention is generated *whenever the action which the speaker is aiming to initiate is indeed a cooperative one*. This is for a very simple reason: when the act of address is part of a legitimate attempt at a cooperative engagement with the addressee, it is an essential ingredient in the life of social creatures like us. But I will argue that there are cases in which the act of address is *not* as it purports to be—cases in which practice of address is *abused*. These are cases in which the producer makes as if she is performing an act of the profile specified above, but in actuality she intends to initiate an action that cannot reasonably be regarded as a legitimate attempt at cooperative engagement. In such cases, the address itself is degenerate, and the speaker is not entitled to expect the sort of respect that I associate with non-degenerate acts of address. Accordingly, the act doesn't generate any reason for the addressee to attend, and so doesn't generate any claim on the addressee's attention. Or so I will be arguing in what follows.

3

My topic, then, is the normative pressures arising out of the act of address. What I am after is an account of the source, nature, and strength of the claim on another's attention generated by the act of addressing him (whether in speech or in some other fashion). I regard such an account to be a crucial first step in any theory which purports to illuminate the sort of pressures generated by conversational participants. Before developing my account, however, I want to make clear both why I regard this as an important topic, and why the topic is not exhausted by work in speech act theory that explores the effects of addressing *particular speech acts* to an audience. I will take these up in order.

Not everyone will see the significance of the normative dimension of address. In particular, those who pursue empirical theories of speech and communication might well have doubts about the significance of the *normative demands* engendered by acts of address. They might argue that once we have an empirically grounded account of how the act of address secures uptake, we have no need for an additional account of the normative dimensions of the address and its uptake. Such a view might be motivated by the thought that any competent act of address will succeed in capturing the attention of the addressee, and that any addressee whose attention has been captured by the speaker[10] has thereby satisfied the speaker's attention-capturing intentions. Alternatively, doubts about the significance of the normative dimension of address might derive from the broadly Relevance-theoretic claim that any communicative act conveys its own relevance to the target;[11] armed with such a view, one might think that there are many ways to account for the reasons the target has for giving his attention to the speaker.[12]

In response I submit that we need an account of the *normative* dimension of the transaction—of the *claim* that the speaker has on the addressee's attention. There are various considerations that can be used to support this contention.

Let's start with the proposal that relevance-theoretic reasons—the anticipated relevance of the communication following an address—are adequate to explain the rationale a target has for attending to the speaker who addresses him. Might such a proposal give us all that we need, so that we can avoid introducing a normative dimension entirely? This seems unlikely, for at least two reasons: the proposal appears to be insufficiently general, and it fails to capture the datum that needs capturing.

This proposal appears to be insufficiently general: while it would appear that you have a reason to attend to one who addresses you *whenever* you are addressed,[13] it is unclear whether the present relevance-theoretic proposal can capture this generality. For example, if you are addressed under conditions in which you are warranted in supposing that the speaker wants to request something from you (and you are warranted in this supposition *prior to* attending to the speaker), in what sense do you have a rationale, deriving from *the anticipated relevance to you* of the subsequent communication, to attend to the speaker? The proponent of the relevance-theoretic model may well be able to make sense of this in particular contexts. For example, if A and B are friends or colleagues, perhaps B has a reason of friendship or colleagiality to attend to what B anticipates will be A's request. (*Mutatis mutandis* if A is B's boss.) More generally, perhaps under conditions of anticipated reciprocity, we can understand B's attending to what

---

[10] Here, and in what follows, I will use 'speaker' to cover the one who addresses another, even when the address itself is not linguistic. (I find this better than using 'addresser'.) Context will make clear when a 'speaker' so-called is not using speech in her address.
[11] See Sperber and Wilson (1996).
[12] I thank Mitch Green and Stefan Kaufmann for urging me (in conversation) to address this matter.
[13] Below I will qualify this, but the qualifications are not relevant to the issue here so I will ignore them.

B anticipates will be A's request: if it is a request and B does as A requests, there is a sense in which A owes B a favour in return, and it is in B's self-interest to collect such favours. We might even anticipate that so long as the target expects something relevant to his perspective, he has a clear rationale to attend to a speaker when she addresses him. But insofar as there is no normativity to acts of address beyond what is found in reasons of these kinds, it seems that we fail to capture the normativity of address in its full generality. For even when A and B are perfect strangers and each might anticipate never again encountering one another, and even when both have reasons to question whether the exchange will be of relevance to each, A's address would appear to make a claim on B's attention (*ceteris paribus*); and what is wanted is an explanation of this general fact.

Might an interest in cooperative exchange itself underwrite the rationale an arbitrary target has for attending to a speaker who addresses him?[14] If so, then perhaps we can respond to the worry about the insufficient generality of the proposal, by explaining that one has a reason to attend to a speaker *whenever* one is addressed. (The explanation would appeal to the assumption that an interest in cooperative exchange is a *generic* interest, one which each of us has all of the time.) But I see three difficulties facing the proponent of the relevance-theoretic account if she responds in this way to the worry about insufficient generality.

First, if it is to enable the relevance theorist to resist the postulation of a normative dimension to address—if it is to enable such a theorist to stick to empirical theorizing—this response faces a dilemma, according to how it construes the claim that everyone has an interest in cooperative exchange. Suppose we construe this as a claim about our *objective* interests—interests which we might, or might not, recognize or acknowledge, but the satisfaction of which *in fact* serves our ends. On such a construal, the claim appears to be of little help to the relevance theorist who hopes to avoid postulating a normative dimension to address. For on this construal, it is unclear how the claim in question—that everyone has an interest in cooperative exchange—relates to our psychology, and so it is unclear how this claim relates to the reasons each of us has to attend to those who address us. To be sure, the relevance theorist might respond by noting that the reasons deriving from what is in one's 'objective' interest are 'objective' or 'external' reasons—thereby making use of the idea, prominent in the metaethics literature, of

---

[14] I thank an anonymous referee from OUP for this suggestion.

'external' or 'objective' reasons for action.[15] Unfortunately, the postulation of 'external' or 'objective' reasons appears to reflect a normative standard by which to determine what is objectively in one's interest. So if it is meant to enable the relevance theorist to stick to empirical theorizing—to *resist* the postulation of a normative dimension to address—this response would appear to be conceding the key point. (Indeed, my own account, in section 4 below, will be a variant on this approach.) To avoid this, the relevance theorist would do better to construe the claim that everyone has an interest in cooperative exchange, as an *empirical* hypothesis—as a claim about human psychology. But on this construal, the claim amounts to a very strong empirical hypothesis, one which would appear to be belied by the facts.

But this is not the only difficulty facing the proposal to appeal to the interest we have in cooperative exchange to account for the rationale we have for attending to a speaker who addresses us. A second difficulty is that this proposal would still appear to be insufficiently general. In particular, it does not cover cases in which one knows in advance that one is not interested in cooperative exchange on this occasion (or with this person). Even if I have a generic interest in cooperative exchange, there might be specific contexts in which I have stronger interest which is in conflict with this generic interest—in which case whatever reasons the generic interest generates will be insufficient to give me an all-things-considered rationale for attending to the speaker who addresses me. For example, suppose I don't like the way you look and so don't want to engage with you. Then even though I have a generic interest in cooperative exchange, my interest in never engaging with you might trump in any context in which you address me. So whenever you address me, I have a reason *not* to attend to you *despite* my generic interest in cooperative exchange. Yet it seems that this is the wrong verdict: if your address was competent and sincere, then it still gives me a reason to attend to you, despite my not wanting to interact with you. The present proposal, it seems, gives us the wrong analysis here; and, more generally, it does not explain why a strong desire not to engage another person does not, by itself, disqualify her addresses from generating reasons for one to attend to her.

Third, insofar as it is an entirely empirical approach to the nature of address, the present proposal on behalf of the relevance theorist doesn't

---

[15] The *locus classicus* for this discussion is Williams (1979).

square well with the idea that, whether or not we *actually* take an interest in cooperative exchange, we *ought* to do so. Perhaps this is unsurprising: to say that we ought to take an interest in cooperative exchange is to make a normative claim, and it is hard to see how to embrace this in entirely empirical terms (having to do with the anticipated relevance of the exchange). To bring this objection out, however, I want to move on, from the current worry (about the insufficient generality of the relevance-theoretic account), to the worry that this account fails to capture a datum that needs to be captured. Simply put, the datum that needs capturing has to do with the *wrongness* (rather than the practical irrationality) of summarily ignoring another person's address.[16]

Suppose that Randy requests something of Frank by addressing him and making the request verbally. There are several likely ways that this scene can proceed from this point. One option would be for Frank to accept the request (agree to honour it); another would be for him to reject it (refuse to honour it). Still another alternative would be for him to follow up by asking Randy further questions, perhaps clarifying what is at issue before deciding whether to accept or reject her request. In each of these scenarios, he would have attended to her request, for he is responding to it in one of the ways that are available to him. But there is another possible scenario. This is the scenario in which Frank summarily *ignores* Randy's request, acting in the way he would normally act under conditions in which Randy was not speaking to him at all. That is, he does not attend to Randy despite having been addressed by her. (Ignoring a request in this way is different from rejecting the request, as the latter involves acknowledging that one was addressed—even as one gives the dispreferred response to having been addressed with a request.[17]) I submit that to ignore a request in this summary way would typically be to *wrong* the speaker. At a minimum, the speaker will *feel* snubbed, wronged, and/or disrespected. This, then, is the datum that needs to be accounted for: the *felt wrongness* of summarily ignoring a speaker who manifestly addresses one.

Now my claim is that the reasons postulated by the relevance-theoretical proposal—reasons deriving from the anticipated relevance to the target of the subsequent communication—are not of the right sort to capture this datum. To see this, suppose that the relevance-theoretic account is correct,

---

[16] With thanks to Paul Bloomfield for indicating the need for addressing the point to follow.
[17] Compare Wanderer (2012), who also distinguishes between the wrongness of ignoring vs. the wrongness of rejecting (albeit in the context of testimony).

so that when one is addressed by another one has reasons (deriving from the anticipated relevance to the target of the subsequent communication) to attend to the speaker. Now if a target ignores (does not act on) these reasons, it would appear that the only person he is harming is himself: he is losing out on an opportunity (for example) to acquire relevant information, receive a promise, etc. It is far from clear that in doing so he is also (thereby) wronging the speaker. Perhaps it will be said in response that insofar as the making of an address presupposes (and at any rate conveys to the target) its own relevance to the target, one who ignores an address that is directed at him thereby makes manifest that his perspective is not aligned with that of the speaker.[18] But it is hard to see how this point, even if correct, underwrites the allegation that the target has wronged the speaker. Not all misalignments wrong the speaker; and while we might rectify this by assuming that it is wrong to fail to align with a speaker who conveys the relevance of her next act, to assume this is already to acknowledge what the proposal was trying to avoid—namely, an normative dimension to the act of address.

4

I have been arguing that the relevance theorist faces two significant difficulties if she aims to resist the significance of the normative dimension of address. If this is so, we should not look to relevance theory in an attempt to avoid having to account for this dimension. In addition, we can defend the importance of the normative dimension of address in other ways as well.

First, even if we assume that all competent addresses succeed in capturing the attention of the addressee, an interest in the normative dimension of the act can be motivated by an interest in normative demands more generally. For example, we might wonder how the normative demands engendered by the act of address fit in with other normative requirements on us (including the ethical requirements we face). Do we require a distinctive account of the normative dimensions of address, or is it a special case of more general principles from some other normative domain (such as ethics)?

Second, not all cases of capturing another's attention—more generally, not all cases of doing something *with the intention* of capturing another's intention—are cases in which one has some claim on that attention, and an

---

[18] I thank Stefan Kaufmann for suggesting this idea to me (in conversation).

account of the normative dimension of address will enable us to say what distinguishes these cases. If, after having had an argument with Francesca, Piotr slams the door in an otherwise quiet house, Piotr will probably capture Francesca's attention, and Piotr may even have intended to do so (and intended as well that Francesca recognize that intention); but this is not a case in which Francesca *owes* it to Piotr to give him her attention. This is important, since if, having given Piotr her attention for a moment, Francesca immediately goes back to what she was doing previously (with the result that Piotr no longer has her attention), there is nothing remiss in this. Contrast the case of addressing another person (whether in speech or not): if the address is both clearly intelligible as an address and is directed to you in a salient way—say, I address you by name in a loud and clear voice—it will capture your attention, but here it seems patent that there is a sense in which your attention is *owed* to me (as the speaker), so that if, having given me your attention for a moment, you then immediately return to doing what you did (subsequently ignoring me), you have wronged me.[19] What explains the difference? Why is one's *ongoing* and *engaged* attention[20] called for when the attention-capturing event is an address? This is something we want to know, and our interest in knowing this remains even if we assume that all addresses succeed in securing uptake.

Third, it is not always true that that competent address secures uptake, and we need an account of the normative dimension of address in order to describe cases in which it doesn't. Consider for example cases in which one hears another speaker perform a speech act under conditions in which one was uncertain whether it was addressed to one. In those cases, one has a reason to determine whether the speaker was addressing one. ('Are you talking to me?') The explanation for this, obviously, lies in the very significance of the act of address itself: if you were addressed, you have a distinctive reason to attend to the speaker, whereas if you were not addressed, you do not have that reason (although you may have other reasons to attend to her). Putting matters in language borrowed from metaethics, we might say that the address itself generates a reason for action, whereas the addressee's recognition of being addressed constitutes the addressee's having that reason. What is more, the standard reaction to an audience who does not act on

---

[19] This is particularly clear in the case of linguistic addresses, but I think it is also true in cases of non-linguistic addresses. I will return to this below.
[20] Of at least enough duration to discern the cooperative activity the speaker is attempting to initiate.

such a reason, and so who does not attend to the address that was directed at him, is the sort of reactive attitude characteristic of someone who has behaved in a way that violates some social or ethical (or other normative) expectation. An account of the normative dimension of address should illuminate these things.

Relatedly, we might want an account of the normativity of address to sort out the proper thing to say about a range of cases in which we have conflicting feelings about the duties and responsibilities of the speaker and the target of the address. Consider these:

1. You are manifestly otherwise occupied on a very important matter which requires the whole of your attention, so that my addressing you fails to have a cognitive impact. (Should I have refrained from addressing you in this circumstance? Do you do me a wrong if you don't respond to me at all, not even to let me know that you are currently occupied?)
2. Your 3-year-old child is constantly addressing you, pulling at your sleeve and requiring all of your attention, so much so that you occasionally tune him out and don't attend at all to his attempts—it becomes mere background noise.
3. Having heard the announcements dozens of times before, you tune out the flight attendant's announcements at the start of the flight ('...a flotation device is located below your seat cushion......'), despite the fact that she is looking right at you as she speaks.[21]
4. You are seated on an international flight next to an extraordinarily garrulous speaker, and as the hours pass and his voice drones on, you succeed at tuning him out.
5. You are driving along the highway and see someone one the side of the road trying to wave you down, where it is clear that he needs help with a flat tyre. Thinking to yourself that you stopped to help someone on the side of the road just yesterday, you drive by without stopping.[22]

---

[21] Some may deny that this is a real case of address, being closer to something like a public service announcement. There are interesting questions that arise when we consider such announcements, though my sense is that these *are* addressed—albeit to the public at large. I will return to such cases below, as they raise interesting issues in their own right.

[22] With thanks to Paul Bloomfield, who suggested I discuss this case. See footnote 35 below, where I address this.

We have the sense that in at least some of these cases you are—or at any rate (if the details are filled out just right) you could be—entitled to ignore the address.[23] But to determine when this is so (and when not), we need to explore the normative dimensions of the act of address itself.

Fourth, pursuing the normativity of address can help us discern what normative constraints (ethical or otherwise) there might be on the *speaker*, that is, on the one who addresses another. One thinks here of an analogue with the phenomenon of trust. As Katherine Hawley (2014b) has aptly noted, trusting another puts normative burdens on the one who is being trusted. As a result, one might not want to be in a relationship in which one is being trusted to do such-and-such, and one might be entitled to explicitly *repudiate* that trust in advance. (Hawley's example is of a someone who is happy to cook dinner for her partner when she gets home from work but does not want the burden of being *trusted* to do so.) Might there be cases in which one does not want the burden of a claim on one's attention, where one is *entitled* to repudiate the attempt in advance? It can seem so. ('Don't talk to me right now. I don't want to hear what you have to say.') As in the case of repudiated trust, so too in the case of repudiated attempts at attention-capture through address, we might hope to illuminate the basis on which repudiation can be legitimate. And this seems to call for an understanding of the basis on which the attention capture itself in cases of address is legitimate. Here the question concerns the normative dimension of the act of address itself.

Fifth, pursuing the basis of the speaker's claim on the addressee's attention can be used to illuminate the status of communication that is not face to face—written and electronic communication, for example. Surely some written and e-communication is addressed to others: written analogues of the act of address can be found in snail-mail letters,[24] emails, instant messaging, facebook tags,[25] and so forth. It is tempting to assimilate these cases to straight cases of being addressed. Still, there are differences—in

---

[23] See section 5.
[24] Indeed, it is no surprise that 'address' is used to designate the uniquely identifying information provided on an envelope, or in an email, which is used to identify the person (or email inbox) to whom the letter or email is to be delivered. Even so, given the possibility of mass mailings and spam, it is no easy matter to determine when a letter or email which is addressed to you in this sense actually addresses you in the sense I am talking about in this chapter. A matter for another time . . .
[25] The pragmatic significance(s) of facebook tagging strikes me as an interesting, and under-explored, question. My speculation is that while some acts of tagging clearly are addresses, others are not (but are merely intended to let the target know of the post without any expectation of further engagement).

them the act of address is not always, or even typically, simultaneous with the act of uptake; the act of uptake is not (always? often?) something that is mutual knowledge; the physical distance prevents the rich back-and-forth signalling between speaker and addressee; the speaker and/or audience might not know one another; the note might be automatically generated; and in general the mutuality of the exchange may be seriously diminished or nonexistent. It would be good to have an understanding of the normative dimension of face-to-face cases if only to be in a position to discern the significance of these differences.

5

This concludes my attempt to motivate the interest of the topic of the normative dimension of address. I move now to my claim that this topic is distinct from, and conceptually prior to, an exploration of the normative dimensions of the various *speech acts* that are addressed to others. That is, it will be very important to me here to distinguish the following two questions:

(A) What is the normative dimension of your being addressed by another person (i.e. the normative demands on the speaker, and the normative demands on the target)?

(B) What is the normative dimension of having observed a speech act X that was manifestly addressed to you (i.e. the normative demands on the speaker, and the normative demands on the target)?

I can imagine someone who questions the value of the distinction here. That is, I can imagine someone who questions whether there is anything to (A) once we have answers to (B) for each of the various kinds of speech act there are. Indeed, this sort of perspective is in keeping with the approach of most of the theorists who have discussed the (normative) significance of address: they have typically approached matters by focusing on some form of question (B).[26] That is, they focus on how particular kinds of speech acts call for particular kinds of response *when these acts are addressed to you*. Thus, there is a huge literature on imperatives and on speech acts that constitute acts of *contracting*, which have the effect of mandating or obligating the parties,

---

[26] The only exceptions to this of whom I know are the philosophers Martin Buber and Emmanuel Levinas.

thereby calling for the responses set forth in the contract;[27] Lance and Kukla (2013) explore the normative demands made by requests, entreaties, and imperatives; and various authors, but most saliently Miranda Fricker, discuss the normative demands that a speaker's testifying makes on her addressees.[28] But to my knowledge none of these authors focuses on the question I am raising here, which is (A). I think we have reason to do so—even if we have complete accounts of (B) in connection with each of the speech act types. I offer three reasons in defence of the need to address (A) even after we have an account of (the various instances of) (B).

First and most importantly, there are forms of address that do not involve language use. Waving one's hand, meaningfully meeting someone's gaze (when the circumstances are right), flagging someone down while stuck on the side of the road with a flat tyre—these are all forms of address, yet none of them employ language.[29] Insofar as we can ask about the normative dimension of such acts, taken as acts of address, it follows that we do not exhaust the normativity of address by focusing on the various instances of (B).

Second and relatedly, by addressing (A), we can determine whether *linguistic* address is a special case of a more general phenomenon (address itself).[30] This is significant, since those who have discussed only (B) typically see the normative dimension of address as deriving from the speech act type in question; but if I am right that there are forms of address that do not involve speech at all, then such views cannot be fully general. But we cannot even bring this question into focus unless we distinguish (A) and (B).

Third, by addressing (A), we can generalize over all speech acts that address, to see how the fact that they are addressed to another affects

---

[27] The locus classicus of this tradition is R. M. Hare (1952). See also Darwall (2006) and Kukla and Lance (2009), who devote a good deal of time to the second-personal dimension of imperatives.

[28] See Fricker 2007. Others include Hinchman (2006), Moran (2006), Dotson (2011) and (2014), and McMyler (2012). In Chapter 4 I will argue that when it comes to the normative pressure that is exerted by an act of testimony, it is a mistake to locate the source of the normative pressure in the act of address itself; my claim will be that testimony exerts the sort of normative pressure Fricker discusses on *anyone* who observes it (including overhearers to whom the testimony was not addressed).

[29] Although for Griceans all of these cases are like language use in that they involve non-natural meaning.

[30] I am going to argue that one of the things distinctive of addresses in speech is that, while the normative demands engendered by addressing another only kick in if the act of address itself was (and was reasonably regarded as) intelligible to the addressee, it is *always* reasonable to regard a linguistic act of address as intelligible to the addressee—at least when one is addressing a colingual. Speech addresses are in this sense fully conventionalized.

matters. Return to the case in which you hear another person say something, but you are uncertain whether you were the one she addressed. Above I said that you have a reason to find out whether you were being addressed, since if you were, you should attend to her (*ceteris paribus*). Notice that this is true whether the speech act was a question, a request, a greeting, a promise, or what have you. So if we are to explain what wants explaining here (namely, why you ought to attend to her), the right degree of generality in our explanation is simply *that you were addressed*; citing the type of speech act performed would be providing too much information, and would fail to capture an important generalization we should want to capture (namely, that *any* type of speech act would have exerted the same normative pressure, namely, that of having a claim on your attention). In this way we can explore a topic that is not explored when we look at speech act types individually: what (if anything) speech act tokens of the various types all have in common when they are addressed to another person.

Fourth, a failure to distinguish between the act of address from the speech act that the speaker addresses to her target will blur a distinction we should want to embrace, that between an audience's *ignoring* a speaker vs. his *improperly rejecting or disregarding* her speech contribution.[31] To be ignored is one thing; to be attended to, only to have one's speech contribution rejected or disregarded on insufficient grounds, is another. This is clear in the case of the sorts of wrongful responses an audience can make in the face of the speech act of telling. For example, when Sally tries to tell Alfred that it's raining, Alfred might simply ignore her (treating the sounds coming from her mouth as mere sounds with no communicative intent behind them), in which case he will proceed as though she made no input into the deliberative process at all; or alternatively he might recognize that she purported to tell him something, but he might improperly downgrade her epistemic authority, and thereby reject or disregard her contribution (Wanderer 2012). The difference between his ignoring Sally and his improperly rejecting or disregarding Sally's speech contribution turns on whether he attended to Sally in the first place. If he did, he didn't ignore her (though he might well have improperly rejected her contribution). These are clearly separate things, and we need to attend to the normative dimension of address to capture the wrong of being ignored.

---

[31] Compare Wanderer's (2012) distinction between having one's testimony be *ignored* and having it be *rejected*.

Fifth, a failure to distinguish between the act of address from the speech act that the speaker addresses to her target will lead to confused analyses of other cases as well. Imagine that the following is heard over a loud speaker at a public event: 'Will the owner of a green minivan, with Illinois license plate B25 OXY, please return to your car immediately?' The *speech act performed* is a query, and indirectly a request, both of which are addressed to the owner of the minivan in question. That much is clear. But if this is all that we say about this and related cases,[32] we will fail to capture the fact that what we might call the 'communicative act' is addressed *to the public at large*, even as the contained query and request is more narrowly addressed to the owner. The evidence for thinking that this speech act is addressed to the public at large is that *everyone in earshot has a reason to attend to it*,[33] even as only the owner (better: the person responsible for that car) has a reason to do as it indirectly requests.

In short, there is a strong case to be made for thinking that we ought to pursue the question of the normative dimension of address, and that pursuing this requires us to go beyond theorizing about the effects of addressing one or the other of the various types of speech act to a given addressee.

---

[32] For example, see the analysis of 'Anyone who is willing to volunteer please raise your hand' in Lance and Kukla (2013: 143). They write that the 'pragmatic function' of this utterance is 'to call upon *you* as *the particular person who was recognized by the call*'. Assuming that the person who was recognized by the call was the person who is willing to volunteer, I fear that this confuses the questions, To whom was this utterance addressed?, and the question, To whom was the request in this utterance made? The answer to the first question is: anyone in earshot (or something like that). The answer to the second is: the person(s) who is (are) willing to volunteer. This confusion between these two questions is encouraged by not separating the act of address from the act of request that was made in that act (and which was addressed to anyone interested in volunteering). See also their earlier analysis of 'Those of you under nine feet tall, please wear this badge' in Kukla and Lance (2009: 23), which I think suffers from the same problem. While they give some indication of being aware of the issue here—they explicitly distinguish between the target of the act and who is called upon to respond (at 2009: 144)—their interest in connecting addresses to the requirements to respond *to the particular speech act performed* makes them overlook the fact that, while only *some people* have a reason to respond to the request or directive, everyone within earshot has a reason to attend to the speech act in which the directive was expressed. This is because even though the act is one in which only some were the target of the request, everyone was addressed in the act.

[33] How does this square with the idea that, at least when it comes to the face-to-face variety, addresses are 'second-personal' in that they are directed at particular targets? In a public address of the sort in this example, it is not the public at large, but each individual within earshot, who is targeted, so that we can think of this as a distributed address, with each individual being targeted. Even so, the request is made only to the owner of the minivan. (With thanks to Paul Bloomfield for indicating the need to address this matter.)

6

What features of an address are responsible for generating a reason for the addressee to attend to the speaker? To answer this it is helpful to start with what I will call the *cognitive mutuality* of the act of addressing someone in face-to-face verbal communication. A competent address is made in such a way that it is manifest to the target that she is being addressed. When this is so, the speaker is entitled to assume that various things are common knowledge between speaker and addressee. I contend that the source of the normativity of address derives from what the speaker is entitled to expect, given what she is entitled to assume.

This last point can be brought out in several steps.

To address oneself to another is to perform an act with the manifest intention that it be recognized by the target(s) as a 'call' for their attention, under conditions in which the (predictive) expectation of success on this score is reasonable. What makes the (predictive) expectation of success reasonable is the fact that competent addresses have three 'appearance' properties. First, the act manifestly appears to be directed at an individual or individuals—the 'target(s)'. Second, the act manifestly appears to be performed with the intention of capturing the target's attention. And third, the act's manifest appearance as having been performed with the intention of capturing the target's attention appears to be in the service of an intention to initiate a (possibly brief) cooperative action with the target. I will call these three properties *apparent targeting, apparent attention-capture,* and *apparent attempt to initiate cooperative action*. To call for another's attention is simply to perform an act with these three appearance properties. And once this is done, various things will be common knowledge between speaker and addressee(s); or at least it will be reasonable (and the speaker will be entitled) to suppose that there will be such common knowledge.

It is at this point that we see why the speaker's act of address not only must have all of the relevant appearance properties, but also must be such that this act can 'reasonably' be expected to succeed. It is not just that an act fails to count as an address if no one would recognize it as such; more importantly, in employing features whose significance can reasonably be regarded as those constituting the relevant appearance properties, the speaker *entitles herself* to assume that they will be recognized as such, and so entitles herself to assume that her act will be ascribed the significance she intends for it to be ascribed. In effect, in performing an act with properties that can 'reasonably' be expected to succeed at the sort of attention-capture associated with the act of address, she both maximizes the chance that her act *will* succeed as an act of address, but also *entitles herself* to assume as much.

Consider now what is mutual knowledge[34] when a speaker addresses her target through the performance of a *speech act*. Here, it is not merely that the speaker is aiming to capture the target's attention, thereby attempting to initiate a cooperative action. At least part of the attempted cooperative action itself will be grasped by the target who attends to the act. This is because it will be common knowledge that, in addressing herself *to you* in speech, the speaker is aiming to initiate a (possibly very brief) speech exchange with you. I do not assume that this requires anything substantial; the 'exchange' might simply be a matter of greeting you, in the expectation that you acknowledge the greeting itself; or it might be that the speaker is passing along information, where uptake is sought after (and expected); or it might be asking a question, with some action on your part made in response (answering; politely declining to answer; saying you don't know; etc.); or again it could be that the speaker is aiming to initiate an ongoing (prolonged) conversation. I use 'speech exchange' to indicate any of these, and other cases. What they all have in common is that they are each a kind of *cooperative and/or joint action* constituted by the speech exchange.[35] If this is correct, then one who addresses you in speech is manifesting her intention to initiate, sustain, or conclude an activity of cooperation where the actions themselves are at least partly a speech exchange.[36] Borrowing a lovely expression from Seana Shiffrin (2013: 150), we might think of this as a matter of instituting, sustaining, or concluding 'bilateral communicative relations' with you.

Herein lies what I take to be the basis for the normativity of address. I submit that when another person makes manifest her intention to be initiating a cooperative action—alternatively: to be instituting 'bilateral communicative relations'—using a method that is (and in any case is

---

[34] In what follows I will speak of what is mutual knowledge when one addresses another— this should be understood to amount to what the speaker is *entitled to assume* is common knowledge.

[35] In suggesting that speech exchanges might be characterized as 'joint actions', I am following the lead of Margaret Gilbert (1989: 294–8, 434) and Herb Clark (1996).

[36] In addition to Gilbert (1989) and Clark (1996), see also Gilbert and Priest (2013). The empirical work on communication makes clear that the hypothesis that speech exchanges are joint actions is well supported; in addition to Clark (1996), see also Streek (1980); Durante (1988); Goodwin (1995).

reasonably regarded as) a recognized method for attaining that end, *she is entitled to expect acknowledgement for her attempt to initiate a cooperative action*. This point is perfectly general; it is not specific to addresses made through speech. The same point holds with respect to *any* act that is intelligible as 'calling' on another's attention for the purpose of initiating (or attempting to initiate) a cooperative action: so long as the attempt is intelligible, or is reasonably regarded as intelligible, as the attempt at initiating a cooperative action, the person initiating the act has a claim on your attention. (Recall the stranded motorist waving his hands frantically in an attempt to draw attention to himself, and in this way to get help.[37]) On this score what is distinctive of speech is that, unlike non-linguistic acts (winks, hand gestures, shrugs, etc.) whose availability for signalling one's intention to initiate a cooperative action often requires prior convention, speech (as a tool for cooperative and joint action) wears its intelligibility on its face.

I just said that a speaker who addresses another is entitled to expect acknowledgement of this, and that the acknowledgement involves (perhaps among other things) attending to her act. The nature of the entitlement here deserves comment. The sort of entitlement I have in mind is that which is associated with conditions in which it is proper to expect another's cooperation. Suppose for example that we have agreed to work together for some common end. Then you and I are entitled to expect of each other that each of us will work to that end. It is not clear whether this entitlement is a moral entitlement; perhaps it would be more accurate to describe it in more generic terms as a social entitlement, as it derives from social norms of cooperation. A speaker who sincerely and competently addresses a target is entitled in *this* sense to expect the target's attention. But whatever we call it, the point is that in performing an act of this type the speaker acquires the *permission* to

---

[37] The contention that he has a claim on your attention should not be confused with the contention that he has a claim on you to help him fix the tyre. Regarding the latter, it is plausible to suppose that the duty to help others is an imperfect duty—one which does not generate duties every time another seeks your help. I submit that the claim on one's attention is different in this regard: we do owe it to anyone who addresses us to give them our attention *at least long enough to discern what cooperative act they aim to initiate*. If we do not stop for each stranded motorist, it may be because, confronted with such a person who is trying to flag us down, we already know what act they want to initiate; and insofar as we are entitled not to help on this occasion (having acted on our imperfect duty on other occasions), we don't bother stopping to tell them this, which would be time- and effort-consuming (and sometimes unsafe, owing to traffic patterns), confident that they will immediately discern our reaction from our failure to stop. (With thanks to Paul Bloomfield for indicating the need to address this case in particular. See also West (2012: 231), who appears to suggest something close to what Bloomfield has in mind.)

expect to have her act acknowledged as the sort of act that it is. If a target fails to do so, the target has thereby wronged her. What supports this contention is the assumption that a speaker who addresses a target is owed the sort of acknowledgement and recognition that is owed to a rational subject when the subject, directing herself to the target, attempts to initiate a cooperative action with him using tools that are (epistemically) reasonably regarded as recognizable as such. This assumption reflects two features of us as moral agents: our rationality, and our sociality.

One normative principle here is that *we owe mutual respect to one another as rational agents*. It may well be that this principle is an ethical one. What is important to me is that it is normative, and that as such it can generate demand-constituting reasons for action. This principle of respect can be used to support the hypothesis that being addressed by another generates a reason for you to attend to her. Insofar as address involves the signalling of an intention to initiate cooperative action, the capacity for addressing another is a capacity of a rational being—a way we have of coordinating with others.[38] Creatures who manifest their attempt to coordinate or to initiate cooperative action with us deserve (and are entitled to expect) our respect.

But the principle of respect owed to other rational agents does not shoulder the entire weight of my argument. We are also ineliminably social beings, and our sociality adds additional support to the idea that being addressed by another generates a reason for you to attend to the speaker. Rational beings who are also social beings must have some way of indicating to others their intention to initiate cooperative actions with them. What is more, since it is crucial to our development as social and rational individuals that we have interactions with others,[39] one's capacity to capture others' attention cannot be left to sheer chance—it cannot simply be a matter of how *de facto* good one is at getting people to attend to one. On the contrary, I submit that every rational being who is also a social being has an entitlement to have the attention of other social rational beings with whom they come into contact, at least in those restricted moments when attempting to initiate what is, and what would be reasonably regarded as, a cooperative action with them. There are of course restrictions on this entitlement; I will

---

[38] See Shiffrin (2014: 9). Schiffrin argues that '... because of its potential for precision and directness, discursive communication plays a special role in our moral lives' (2014: 79), and that we have reason to protect our ability to use this role.

[39] This is a common theme in much of the ethics and developmental psychology literature. For two recent examples, see Shiffrin (2014) and Jones (2016).

discuss these below, in the context of what I will call the *misuse* and *abuse* of the act of address. But these are special cases; in ordinary cases there is a normative expectation to another's attention when attempting to initiate a cooperative action by way of addressing him.[40]

With this as our foundation, we can now go on to discern how addressing another in speech generates a distinctive reason for the addressee to attend to the address. One who addresses you in speech is doing something which generates a reason to regard her as attempting to initiate a cooperative activity with you; insofar as she is a rational being (as confirmed by her use of speech), she is entitled to expect the respect due to a rational being who is recognized as having attempted to initiate a cooperative activity; and the respect due to such a person is to recognize her as having aimed to initiate a cooperative action. In short: acts of addressing another in speech generate a claim on our attention, in a way that is conceptually prior to the recognition we owe once we have recognized the particular speech act they have performed. This, I submit, is the fundamental basis of the answer to (A). That is, it is the basis of the normative dimension of address.

Of course, once the target/addressee has attended to and recognized the speech act for what it is, the target/addressee then owes any *additional* regard that is due to acts of that kind. It is on this point that I think Lance and Kukla are exactly right when they say that

> ... [W]hile all calls give their targets reasons to act, *different kinds of calls create different kinds of reasons*, and these kinds often cannot be understood except in relation to the types of second-personal transactions that institute them. (Lance and Kukla 2013: 462)

> Since calls [= second-person addresses] are targeted events that essentially call for uptake, they have a special normative impact upon their targeted audience; there are norms of discursive pragmatics that govern what counts as an appropriate way of acknowledging and responding to a particular call, and the call mobilizes these norms.... Once a call is recognized by its target, even inaction counts as a response, since the call calls for uptake. (Lance and Kukla 2013: 468)

---

[40] Somewhat speculatively, we might think of the infant's anguished cry (when dirty or cold or hungry) as nature's way of building in a 'call' to another for help—a way of capturing another's attention before one has the cognitive maturity to do so by addressing them.

These are what I would call the *downstream* claims on one, generated by being addressed by another in speech. Prior to these downstream claims is the claim on your attention that is generated by the very fact of being addressed. Once you have honoured that prior claim, and so have attended to the speaker, you then face the downstream claims generated by the type of act that is at issue.

7

My contentions so far have been two: an address purports to be an attempt by the speaker to capture a target's attention, and therein to initiate a cooperative action with the target; and that insofar as it is as it purports to be, such an act generates a reason for the addressee to attend to the speaker, at least long enough to discern what the proposed cooperative action is. When the speaker does her part, the reason is generated, and the addressee owes it to her to attend to her in this way. But there are at least two types of case in which the speaker does not do her part. I will call these, respectively, *misuses* and *abuses* of the act of address.

Let us describe a speaker as *misusing* the practice of address whenever her address (and any allegedly cooperative action she is intending to initiate) is not part of a cooperative engagement with the would-be addressee. Misuses need not be deliberate; sometimes people are incompetent or interpersonally insensitive (but not maliciously so). I will call such cases *mere* misuses of the practice of address. But when a speaker is deliberate in her misuse of the practice of address—say, she is addressing others and then aiming to engage with them with the intention merely to waste their time for the sheer fun of it (or out of some other malicious or otherwise uncooperative[41] motive)—in that case we can describe her as *abusing* the practice. In particular, a speaker counts as abusing the practice of address just in case it is *by intention* that her would-be address (and any further action she is intending to initiate) is not part of a cooperative engagement with the would-be addressee.

In broad outline, the model I propose for cases of misuse depends on whether the case is one of abuse. In cases of an abuse of the practice—the

---

[41] It is to be borne in mind throughout that the sort of cooperativity I have in mind is that which I characterized at the outset of this chapter: an activity involving more than one subject is *cooperative* in the relevant sense when it is structured around a common interest (often, though not always, a jointly accepted aim), such that having this common interest gives each party reasons to act in certain ways and not others at various points throughout the activity itself.

speaker who is doing the addressing is not cooperative in the relevant sense, and the lack of cooperativity is deliberate—the speaker is not entitled to expect to be attended to, and so her address fails to generate any reason at all for the target to attend to her. However, when the speaker is *merely* misusing the practice of address—although the promise of cooperativity is not met, this occurs without any malicious or hidden motive—the speaker's address continues to generate a claim on the addressee's attention even if the addressee knows of the speaker's misuse of the practice. The proper remedy here is to try to educate the speaker as to the mutuality of the practice of address. My reason for thinking this again reflects the importance of the need for a practice that lets each of us call on the attention of another as something owed to one: so important is the practice, and the presumption of cooperation, that if a speaker is engaging in the practice incompetently but not maliciously, the proper remedy is to attend to her while simultaneously enculturating her into proper practice. Indeed, it is plausible to think that cases of this (mere misuse) sort are much more common than cases in which a speaker abuses the practice. As evidence for this contention, I note that even those who choose to ignore a speaker with a bad track record will feel some twinge of remorse, and feel as though they owe him some sort of acknowledgement—even if not the sort he was seeking in his speech act.[42]

One other point is in order before I proceed to apply this account to cases. The point concerns what we might call the epistemology of address. The need for the point arises because targets typically don't have access to the facts that determine a speaker's cooperativity in addressing them. For this reason we also need an account of the conditions on which an addressee would be *excused* for not having attended to the speaker when he should have done so. I submit that this can be given in terms of the adequacy of his (epistemic) reasons for suspecting non-cooperativity: if these reasons are adequate, he is excused, but if not, he is not. I would add that in the absence of reasons bearing on the speaker's cooperativity, a speaker is to be *presumed* cooperative; this ensures that mere lack of reasons confirming cooperativity is not a sufficient basis for properly ignoring one who has addressed you. The epistemology of the normativity of address, then, turns on the

---

[42] Interestingly, this appears to be true even in cases in which people are approached on the street by panhandlers. See e.g. Nielsen (2012: 167).

defeasibility of the presumption of cooperativity, as it bears on the act of address itself.[43]

With this as the proposed model for cases of misuse, I now want to go on to apply this model to four types of situation in which there might be doubts as to whether a would-be act of address generates a claim on the addressee's attention. These include cases involving *impractically many addresses*, addresses by speakers with a *bad track record*, addresses made in an *inappropriate context*, or addresses involving *questionable, self-serving, or otherwise bad motives*. My claim will be that it is only when the tool of address is abused that there is no claim on the addressee's attention at all.

I begin with cases in which there are *impractically many addresses* at once, so that the addressee herself cannot respond to all of them (at least not in this context, and possibly not at all). Here one might be tempted to appeal to the principle that '*ought' implies 'can'* to argue that it isn't the case that every one of these addresses generates a claim on the addressee's attention. But I think we can drill deeper by considering a concrete case. I offer the case of Madonna. Madonna is a famous pop star. One day, as she is leaving her hotel, she is mobbed by her fans who all address her by name, wanting desperately to speak with her—if only for a moment! There is no way she can attend to any but a select few. And she is not particularly keen on doing even that; she wants her privacy. What, if anything, does she owe her screaming fans?

I offer two responses, one of which questions the assumption that her fans' actions count as acts of addressing her, the other of which grants this assumption.

In order for each of these acts by her fans to count as an address, it must be true that each of these acts can reasonably be regarded as an address. This can be doubted. Perhaps for a good many people in the crowd, it would be unreasonable for that person to suppose that Madonna could succeed in ascribing such a significance to his particular would-be act of address, for the simple reason that Madonna has only limited attention and so is unlikely to observe his particular attempt to call to her. (Each of her fans might be

---

[43] If we allow that it is defeasible, the presumption of cooperativity would appear to be a principle in place whenever we engage with others at all. It is also a presumption that appears to loom large in speech act theory itself. Marina Sbisà notes that in ordinary conversational exchanges 'The satisfaction of felicity conditions is assumed by default, that is, as a first option and without raising the issue explicitly. Like other default assumptions, this too is defeasible: it is suspended as soon as doubts arise and if it is discovered not to hold, the speech act is either evaluated as infelicitous or is redescribed.' (Sbisà 2002: 425). She goes on (same page) to note that the same is true of presuppositions. (See also Sbisà 2001: 1796–97, fn. 5, and 1800–1.)

trying to capture her attention, but this wouldn't be sufficient for each of their individual acts to count as addressing her.) If this is correct, then at best only a limited number of (lucky!) fans can reasonably expect[44] Madonna to regard their act as an address. In that case, only the acts of these lucky few count as addresses, only they are entitled to expect her attention, and so it is only in their case that the acts generate a claim on Madonna's attention (the multitude of others would have no such claim).

But suppose that we waive this first response and agree to treat all of these acts as addresses. What should be said about this case? Well, Madonna is savvy and knows all about her fans; she knows that many of them merely want to speak to her (to be able to say that they've done so), or to catch her eye (merely to brag to others that she looked at them). What is more, she also knows, and knows that her screaming fans know, that under the circumstances the prospects of a serious engagement with any one of them is nil. The best that they can reasonably hope for is a wave or a 'hello'. Given what Madonna knows, she knows that it would not be reasonable for any of her fans to intend to initiate a cooperative action that is more demanding than this—that insofar as a fan would propose anything more than this, it would no longer have the sort of mutuality characteristic of cooperation. In this case I am inclined to say that Madonna is under normative pressure only to acknowledge the collection of fans as such, rather than any single fan. This is supported by the model: Madonna's knowledge ensures that anything more demanding on their part would be manifestly uncooperative, and so would cancel the presumption of cooperativity, and so would generate no claim at all.

I submit that other cases of impractically many addresses can be handled similarly.

It is worth noting that this analysis, which has been offered for cases involving too many would-be addresses *at a given time*, can be generalized to cases of too many would-be addresses *over time*.[45] Madonna is burdened not only by being swamped whenever she leaves her hotel, but also by being accosted whenever she is in public virtually anywhere. The slow but persistent drip-drip-drip of autograph seekers and fans is enough to drive anyone crazy. But insofar as this is common knowledge, it places a restriction on what anyone can reasonably expect from Madonna. Once again she knows, and knows that her many fans know, that under the circumstances the

---

[44] This is the predictive sense of 'expect' here.
[45] I thank Duncan Pritchard for indicating the need to address this case too.

prospects of a serious engagement with any one of them is nil. In fact, insofar as all of them should recognize that she is entitled to some privacy herself, the best that they can reasonably hope for is that she will from time to time acknowledge her fans. Given what Madonna knows, she knows that no fan can reasonably intend to initiate a cooperative action that is more demanding than this—that insofar as a fan does propose anything more than this, it would no longer have the sort of mutuality characteristic of cooperation. Then we might think that insofar as Madonna has good reason to think that a particular would-be address comes from a fan seeking to capture her attention for no further purpose than for the thrill of having done so, she is within her rights not to attend (on grounds that this is not part of a cooperative endeavour). Alternatively, we might think that the duty to attend to her fans is, given her fame, an imperfect one: she is under normative pressure to acknowledge only some of her many fans' calls over the years. (Matters remain otherwise, of course, when Madonna is being addressed under conditions in which she has no reason to suppose that she is being addressed as a celebrity by a fan; in that case she is as the non-famous are, i.e. she ought to presume the speaker's cooperativity.)[46]

Next, I move on to cases in which an address is made by a speaker with a bad track record. These sorts of case might seem analogous to the 'boy who cries wolf'. To this end consider the case of Jones. Jones always seeks to capture other people's attention by addressing them by name, but when attended to he never has anything that has any relevance or interest to anyone else, and the (allegedly) cooperative actions he tries to initiate never are the sorts that anyone would be interested in participating in (or would willingly agree to participate in). What is more, his requests are inappropriate, he greets people at inapt times, he asks irritating questions which

---

[46] Madonna is protected by the mutual familiarity of her fame, but what should be said of cases where the target of the multiple simultaneous addresses is not famous? Imagine a case in which a worker receives multiple email requests at the same time, where it is the worker's job to respond to each individually. Here I think that the reasonableness criterion continues to cut ice: since it is unreasonable to request something that it would be practically impossible for the requestee to do, it is unreasonable to expect any such request to be met. Of course, what is practically impossible is for the worker to respond to all requests *at once*; this does not mean that he is under no obligation to respond to each them at some point in the future, so long as doing so is reasonably expected of one in his position (and is compatible with his performing his other job duties). Madonna's case differs only in that the practical impossibility of her responding to everyone is something that will be known in advance (given her fame), whereas the practical impossibility of the worker's responding to everyone at the same time is something that others may only come to learn after the delay in her response. (I thank an anonymous referee for OUP for encouraging me to consider this case.)

manifest profound misunderstanding of the issue under discussion and a failure to track salient presuppositions of the conversation, he issues unauthorized demands, he apologizes when he hasn't done anything wrong, and so forth. In light of this, some might think that audiences who know this of him are entitled to ignore his future attempts to capture their attention when he addresses them in speech. His addresses, it is alleged, no longer make any claim on the knowledgeable addressee's attention.

The proper analysis of this case, I submit, depends on whether we imagine the behaviour to be intentional or not, since this will determine whether he is abusing the practice of address or merely misusing it. If it is a case of mere misuse, where the promise of cooperativity is not met but where this is not the result of any malicious or hidden motive on the speaker's part, then the address does generate a reason to attend—with the proper remedy being to educate the speaker in the practice of competent address. But if it is a case of abuse, then the would-be address generates no reason for the target to attend. This sort of analysis can be applied to other cases involving a bad track record. For example, consider a case involving a person whose speech acts regularly undermine or sabotage group discourse: if the sabotaging is intentional, then the case is one of abuse and there is no reason to attend; but if this is not intentional (we have an oblivious speaker), then a reason to attend is generated. In the latter case, the addressee's recourse is to acknowledge the claim on his attention and attempt to bring the speaker into competence in the practice.

Bad track record cases point to an interesting *mutuality* in the normativity of address. I have been emphasizing that an addressee who ignores an address directed to him under conditions in which the speaker was in fact cooperative disrespects the speaker (although he might be excused for doing so if he had adequate but misleading grounds to suspect a lack of cooperation on the speaker's part). But it is also worth emphasizing, with the example above, that a speaker whose addresses are inappropriate in the manner just described *disrespects his addressee*. To generate a reason for another to attend to you, and to do so by way of a second-personal address, you ought to have something it would be reasonable to assume is worth his attending to; if you don't, this is itself a form of disrespect—of not properly valuing his time and attention (as well as the effort it takes to comprehend your address). In effect, when you address another person in speech, you are changing the normative landscape in such a way that his giving you his attention is something that *he owes you*. If you don't have a proper reason for doing so—if you don't have a proper reason for exerting normative pressure on him to attend to you—then you have disrespected him as an autonomous subject.[47] If your doing so was intentional, you have no claim on his attention; if your doing so was the result of obliviousness, then while you have a claim on his attention, he is entitled to redirect how you participate in the practice of address in the future. It is for this reason that over time bad track record cases are likely to degenerate into cases of abuse: once one has been given ample opportunity to become competent in the practice, subsequent failure to engage cooperatively with others is best explained as a form of abuse, not a mere misuse, of the practice.

A third type of case to consider, where it appears that the speaker's address of an audience makes no claim on the audience's attention, is one in which the address happens in *inappropriate contexts*. I can imagine two subclasses of case of this sort; they are different enough that they demand separate treatment.

One sort of inappropriate context is one in which the would-be addressee is manifestly otherwise occupied on something taking all of her attention. (These are the sorts of case in which politeness requires the address be of the explicit form 'Excuse me' or 'Can I have your attention for a moment?') It is easy to see how to handle such cases in a way that is consistent with the hypothesis that they continue to make a claim on the addressee's attention: they are cases in which, having addressed you in this way, the speaker does have some claim on your attention, but the reason you have for attending to her right now (beyond giving her a 'Not now!' reply) can be outweighed by the reasons you have to continue with the urgent task you are currently working on. That is, I would analyse such cases as ones in which there is a claim on your attention, but you are entitled to postpone responding in any way beyond saying 'Not now, can't you see I'm busy?'

I can imagine theorists who would object to this analysis as follows. Insofar as you would be within your rights to respond with a baldly dismissive 'Shhh, not now!', this suggests that the speaker was not within her rights to address you at this moment; and if the speaker was not within her rights to address you at this moment, then she has no entitlement to expect your attention, and so generates no reason for you—no claim on you—to attend to her right now.

---

[47] I don't want to overstate this wrong here—it's rather minor in the grand scheme of things.

But various considerations can be offered against this analysis. I offer three, all of which support the idea that even in such cases the speaker's addressing you generates a claim on your attention.

First, the very fact that one feels the need to reply at all—that one doesn't simply ignore the addressee altogether until she goes away, but explains or makes manifest that one is busy—indicates the felt need for attending to her, at least *minimally* in the sense of offering an indication of the reason that the address cannot be further attended to at the moment. The basis of the felt need to attend to her (at least in this minimal sense) in such cases cannot be that we do so only to get the speaker to stop addressing us, for one feels the need to respond even in cases in which one has great confidence that the speaker will go away quickly even if ignored. The felt need to respond indicates our recognition that the speaker has a claim on our attention.

Second, in cases in which one's current activity will end quickly, one's reason to continue doing what one is doing is a reason to *postpone* giving one's attention to the addressee, rather than a reason to ignore her entirely (even after one has completed one's task). This suggests that the address itself did give one a reason to attend after all.

Third, my proposed analysis is also favoured by cases in which, unbeknownst to you in the moment, it turns out that the speaker has a compelling reason to interrupt you after all. Suppose that the speaker responds to your 'Shhhh! Not now, I'm busy!' with, 'Yes, I know you are busy, but your house is on fire!' (Or let it be anything that is urgent and whose urgency would be such that it would be reasonable to assume that you would value it more than you value what you are currently doing.) Then I would take it that you owe the speaker an apology. Here, you are apologizing for not having properly attended to her original claim on your attention: had you done so, you would have come to know of the urgency of what she had to say to you. Might a theorist who is pressing the current objection respond by claiming that the apology is owed, not for your failure to attend properly to her claim on your attention, but for not accepting the help that she was offering you? But this cannot be the whole of the story, since at the moment of address you might not have known what she was trying to get your attention for; so your subsequent apology to her for your dismissive response, once you found out why she wanted your attention, couldn't be an apology for not taking help that was being offered. It seems that there is nothing you could be apologizing to her *for*, other than for not having taken up her claim on your attention.

I conclude, then, that these sorts of cases—cases in which you do not give your attention to another's address because you are currently occupied by an important matter—are best handled as cases in which, while the speaker did have a claim on your attention in virtue of addressing you in speech, you might well have a stronger reason to postpone attending to her, in order to continue doing as you are doing. When the dismissive response ('Shhhh! Not now!') is called for, what underwrites it is not that the speaker had no claim on one's attention, but rather that one expects others to recognize when one is busy, and expects that others take one's being busy as a reason not to interrupt one (unless the matter is urgent).

The other sort of inappropriate context I want to consider involves discursive contexts in which the various parties' contributions to the speech exchange are highly regulated. In this connection we might think of courtroom settings, or the classroom, or meetings run by Robert's Rules (or some other set of rules and procedures) etc. Here there is such a thing as 'speaking out of turn'. And it is easy to imagine an objection which holds that if one were to address another person in speech in such a way that one is, or would be, speaking out of turn, one's address then generates *no* claim on the addressee's attention. The reason is simply that (by the prevailing norms in play) one wasn't entitled to speak at that point to begin with; and presumably performing an act one wasn't entitled to perform in the first place does not entitle one to expect another's attention, and so does not generate a reason for the other person to attend to one.

While I can see the case for thinking that an out-of-order address of this sort cannot make any claim on another's attention, I think we should resist this. But first I want to make a few preliminary points. In a context in which speech exchanges are regulated, ordinarily this is common knowledge, so that one who performs a speech act that is 'out of turn' is doing something which, on the face of it, is not consistent with the rules governing the exchange, and so to that extent is being uncooperative.[48] This will immediately give a would-be addressee a reason to question the cooperativity of the speaker on this occasion. However, the addressee may also reason that since the speaker could be expected to have been aware of all of this, she may have a valid overriding reason behind her address. This highlights the prospect for two types of case. In one, the speaker does *not* have any valid overriding reason behind her address; in that case I think it should be analysed

---

[48] This assumes that the practice itself, and the regulations on speech it imposes, is legitimate.

according to whether it was a case of abuse or merely of misuse of address. In the other, though, the speaker does have a valid overriding reason behind her address, and so remains cooperative. But since the speaker is being cooperative, the claim on the addressee's attention is generated. (A target who nevertheless ignores the address, regarding the speaker as speaking out of turn, might then be excused if his reasons for doing so, though misleading, were sufficiently good.)

I think this analysis is independently plausible. When one speaks out of turn in a context in which there is a justified regime involving the regulation of speech exchanges, thereby interrupting the official record (i.e. this is not a case of a quiet address on the side), one's speech act is impermissible in that context. The rules forbid it, and they may allow for appropriate forms of punishment (i.e. being held in contempt of court, being forcibly escorted from the courtroom). But it is worth noting that these contexts are not utterly sealed off from everyday life. Suppose for example that the defendant in a courtroom all of a sudden starts to be overcome with dizziness; presumably he can speak up then, addressing himself to the judge to let her know of this. No doubt, there are other matters on which he might 'speak out of turn' and yet do so in a way that makes a legitimate claim on another's attention. Any regime of regulation ought to tolerate 'exceptional' addresses like this.[49] In fact, I would speculate that this is part of the legitimacy and justification of any regime of speech regulation in context: it must allow for legitimate exceptions (e.g. in the case of the health or well-being of participants, emergency matters, etc.). What such regulated contexts do, I submit, is to *raise the bar for counting as being cooperative*: in such a context, one's addressing another in ways that contravene the regulations on speech exchanges require one's reason being sufficiently important that it justifies the violation. Anything less than this is will count as uncooperative, and hence as an abuse (if intentional) and a misuse (if not).

Indeed we might even think of ordinary conversations as a speech context in which exchanges are regulated, albeit weakly. There is a loose but significant structure to ordinary speech exchanges: we take turns, we do not monopolize the floor, we interrupt only when needed, we indicate our ongoing attention to the other participants, we keep our comments relevant, and so forth. It is plausible to think that there is a loose collection of soft rules that regulate these exchanges, and that these are common knowledge

---

[49] This appears to be recognized by Lance and Kukla (2013: 140), at least in cases in which the addressee was already occupied, although they note this without offering an explanation.

(Clark 1996). If this is so, then the foregoing analysis of the more strictly regulated speech contexts applies, albeit with accommodation made for the looser, softer rules in place. If in the course of an ordinary conversation you interrupt another's speech by addressing her—or if you do so by addressing another, but you do so in a way that interrupts the ability of others to attend to what she was saying—you are like the person who interrupts a court proceeding with an address. This *can* be a cooperative act, but it is cooperative *only if* the reason for the interrupting address is sufficiently weighty that it captures something that it is reasonable to think would be valued by the other participants, and especially by the speaker, more than they value the conversational contribution(s) they are currently making/observing. If this condition is not met, the interrupting address is either a misuse of the practice (if one's lack of cooperativity is not intentional), or it is an abuse if it is intentional.

I turn, finally, to the fourth type of case to be considered: cases in which the speaker's *intentions are questionable, entirely self-serving, or malicious*. While there are many varieties within this category, I will describe four distinct cases, from the relatively innocuous (if irritating) to the downright evil. Whether these are cases in which the address generates a reason for the target to attend, I submit, is determined by whether the speaker's address was part of an attempt at cooperative engagement with him, and if not whether this was intentional.

The first sort of case I want to discuss in this connection is cases involving addresses in which the speaker's intentions are *narrowly commercial*.[50] Imagine walking the aisles of your local supermarket only to encounter a person who starts trying to get you to buy a particular product he is hawking. Does his addressing you in this way ('Try the Sudsie Brand of dish soap! It's great!') really generate a claim on your attention? Suppose you were to discern his intent ahead of time—say, he is wearing an official uniform of the company, and is standing behind a table containing samples. Do you really owe him your attention merely because he addressed you? I want to say: on the plausible assumption that commercial transactions are not *ipso facto* uncooperative, then yes, you do. Two things recommend such a treatment of this sort of case.

First, this treatment can explain why it is that many of us are *frustrated and irritated* by being addressed in this way, or why we experience one or

---

[50] With thanks to my son Gideon, for urging me to consider this sort of case.

another of the negative reactive attitudes. The explanation, I submit, is twofold. An initial point is that we feel that the speaker is addressing us without any serious consideration for our perspective or our interests, beyond thinking of us as potential consumers. Some theorists will think this suffices to show that the speaker's address is not part of a cooperative engagement; but I don't agree. I think this sort of case is not all that much different from ordinary commercial transactions, which I regard as cooperative even when entirely transactional. Still, the speaker is less vested in incorporating our perspective into her action, and this is something of which we are aware. A second supplemental point is that, in light of the narrowly commercial interests of the speaker, we feel that he is *manipulating* the practice of address. His action is seen as manipulative, precisely because he is exploiting the pinch we feel to attend; the fact that he is doing so without any serious consideration for our perspective or our interests, beyond thinking of us as potential consumers, makes this seem like a manipulation of the practice. But this explanation sees this type of address as a manipulation *of the practice*—that is, as a manipulation of the tool that linguistic address affords us, as a way of generating a claim on another's attention. Here I note that if his addressing us had no claim on our attention, it is hard to see why we would ever feel this way, as opposed simply to being irritated by his behaviour—as we might in a case in which someone makes an irritating (but non-linguistic) noise in our presence.

Second, most people feel that even in cases of this sort, the addressee owes a polite response ('No thank you'). Why this should be, if the address itself had no claim on one's attention in the first place, is mysterious.[51] After all, if one need not have attended to the address at all, it is hard to see why one need have responded to the speaker at all. And yet we feel some (albeit minimal) response is called for. Again, this suggests that we see the fact that we were addressed as having generated a claim on our attention. For insofar as it does, and insofar as our attending leads inevitably to our apprehending the speech act she performed, the norms of the act he performed kick in,[52] and we are put under normative pressure to respond.[53]

---

[51] Compare again the standard reaction to panhandlers on the street, as described in Nielsen (2012: 167).

[52] This is the topic of my subsequent chapters; here I merely assume that the performance of a speech act alters the normative environment of the speaker and addressee. For a discussion, see Lance and Kukla (2013).

[53] An interesting case like this one is the case of unsolicited commercial mail and email. There I don't think there is any claim on our attention. Suppose that there were a filter that screened all such emails and placed them into a single file, and that I know this. Then there is no

For a second sort of case in which the speaker's intentions in addressing another are questionable, self-serving, or malicious, take a case of a speaker who persists in addressing another long after having been made aware of the other's desire not to engage. (Let us assume here that the would-be target's desire not to engage is legitimate, it is not just a case of a desire to ignore someone out of spite etc.) Here, unless the speaker's persistent addresses are backed by reasons which are sufficiently weighty to outweigh the reason he (the speaker) was given by the addressee not to engage with her, this is a clear case of abuse. What is more, the weight of the reasons that the speaker must have will have to be regarded, not from his perspective, but from that of his would-be addressee. After all, it is her attention that he seeks to capture, and thereby to attempt to initiate a cooperative action. So if this is to generate a reason for her to attend, the reason has to be sufficiently weighty from her perspective. If not, the address generates no reason for the addressee to attend, since in that case the practice is being abused (he knew of her desire not to engage, and yet he persisted without good reason, and so was not entitled to expect her attention).

For a third sort of case in which the speaker's intentions in addressing another are questionable, self-serving, or bad, consider the catcall.[54] Imagine several men standing by the side of the road who start addressing themselves to a woman who is walking by them, making lewd, sexist, and other inappropriate comments to her. Should we see the men's addressing her in this way as making a claim on her attention? Clearly not; their intention in targeting her as they do is not part of a cooperative engagement with her, they are not entitled to expect her attention, and so there is no claim on her attention generated. I submit that this claim of non-cooperativity holds even restricting ourselves to the Gricean sense of cooperativity (that which is presumed to be in play conversations). Here it is worth bearing in mind Grice's own characterization. He had in mind 'the standard type of conversational practice' in which participants could be presumed to '[care] about

---

claim on me to read any of that file, even if the individual emails are addressed to me personally. Part of the explanation is that the case of mail and email differs from the face-to-face case I am discussing here: the ethics and norms of written address differ. While I do think that letters and email, including unsolicited letters and unsolicited email, can have a claim on one's attention, I think the source of the claim is a bit more complex, and that the practices that have evolved with mailings and emailings make it permissible to ignore commercial letters and emails even when they are addressed to one. Making the case for this, however, would require more space to suss out the differences. I hope to return to this at a future time.

[54] This case is briefly discussed in Kukla and Lance (2009: 143 n. 13).

the goals that are central to conversation/communication (such as giving and receiving information, influencing and being influence by others)'. Regarding such participants he wrote that they

> must be expected to have an interest, given suitable circumstances, in participation in talk exchanges that will be profitable only on the assumption that they are conducted in general accordance with the Cooperative Principle and the maxims. (Grice 1968/1989: 29–30)

My claim here is that those who catcall are not properly regarded as '[caring] about the goals that are central to conversation/communication', but rather are properly seen as abusing the tools that are used by those who *are* properly so regarded. Simply put, the very act of catcalling manifests a perspective in which one's addressees are being targeted in ways that manifest a fundamental lack of respect. Here the presumption of mutuality is destroyed, and where there is no mutuality, the act of address generates no reason to attend.

It is tempting to think of the case of the catcall, and (more generally) of the prevalence of sexist practices of address, as undermining my claim that the assumption of cooperativity ought to be ascribed a default status.[55] But I think we do better to treat the prevalence of sexist practices as a (generic) reason to suspect non-cooperativity, and so as something that potentially defeats the presumption of cooperativity. Whether this reason is sufficiently weighty in any case to defeat the presumption will depend on features of context. My general reason for preferring this analysis reflects the overarching centrality of our need to interact with others, and of the need to coordinate with them to this end (which need minimally involves having their attention).[56]

The final sort of case in which the speaker's intentions in addressing another are questionable, self-serving, or malicious, is cases in which the speaker manifestly aims to do harm to her addressee. Suppose that you know that Smith is out to do you grave harm, and that she is looking for you. She knows you are in the forest, but does not know your exact location. You are hiding from her, currently out of sight but not out of earshot. You hear her call out to you: 'Where are you? I know you are here somewhere.' Does her addressing you have a claim on your attention? Do you *owe it* to her to

---

[55] With thanks to an anonymous referee for urging that I consider this.
[56] See Chapter 8 for more detailed discussion.

attend to her address? I submit that this case is best analysed as an abuse: insofar as the speaker's act of address is not part of a cooperative engagement, and that this is intentional, the address generates no reason to attend.

I believe that the various examples I've considered in this section point to an important lesson about the nature of the act of addressing another person. Addresses, I submit, are perhaps the fundamental way we have of initiating cooperation and joint action[57] with others, and they work by making manifest to one's target(s) one's intention to do just that. It is because this tool for the initiation of cooperative action is so fundamental that its use generates a claim on the target's (targets') attention. This claim is backed by the presumption of cooperativity that must be part of our engagement with others, given that we are social by nature and that we have a deep and abiding interest in cooperating. However, there are cases in which others aren't cooperative, and when this is so in a context in which another is addressing us, they have no claim on our attention: their address is not part of a cooperative engagement, and so, since they are not entitled to expect our attention in such cases, their act generates no reason for us to attend.

8

The model I propose, then, holds that being addressed by another in speech, when it is part of a cooperative engagement with you, generates a claim on your attention (by generating a reason for you to attend to their attempt to initiate a cooperative or joint action). This model can be used to explain various familiar phenomena.

It can explain the phenomenon of feeling *put upon* when another attempts to engage us in conversation when we are not interested in doing so. In effect, in the very act of addressing us in speech, they are generating (or purporting to generate) a claim on our attention; and insofar as we honour that claim and comprehend the act they have performed, we then owe them whatever kind of response is appropriate to speech acts of that kind. If you are not interested in conversing with me, my asking you where you are from can feel intrusive: you just want to be left alone, and I have

---

[57] Minimally, the joint action in question involves the subsequent conversation itself; but on those occasions when the conversation has a practical upshot, it will also involve whatever other activities are jointly planned in the course of the conversation.

forced you into a situation in which either you must respond or be (seen as) rude, at least by conventional standards.

Relatedly, the proposed model can help us understand why there are often elaborate, non-verbal practices whereby two individuals not previously known to each other might try to signal their interest, or lack of interest, in initiating a conversation whose purpose is not narrowly practical. Addressing another in such a case is a somewhat high-cost way to manifest one's intention to initiate a conversation: one is making a claim on the addressee's attention. We might think that there would be occasions, then, when one wanted to ascertain the interest of one's potential addressee *prior* to addressing him. And sure enough we find a variety of low-cost ways of trying to discern whether the very act of manifesting one's attempt to initiate a joint action will be welcomed. The existence of these ways makes sense, as employing them in this way would expose one to less social risk than what is associated with an explicit and public act of address.

We can make sense, too, of the idea that the injunction to be considerate of others (if not of some stronger moral principle) places some constraints on initiating a conversation with a person not known to you. In particular, the requirement to be considerate of others puts some pressure on us not to put others in the position of either having to respond or be seen as conventionally rude, without having some appropriately compensating reason for doing so. (I have no doubt that insensitivity along this dimension dooms a good many attempts at conversation.)

Our model can also make sense of the a certain kind of conversational obliviousness: there are many who, when considering whether they have an 'appropriately compensating' reason for addressing another in speech (and thereby putting pressure on them to respond appropriately), always take only their own point of view into account, initiating conversation whenever it suits their needs but with no consideration at all for those whom they address. This kind of obliviousness fails to come to proper terms with the *cooperative* nature of conversation, and with the fact that one has already put pressure on one's addressee in the very act of addressing him. Even worse in some ways is the speaker who regards himself[58] as having his interlocutor's interests in mind, but who thinks of these interests entirely

---

[58] Here I have switched in my use of the gender of the pronoun of the speaker: I use male, rather than female, if only because I suspect that the phenomenon I am describing is highly gendered (and that men are more guilty of this conversational self-centeredness than women are).

from a perspective that is dominated by his own interests. (I do not mean to be overly moralizing here; the anticipated pleasure of an imagined conversation can be an appropriate reason to attempt to initiate a conversation with a partner not previously known to one; but it can also happen that what one thinks of as the anticipated pleasure is really an entirely one-sided affair.)

The model can also explain a certain asymmetry between the normative situation in cases involving speech acts which *initiate* a speech exchange and those that merely *extend* an already-ongoing speech exchange. One attempts to initiate a speech exchange with another by addressing oneself to that person—thereby manifesting to the addressee one's intention to initiate a conversation. According to the model, this act of address generates a reason for him to attend to one's attempt to initiate a cooperative action. To be sure, one who recognizes the interlocutor's attempt to engage one in conversation need not take up the offer; one may wish to beg off (politely). But suppose one takes up the speaker's attempt at (the cooperative act of) conversing, and so begins to converse with the speaker. In that case, one has already made manifest a willingness to engage in the cooperative action. This entitles the original speaker to expect that the two of them will participate until the conclusion of the cooperative action itself.[59] And while there may be (and often is) some indeterminacy at the outset of how long the conversation will last, even so the entitlement the speaker has to expect completion places an additional distinctive kind of pressure on the addressee once the conversation has been initiated.[60]

Other familiar phenomena can also be made sense of in this model.

---

[59] Precisely how should we understand the move to conclude a conversation? What are the expectations to which participants are entitled, given that they are presently engaged in a conversation? These are hard questions which I hope to address at greater length elsewhere. But here I can register my sense that there is an asymmetry between initiating and concluding a conversation: the latter places fewer demands on one than does the former. This seems to be a feature of cooperative activity more generally. (With thanks to an anonymous referee for suggesting that I address this issue.)

[60] My sense is that this pressure can increase during the course of the conversation: while it may be easy to back out from a brief exchange with a stranger, and to bring such an exchange to a jointly acceptable conclusion rather quickly, once the conversation is ongoing, it can lead one or both of the participants to expect a more substantial exchange—increasing the pressure on one or both of the parties to do so. Of course, it often happens that parties do not have the same level of enjoyment of the exchange, leading to asymmetric motives regarding when to conclude the conversation, and these can be tricky to manage without giving offence. The sense of offence might arise when one party concludes the conversation in a way that strikes the other party as premature, as terminating before the joint action reached what *they* see as its proper conclusion. Of course, parties can also be overly demanding, or overly sensitive, in these matters as well. (I wish I had more insightful things to say about this.)

For example, we might anticipate that in cultures that place great emphasis on social hierarchies, there will be elaborate norms regulating both the circumstances and the manner of address. This can be explained by noting that if a culture takes an interest in protecting these hierarchies, it may well take an interest in regulating when (if at all) 'low-ranking' members can make a claim on 'higher-ranking' members, and if it does it may take an interest in regulating the conditions under which the former can address the latter. In addition such a society may want to regulate *how* the higher-ranking member is to be addressed ('Your Royal Highness,' 'Distinguished Professor X,' 'Ms. President,' 'Dr. So-and-so', etc.).[61] Similarly, we might also anticipate that in cultures that place great emphasis on social equality, there will be few or no such norms, and forms of address will be more equitable ('Comrade') or else informal (first-name basis). This is in keeping with the value such societies place on the equality of its members: any member can generate a claim on the attention of any other member at any (reasonable) time. Unlike Lance and Kukla (2013: 140), who appear to think of the practice of second-person address as constituted differently by different culture-specific practices,[62] I see cultural practices such as the ones just described as operating on a prior, more fundamental human practice—a practice whose rationale reflects *any* human being's need to be able to call for another's attention, as part of an attempt at cooperative engagement with them.

This model can explain the potential to be placed in a normatively compromised position by people who address one in the course of asking for money on the street: in addressing you, they are performing an act that gives you a reason to attend to them. Once they have addressed you, your only options are (i) to give them money or some other good, (ii) to ignore them, and so to ignore the request, entirely, or (iii) to respond with a polite refusal. Those not inclined to (i) are in a normatively compromised position, since either way their response would appear to be normatively tainted: (ii) directly so, and (iii) insofar as one is forced to acknowledge (to oneself as well as to the addressee) that one is refusing a request for help.[63]

---

[61] See again Morand (1996), Dickey (1997), Benatar (2011), and Olson (2011).

[62] They write, 'the *neutral* hail [second-personal address] is an illusion sustainable only in a relatively lax and ritualistically flexible society such as ours'.

[63] Compare Kukla and Lance (2009: 141); and for an interesting discussion of standard responses to those who beg on the street, see Nielsen (2012).

Finally, this model can also explain the distinctly moral flavour of *snubbing*, whether speaker-directed or audience-directed.[64] A would-be target snubs a speaker when the speaker targets him in an address and he ignores it (under conditions in which there was no basis for questioning the cooperativity of the address). This is a snub precisely because in addressing him she has a claim on his attention and he refuses to acknowledge that claim. What makes this a snub is precisely the sense that he is refusing to see her as having generated a claim on him when in fact she has—as if he is failing to acknowledge her as a 'source of claims' (Rawls 1980). Notice that if addresses didn't generate claims on another's attention, it is hard to reconstruct the distinctly normative flavour of the snub. It is not merely that the would-be addressee isn't responding to the manifest desire of the speaker to be attended to; not all failures to respond to another's manifest desires have a sense of wrongness about them. It is rather that the speaker is *entitled* to be attended to, and the would-be addressee refuses to acknowledge this entitlement. So too with addressee-directed snubs. A speaker snubs her addressee when, having captured his attention by way his recognition of her having addressed him, she reveals that she has no further cooperative action to initiate, and that this was intentional. ('Francisco!' 'Yes?' 'Oh, nothing.') This is a snub precisely because one exploited a claim on another's attention merely to make manifest one's capacity to generate such a claim, not—as with the public significance of an address—to attempt to initiate a joint action. Again, the sense of wrongness of this is lost if we don't see addresses as generating claims on another's attention.

9

In this chapter I have argued that we exert a kind of 'conversational pressure' on others when we address them in speech: in the very act of addressing them (in a cooperative spirit), we are entitled to expect their attention, thereby generating a reason for them to attend to us. This underwrites the sort of wrong one does another speaker when one ignores her despite being addressed by her. But once we attend to a speaker who has addressed us, and so come to comprehend the type of speech act she has performed, we will then owe her the sort of response that is called for by her act. Responding

---

[64] With thanks to Aleta Quinn, for suggesting this point to me (in conversation). Compare this treatment to that in Kukla and Lance (2009: 147).

properly to one who has told you something is one thing; responding properly to one who has made a request of you is another; responding properly to one who has issued you a directive is still another; and so forth.

In the remainder of this book I will be focusing primarily on the conversational pressures that are generated by the speech act(s) of asserting and telling. I do so because I think this type of act has been misunderstood in ways that derive from limited theories: ethicists tend to think of asserting and telling from the point of view of the ethical dimension of these acts, and so tend to ignore or (more often still) to mischaracterize the epistemological dimension; whereas epistemologists tend to think of asserting and telling from the point of view of the epistemological dimension of these acts, and so tend to mischaracterize or (more often still) to ignore normative dimensions beyond the epistemic. What I will try to do in what follows is over a unified account of both dimensions. I will begin simply by laying out what I take those dimensions to be.

Appendix to Chapter 2

Yo Kukla and Lance!

In their 2009 book *'Yo!' and 'Lo!'*, Quill Kukla (writing as Rebecca Kukla) and Mark Lance draw our attention to the underappreciated speech act of the vocative—the act by which we 'call' another person. Their paradigmatic examples are cases of utterances such as 'Yo Mark!' and 'Hey Quill!' They designate these as 'calls' and offer an analysis of them. In this appendix I argue that their analysis is wrong in a most ironic way: they fail to appreciate that the fact that vocatives are acts which speakers direct at particular individuals—the target(s)—means that these acts do not single out their target *by identification*, but rather do so in a way that is similar to how a speaker singles out an object as her intended reference. Donnellan taught us about the referential use of definite descriptions; I'd like to suggest that there are Donnellan cases for vocatives too.

I begin with the account Kukla and Lance offer. They write that the vocative—the act of calling another person central to the act of addressing them—is an act in which the speaker 'call[s] upon [the target] to recognize that he has been properly recognized'. (138) In this respect an act such as the utterance of 'Hey Quill!' is an instance of what they call a 'recognitive', a speech act 'that serves to express recognition of something that makes itself present to the receptive faculties of the speaker' (137). This element of recognition goes hand in hand with their idea that in performing a speech act of this sort, one identifies the target. Thus—using 'hail' as a stand-in for 'call'—they write,

> You cannot hail someone unless you recognize that he is there to be hailed, and part of what your hail expresses is this very recognition. (138)

Recognizing the hail [directed at me] involves recognizing not just its presence but its target, it source, and its binding force, which is inseparable from taking it as really aimed *at me*—as making a real claim [of acknowledgement] on me *in virtue of having correctly identified me*. (139; second italics mine)

There is much to recommend this sort of analysis: the claim that calls (hails; vocatives) call for acknowledgement, and that they are essentially second-personal (2009: 151–2), strike me as important insights about the nature of the phenomenon. But the inclusion of an identificatory element in the call, I want to argue, is importantly mistaken.

Since I want to give a counterexample to their thesis that the phenomenon at issue—the call—involves an identificatory element, it will be important to make sure that we can agree on the extent of the phenomenon itself. The subject matter they aim to be talking about under the rubric of the 'call' is the act wherein one person directs herself to another and 'calls upon the target to recognize that he has been properly recognized'. In keeping with the vocabulary of Chapter 2 I might favour the expression 'address' instead of 'call', but I won't insist on this. What I would like to insist on is that such speech acts need not have an identificational element, and indeed that they can succeed even when they have an identificational element that fails to pick out the right person (in a way made familiar by Donnellan (1966)).

I begin with an example in which one subject successfully hails another despite misidentifying the target. Consider: you are at the local store, and seeing someone you take to be Bob, you call out 'Hey Bob!' Only it's not Bob; it's Tom. I submit that if it is mutually manifest that you have targeted him—you are looking him in the eye, your wave is directed to him, you are starting to walk over to him—then you have succeeded in 'hailing' Tom, in 'calling' him, in 'addressing' him. Evidence for this comes from the fact that the sort of normative demands that Kukla and Lance associate with the call—the need to acknowledge having been the target of the act, and the need to respond—are both present here in connection with Tom. He ought to acknowledge that you have hailed him, albeit under the misimpression that he is Bob. Thus he might respond with, 'Sorry, you got the wrong person.' Still, he ought to respond; again, assuming that it is mutually manifest that you are looking him in the eye etc., it would be wrong for him simply to ignore the call. This is evidence that you succeeded in addressing (alternatively: hailing) him even though you mistook him for Bob.

Indeed, we can even find examples in which the identificational element does succeed in singling someone out, albeit not the person who was the intended target of the hail, where it is the intended target, not the person singled out by the identificational element, who is hailed. (These cases have a decidedly Donnellan-like feel to them.[65]) Suppose that it is common knowledge that all employees in the shop are to be hailed with 'Kind Employee'. ('Oh Kind Employee, will you help me find the chargers?') Now suppose you are in the shop, needing help from a shop employee, and, mistaking a fellow in a bright red shirt for an employee, you say, 'Kind

---

[65] This example is owed to Todd Nagel, who suggested it to me, in conversation.

Employee, would you help me find the basinettes?' Here it is mutually manifest to everyone that you mistook him for a shop employee. Even so, you have addressed him, called him, hailed him. You have done so under the misimpression that he is a shop employee, to be sure, but you have hailed him nevertheless. Indeed, this remains true even if, unbeknownst to you, there was a shop employee just out of visual contact, who heard your request and recognized your error and immediately came to your aid. You didn't address *that* person, even though she was both the nearest employee and the only employee to have overheard your request.

It might be thought that neither of these counts as a hail. After all, the speaker mistook the individual in question for someone else, or for someone who was an employee. But this response is implausible on its face—given these examples, why think that to hail someone you need to correctly identify them? Even waiving this point, though, it is a trivial matter to extend the cases so that there can be no doubt at all about the success of the hail. In the first case, you mistook Tom for Bob, but the point of your hailing *him* was to tell him that he is tracking mud all over the store—something you can do even having misidentified him, and something which requires your having hailed *him* (whoever he happens to be).[66] In the second case, you mistook that poor fellow for a shop employee, but you are the sort of person that doesn't care from whom you get the help—whether the person is an employee or not. What you care about is to be able to request help from *him*—something you can do even having misidentified him as an employee, and something which requires that it be *him* whom you have hailed (even if he isn't an employee). I can't see how it can be reasonably maintained that these are not successful hails.

Notice that in neither of these cases is there any recognition required to succeed in hailing or calling the target—or at least no recognition of the sort Kukla and Lance think is essential to vocatives. (This is the sort of recognition corresponding to what they allege is the identificatory dimension of the hail.) It may be that one needs to recognize the target as a proper object of a call: you can't hail a rock, or a tree, or a lemon. But you don't need to recognize *the particular individual* in question. You can succeed in calling an individual whom you mistake for someone else, just as you can succeed in calling an individual whose role you misconstrue. All that you need to do to succeed in calling an individual is to make manifest to the target that you are targeting him/her/them in an act which you intend them to recognize as having the significance of a call directed at them. Regarding what significance that is, I am inclined to think that Kukla and Lance have it broadly correct,[67] save in their insistence that an identification (and corresponding recognition) are required.

It is curious that Kukla and Lance should be open to this criticism. After all, few theorists have stressed the importance of our attending to the pragmatics of

---

[66] This parenthetical remark has two purposes. First, and most obviously, it is to make clear that the semantic condition set down by the identificational element of the act need not be satisfied if the act is to succeed as a hail. But second, and less obviously, it is to make clear that, as with cases of speaker reference generally, the act of securing a (speaker) reference need not proceed by identification (by description or by name) in the first place, but instead can be a matter of what is mutually contextually salient to speaker and would-be addressee.

[67] See Kukla and Lance (2009: 138–45).

second-person calls more than they have.[68] What is more, they are keen throughout their (2009) not to make fallacious inferences from false assumptions about the centrality of semantics over pragmatics, or false assumptions about the centrality of declaratives among types of speech act. In effect, I am accusing them of making an error in this very ballpark: they are insisting on the semantic content of a description, or the semantic value of name, as a semantic condition on successful calling. So to them I say: Hey you two, that's not so!

---

[68] In addition to Kukla and Lance (2009), see also Lance and Kukla (2013).

PART II
THE SPEECH ACT: PERFORMANCE AND UPTAKE

3
Conversational Pressures, Interpersonal and Epistemic

1

This chapter develops a challenge that arises when we try to understand the normative dimensions of the speech acts in which a speaker advances a claim—the sort of act in which a speaker makes a statement, gives testimony, tells another something, makes an assertion, and so forth. On the one hand, there are epistemically proper ways to respond to an observed act of this kind: audiences who violate epistemic standards in their doxastic response to being told something are described, alternatively, as being *not epistemically entitled* to have accepted the testimony, or as having formed a testimonial belief that is *unwarranted* or *unjustified*.[1] On the other, there are interpersonally proper ways of responding to an act of this kind: audiences who respond in certain (inappropriate) ways to being told something are described, alternatively, as *wronging, harming, insulting, abusing, slighting, rebuffing,* or *disrespecting* the speaker.[2] The challenge is to see how these two kinds of normative assessment relate to one another, and how the two associated normative pressures interact.

There need be no mystery in the thought that, when an audience responds to a telling, he is under conversational pressure that is at one and the same time both epistemic and interpersonal. But there are some thorny questions theorists must face as we seek to understand these sources of normativity in conversation. What, precisely, is the nature of the interpersonal and epistemic dimensions of conversational pressure? What are the mechanisms by which these types of normative pressure are brought to bear on conversational participants? Do these sources of normativity ever pull in opposing directions?

---

[1] This is the domain of the epistemology of testimony, for which see the references below.
[2] This is a domain that includes issues of epistemic injustice, for which see the references below.

This chapter is the first of several in which I address these matters. My main ambition here is merely to characterize these types of conversational pressure, and to identify the questions that must be answered if we are to have an adequate characterization of them. This will pave the way for the next two chapters, where I evaluate and reject several extant accounts (Chapter 4) and go on to give my own preferred account (Chapter 5).

2

It should come as no surprise that epistemology is a source for one sort of pressure that arises in connection with acts of telling. However, since a proper account of this pressure will require delving into matters that are controversial, care needs to be used in bringing the point out.

Consider an audience's epistemic perspective just prior to, and then on observing, a speaker's telling her that p. At a minimum, an audience who observes this has a new piece of evidence, corresponding to her observing of this act of telling. Some epistemologists will go further and will say that an act of telling someone something is no (mere) piece of evidence, but functions in a different way from other (non-testimonial) evidence she has.[3] But however we represent the contribution to the addressee's epistemic perspective when she observes another speaker tell her that p, her epistemic perspective has changed. It may be that certain things that were unreasonable to believe before the observed telling become reasonable afterwards; it may be that the addressee thereby acquires the basis for a justified or perhaps even knowledgeable belief that p; and so forth. Epistemic norms provide the standards for transitions of this kind. Some of these transitions are rational, or result in justified belief and knowledge; others are irrational, and result in unjustified belief. But there can be little doubt but that epistemic norms bear on how one reacts to observing another speaker tell one that p. We might call the pressure that derives from these norms *rational* or *epistemic* pressure: insofar as some doxastic reactions to the observation of the telling conform to these norms while other reactions do not, *one is under rational or epistemic pressure to ensure that one's doxastic reactions conform to epistemological standards.*

---

[3] See e.g. Hinchman (2005), Moran (2006).

Precisely what does epistemology tell us about the proper or permissible way to respond to another speaker's telling us that p? This is one of the central questions in the epistemology of testimony. I will not go into details here, save to identify two main competing views. One of them, the so-called *reductionist* view, holds that it is not epistemically permissible—alternatively, one is not epistemically entitled—to accept another's telling unless one has reasons, independent of the telling, to regard this act as credible (sincere and reliable). Another, the so-called *anti-reductionist* view, holds that it is epistemically permissible—alternatively, one is epistemically entitled—to accept another's telling so long as one lacks reasons for doubt (whether about the sincerity or competence of the speaker, or the truth of the attested proposition). This view is called anti-reductionism insofar as it does not construe one's permission to accept the telling as reducible to one's other reasons to regard that testimony as credible.

For my purposes in this chapter, it does not matter which of these is the correct view. Either way, epistemology yields norms for the proper or permissible doxastic reaction to an observed telling, and an audience who observes a telling addressed to him is thereby under epistemic or rational pressure to conform to the norm(s) in question.

This point can be generalized along two different dimensions.

First, while I have been speaking about the speech act of *telling*, the point would appear to hold for all cases of *assertion* and *testimony* more generally. Here is how I propose to talk about these speech act categories. The most general category is that of an assertion, and we can think of tellings and testimonies as special cases. A *telling* is an assertion that is made with the manifest intention of informing an audience of the truth. Not all assertions are tellings: a student might assert the answer to a question posed by her teacher, but does not thereby intend to inform the teacher (or perhaps anyone else for that matter); a liar asserts in the hope that she is taken to be trying to inform, but typically her real intention is to deceive (either about the facts or about her beliefs); etc. In addition to *tellings* and *assertings*, some authors speak of *testimony* and *testimonies*. This too can be characterized as a subclass of assertions. Take the members of the class of assertions that p; identify those that either purport to be providing epistemically high-quality information to an audience, or else which can be treated by an audience as so purporting; and call this the class of testimonies. For my purposes here, however, I will use 'assertion' and 'testimony' interchangeably.

Epistemic norms would appear to cover all three types of speech act (asserting, telling, testifying). It may be that the norms differ according to whether one can discern that the speaker's aim is to inform;[4] but even if this is so, for any case in which an assertion is made, there are epistemically proper ways for an audience to respond, and epistemically improper ways for an audience to respond. So it would seem that there will be epistemic pressure in any case involving assertion, whether or not it is a case of telling.

The second way in which my present point can be generalized is this. While I have been speaking about cases in which the audience is the addressee, it seems that this is not crucial to the present point I am making. For the present point is that for any observed assertion, there are epistemically proper ways to respond and epistemically improper ways to respond. This is so even if there is an epistemic difference in what is proper, according to whether one is an addressee or a mere overhearer. The present point is important as it makes clear that testimonies (and not just tellings) will generate epistemic pressure on anyone who attends to them.

3

It should also come as no surprise that, in cases in which one is the addressee of another's testimony that p, there is an interpersonal dimension to conversational pressure in addition to the epistemic dimension just described. (I will go on to argue that the basic point holds for *anyone* who observes a speaker give testimony, whether the audience is the addressee or a mere overhearer; but I begin with the case in which one is addressed, as this is the easier and less controversial case.) The point here is not that when another tells us something we are under pressure not to be rude or insulting. This is of course true (ordinarily). The relevant point is rather that there would appear to be a distinctively interpersonal set of norms or demands that come into play in speech contexts in which another speaker tells us something.

This point has been noted by a good many philosophers. Many have remarked that when a speaker tells an audience something, the speaker can feel hurt if she is not believed. Thus Elizabeth Anscombe noted that

> It is an insult and may be an injury not to be believed. At least it is an insult if one is oneself made aware of the refusal, and it may be an injury if others are. (Anscombe 1979: 9)

---

[4] This hypothesis has been defended by E. Fricker (2012, 2017), though I myself have raised doubts (Goldberg (2011b, 2015b)).

While Anscombe speaks of the 'insult' and potential 'injury' of not being believed, her more general point might be taken to be that there is an interpersonal normative dimension to an audience's response to a speaker's say-so. This is a theme echoed in more recent work as well. Ted Hinchman describes the speech act of telling itself as involving a kind of 'invitation to trust', such that if the audience improperly gives no credence to what he was told this amounts a kind of 'slight' or 'rebuff' to, and even a kind of 'abuse' of, the speaker (Hinchman 2005: 565, 568). Richard Moran speaks of the 'offense' that is committed by hearers who do not react appropriately to tellings (Moran 2006: 301). And Thomas Simpson underscores Anscombe's original point by flatly asserting that '[i]t is an insult to refuse to trust' (Simpson 2012: 562).

The authors just quoted appear to have in mind the sort of case in which a speaker tells an audience something, and they appear to think that the interpersonal dimension of the conversational pressure trades on the face-to-face and second-personal nature of the situation in which one speaker addresses another. It is in this context that language like 'insult,' 'slight,' and 'rebuff' make sense; and it is also in this context that conceiving of the speech act itself as an 'invitation to trust' can seem apt. But it is important to note as well that there is also a tradition that appears to be conceiving of the interpersonal dimension as pertaining to any case of testimony whatsoever—that is, any case in which one person, the audience, observes another person, the speaker, state (assert; avow; inform; testify; etc.) that p. This tradition, which became broadly known with the publication of Miranda Fricker's 2007 book *Epistemic Injustice*, has long been developed in interesting and novel ways by feminists and race theorists. Fricker's own way of presenting the matter is to draw our attention to cases of 'testimonial injustice', in which 'prejudice on the hearer's part causes him to give the speaker less credibility than he would otherwise have given', thereby 'wrong[ing] a speaker in his capacity as a giver of knowledge, as an informant' (Fricker 2007: 4, 5). While Fricker herself often speaks of the face-to-face second-personal encounter in which one tells another something, it is important—and below I will be arguing—that this is not central to the normative feature she is most interested in. On the contrary, her point about epistemic injustice would seem to hold whether or not one is the addressee: so long as another offers her testimony, her audience would appear to owe it to her not to treat her, and so her testimony, unjustly. This point is picked up by Jeremy Wanderer, who speaks of the 'testimonial insult' of not having one's say-so taken seriously, as when it is not treated 'as a genuine input to the deliberative process' (Wanderer 2012: 16). Failing to treat another's say-so 'as a genuine input to the deliberative process' is something one can do whether or not one was addressed by that say-so.

I just noted that these authors appear to focus on different sorts of case: face-to-face tellings, and testimonies more generally. Unsurprisingly, it is not entirely obvious that the interpersonal harms that these authors identify are the same: perhaps there is one sort of harm perpetrated in face-to-face cases in which an addressee reacts in an interpersonally improper fashion to being told something, and another sort of harm perpetrated in cases in which one reacts in an interpersonally improper fashion to *overhearing* a telling addressed to another. This is something that must be sorted out in any complete account of the interpersonal pressure involved in these cases.[5] Even so, it is important not to lose sight of what these authors agree on. For whatever their ultimate analysis of the source and nature of these harms is, they appear agreed that there are ways of reacting to a speaker's testimony[6] whereby an addressee or audience who responds in one of these ways thereby *wrongs* the speaker in her capacity as a testifier. If this is so, then an account of the nature of this wrong (or these wrongs) is an account of another kind of normative pressure on an audience who observes another's testimony: interpersonal norms mandate that the audience not react in these ways, on pain of exhibiting one or another of the sorts of wrong described by the authors above. This is so whether the interpersonal norms in question are those of ethics or justice, or they are more broadly social norms.

4

On the face of it, then, the case of telling would appear to be a curiosity: an audience who is addressed by a speaker who tells the audience something is under a combination of *epistemological* and *interpersonal* normative pressure to respond appropriately.

I think that a good many authors in this literature have been less impressed by the theoretical task here than they ought to be. To be sure, a good many people writing in the literature have observed, and have tried to theorize about, the potential clash of interpersonal and epistemic norms in speech encounters *as these arise in specific domains*. For example, there is a

---

[5] I will be developing my own positive account in Chapter 5 of this book.
[6] Let this cover the cases involving tellings as well.

cottage industry of people who worry about how interpersonal and epistemic norms interact in cases in which one is encountering new testimony about a friend (whether from the friend herself or from some third party): these theorists address the worry that one may have an interpersonal duty of friendship to be epistemically partial towards one's friends, in which case the norms of friendship clash with the epistemic norms of belief. (I will address this issue at length in Chapter 7.) But if I am right, this is a special case of a perfectly general phenomenon: any case in which a speaker states that p, and an audience observes this, the audience is under a combination of interpersonal and epistemic conversational pressures to respond appropriately.

It follows that many of the same questions that have been asked regarding the more specific subdomain of epistemic trust in friendship can be posed in connection with the general phenomenon itself. For example, what in general is owed, both interpersonally and from an epistemological perspective, to a speaker who testifies that p? Can it happen that the interpersonal and epistemic demands pull in different directions in a particular case? That is, can there be cases in which the interpersonal relationship between speaker and audience makes it so that the audience owes it to the speaker to respond in one way, but where this interpersonally required response involves a doxastic reaction that epistemology itself *forbids* (as irrational, unjustified, unwarranted, or what-have-you)? If we think this can't happen, what guarantees this? And why does it seem (to some people, anyway) as though this can happen?

5

I believe that we can use the foregoing as a way to impose several adequacy constraints on any theory of conversational pressure that hopes to illuminate the case of testimony and telling. In particular, there are several things that must be accounted for in this domain. The foregoing makes clear that, when a speaker testifies or tells another something, she has normative expectations for being treated properly, where this is a matter of proper treatment relative to the interpersonal norms in play (whether of ethics and justice, or social norms more generally); and insofar as a speaker is entitled to these expectations, they place audiences under normative pressure to respond appropriately. But the foregoing also makes clear that, as they react to the speaker's say-so, audiences face another source of distinctly epistemological pressure as well: their doxastic reactions must conform to epistemic standards. Both of these sources of pressure must be adequately explained. I believe that doing so will require an adequate answer to no less than five distinct questions.

To begin, we would like to characterize the *scope* of what I will call the *speaker's expectation of proper treatment*. By this I will understand the speaker's normative expectation *not* to be treated in any of the (interpersonally improper) ways described above. Clearly, the scope is restricted to that subset of speech exchanges involving acts in which a speaker *advances a claim with a particular content*. Still, we might wonder whether the expectation of proper treatment holds only in those cases involving tellings directed at an addressee (or addressees), or whether it holds more generally in any case in which a speaker's testimony is observed by an audience (whether addressed or as mere overhearers). I will call this the **scope question**.

Second, we would like to discern the *source* of the phenomenon of the speaker's expectation of proper treatment. Here we should distinguish two questions. The first is the *descriptive source question*: why is it that, as a matter of fact and often enough, speakers who make claims do expect proper treatment? The other is the *normative source question(s)*: in virtue of what (and in what sense) are such expectations appropriate, and what entitles speakers to have them? In this book I will be interested primarily in the **normative source question**(s), though I will have things to say about the **descriptive source question**.

Third, we would like to articulate *the content* of the expectation of proper treatment: precisely what is a speaker entitled to expect when, having advanced a claim of the relevant sort, she expects proper treatment by her audience? Here it is natural to think that our answer will be intimately related to our answer to the normative source question: whatever it is that generates a speaker's entitlement to expect proper treatment will determine what proper treatment involves, and so will determine the precise content of the expectation to which the speaker is entitled. I will call this the **content question**.

Fourth, and relatedly, we would like to identify the *nature of the wrong* that is done to a speaker when the expectation of proper treatment is violated. Here it is plausible to think that we can use the content of the expectation, together with the nature of her entitlement to have such an expectation, to identify the relevant kind(s) of wrong. I will call this the **nature of the interpersonal demand question**, since in effect what is demanded is that these wrongs not be committed.

Finally, we would like to know how the interpersonal normative pressure on an audience, as he reacts to a speaker's claim, is related to the *epistemological dimension* of the question whether to accept her claim. It is plausible to suppose that whether to accept a speaker's claim on a given occasion turns on whether it is epistemically proper to do so.[7] If this supposition is false, we would like to know why; and if it is true, we would like to know how the speaker's expectation of proper treatment bears on the epistemology of testimony. I will call this the **epistemological question**.

In light of what we would like explained and how these topics relate to one another, I submit that any adequate account of the phenomenon will have to satisfy five distinct constraints, as follows:

SCOPE: identify the domain of claimings in which the speaker will have, and is entitled to have, an expectation of proper treatment, where this expectation is the sort that in play in the four other constraints.

ENTITLEMENT: identify what generates the speaker's entitlement to expect proper treatment (when she advances a claim);

CONTENT: characterize the content of the expectation of proper treatment;

INTERPERSONAL DEMAND: specify the nature of the wrong that is done when an audience violates this expectation;

EPISTEMOLOGY: show how the speaker's expectation of proper treatment coheres with an acceptable account of the epistemology of testimony.

The satisfaction of each constraint is necessary for adequacy, in that the failure to satisfy any one of them will leave us without an explanation of one or more of the above; and the satisfaction of all five is sufficient for adequacy, in that if they are all satisfied then we will have a full account of the phenomenon we are seeking to understand.

---

[7] As we saw above, not everyone agrees that this is the *only* thing that should determine whether it is proper for the audience to accept the speaker's claim. Some think that in cases in which the speaker and audience are intimates (close friends or family members), considerations of friendship can enter into the question whether it is proper to accept what one is told. Others think that the very act of telling is itself an act with a salient interpersonal dimension, and the morality of this act itself underwrites a kind of ('second-personal') reason for belief. I disagree with both of these views. I will be returning to discuss the latter below, and the former in Chapter 5.

6

In this chapter I have begun to lay out the demands on a theory that would account for the conversational pressure that is generated by speech acts in which a speaker advances a claim. While the precise scope of the inquiry is itself something to be settled in the course of theorizing, we can fix the contours by asking: what sort of conversational pressure is there on one in connection with one's attitude towards the proposition that p, when one encounters the relevant sort of speech act in which the speaker claims that p? I have argued that there are (at least) two sources to this conversational pressure, one interpersonal, and one epistemic. I have also argued that any adequate account of this pressure must be able to answer five distinct questions: in addition to the question about the scope of the phenomenon, there are also questions as to the speaker's expectation of proper treatment (the content of this expectation, the basis for the speaker's entitlement to it, and the nature of the wrong that is done when it is violated), as well as questions about how all of this fits into the epistemological dimension of accepting another person's say-so.

4
The Speaker's Expectation of Trust
Some False Starts

1

In Chapter 3, I argued that acts in the class that consist of assertions, statements, tellings, informing, reportings, avowings, and so forth generate conversational pressure on the relevant audience, and that this pressure has at least two dimensions—an interpersonal one and an epistemological one. The interpersonal dimension of the normative pressure in conversation arises because it is possible to react to another's speech act in such a way as to wrong the speaker, and speakers are entitled to expect not to be wronged in these ways—so that audiences are under (interpersonal) normative pressure not to do so. The epistemological pressure arises because there are epistemically proper and improper ways to respond to another's of assertion (or report or . . .), such that audiences are under epistemic pressure to respond doxastically in a way that conforms to the norms of epistemology.

I argued, too, that any adequate account of conversational pressure in these cases must satisfy five distinct adequacy conditions. It must

> identify the domain of claimings in which the speaker will have, and is entitled to have, an expectation of proper treatment, where this expectation is the sort that is in play in the four other constraints [the SCOPE constraint];
>
> identify what generates the speaker's entitlement to expect proper treatment (when she advances a claim) [the ENTITLEMENT constraint];
>
> characterize the content of the expectation of proper treatment [the CONTENT constraint];
>
> specify the nature of the wrong that is done when an audience violates this expectation [the INTERPERSONAL DEMAND constraint];

show how the speaker's expectation of proper treatment coheres with an acceptable account of the epistemology of testimony [the EPISTEMOLOGY constraint].

To the best of my knowledge, no single account to date has explicitly addressed itself to all five constraints. (While several extant accounts are explicit in addressing one or two of them, and a few are explicit in addressing three or four, none explicitly addresses all five.) In an attempt to see whether one or another of these extant accounts can be made to address all five constraints adequately, I will be developing these accounts in ways that go beyond what their original authors said in developing them. My hope is that even if I do so in ways that their own authors would reject, the lessons that I will be drawing will still be of general interest. For it is the aim of this chapter to argue that certain currently popular ways of addressing some of the constrains above will force our hand in how we address others. This is true, I argue, even if the way I develop the accounts discussed here would be rejected by the original authors of the accounts.

2

I want to begin by considering several proposals that appeal to aspects of speech act theory in an attempt to address something in the neighbourhood of the set of constraints just described. I believe these accounts do not succeed, as they fail to have an eye on the epistemological dimension of the transaction. Bringing this out will put us in a position to better assess those accounts that purport to have a handle on the epistemology—something that I will do in the sections to follow.

I begin with a proposal by Allan Gibbard (from whom I borrow the phrase which is the title of this book). Recognizing the 'implicit demands and pressures' that a speaker puts on an audience in the course of conversation, Gibbard suggests that we understand these in terms of the act of *demanding*. Thus, describing the act wherein a speaker expounds on a topic, Gibbard writes,

> conversation is full of implicit demands and pressures. Suppose I confidently expound astrology, and you give no credence. The result will be discomfort: in effect, *I demand that what I say be accepted, and you will not accede.* (Gibbard, 1990: 172; italics added)

Following in the spirit of Gibbard, suppose we construe the act of making an assertion as involving a secondary act wherein one *demands* that one's audience accept what one asserted. Might we use such a model to provide an adequate account of each of the five constraints above?

I begin with SCOPE. Insofar as Gibbard's account characterizes the pressure on an audience (to accept what is asserted) as the pressure to satisfy a *demand*, this account would appear to conceive of the scope of the phenomenon as including only those encounters in which it is manifest that one of the speaker's overarching aims in advancing her claim is that what she asserts be accepted. That is, Gibbard's account would appear to restrict the phenomenon to cases of tellings addressed to a specific audience. For *demands* are speech acts with a clearly second-personal dimension: one demands something of another person, and directs the demand specifically to her, with the intention that she recognize that she is the target of the demand (and acknowledge this accordingly).[1]

If this is the scope of the phenomenon, what is the source of the speaker's entitlement to *make* such a demand, and what is the content of the speaker's expectation on this score? Starting with the latter (content) question first, Gibbard appears to construe the expectation of proper treatment as the expectation *to be believed*. This is a very strong expectation. What entitles a speaker to this? That is, how might Gibbard's account satisfy the ENTITLEMENT constraint, given its answer to CONTENT? Well, there is one aspect of Gibbard's account that strikes me as on the right track: if you demand something of me, you expect me to comply. This much reflects the nature of the act of *demanding* something of someone. The difficulty, though, is in seeing what *entitles* a speaker to the expectation to be believed. This is where I think Gibbard's account breaks down. This is because, at least on the face of things, the authority behind the act of telling someone something is supposed to be *epistemic* authority, whereas the sort of authority that legitimizes a demand—the sort of authority that legitimizes the expectation that one's demand be met—would appear to be a species of *practical* authority. Insofar as practical authority does not entitle one to expect *to be believed* (i.e. to have one's say-so accepted), the demand model appears on the wrong foot from the start.[2]

---

[1] For a particularly clear analysis of the second-personal dimension of this, see Darwall (2005), Kukla and Lance (2009), and Lance and Kukla (2013).
[2] This is a point Stephen Darwall appreciates when he contrasts the sort of practical authority involved in making a claim on another person in the sort of second-personal relationships he is interested in, with the sort of epistemic authority involved in making claims about the world. He

Before considering how the demand model might be modified to deal with this worry (and I think some version of it can do so), I want to consider an alternative proposal by Michael Ridge, as Ridge's proposal avoids this problem altogether. Like Gibbard before him, Ridge is motivated to explain the 'conversational pressure' exerted on an addressed audience by one who claims that p. Ridge appear to agree with Gibbard about the scope of the phenomenon: like Gibbard, Ridge appears to think that a speaker performs the relevant speech act when she makes an assertion and addresses this assertion to another person. But Ridge regards the relevant sort of pressure differently from Gibbard, and so presumably his account has a different approach to addressing the ENTITLEMENT and CONTENT constraints. Ridge explains:

> to assert that p is not only to express the belief that p; it is also to exert a kind of conversational pressure on one's interlocutor to adopt the belief that p.... Moreover, the form of conversational pressure involved here constitutes a way of *advising* someone to believe that p, and is not simply goading or manipulation. (Ridge 2013: 58; italics added.)

Ridge's view would thus appear better suited than Gibbard's in addressing the combination of CONTENT and ENTITLEMENT. To see why, consider a speaker S who *advises* A to believe that p. Like demanding, advising is an act with a distinctly second-personal dimension: one advises another, targeting that person and expecting her to recognize being so targeted, and to acknowledge this accordingly. Only the acknowledgement one expects from an addressee when one *advises* him to do something is very different from the acknowledgement one expects when one makes a *demand* of him. To demand that another do such-and-such is to expect him to recognize one's authority in making this demand. This was why Gibbard's account seemed off on the wrong foot, since ordinarily the authority for making a demand is a practical authority, and yet the sort of authority relevant to acts of telling is epistemic authority. But now consider the sort of acknowledgement one expects from an addressee when one *advises* him to do such-and-such. Here, one expects to be recognized by the addressee as having presented his doing such-and-such as something that is *advisable*, that *it is in his interests to do*.

---

writes, 'by its very nature, belief is responsible to an independent order of fact, which it aims to represent in a believer-neutral way' (Darwall 2006: 56), so that epistemic authority 'is not second-personal all the way down' (57). This contrasts with the sort of authority involved in the practical sphere, which 'derives from normative relations that reciprocally recognizing persons assume to exist between them' (60).

In at least some respects, this advising model has better prospects of satisfying the various constraints above. Insofar as the generation of conversational pressure by an assertion is modelled on the act of *advising* the addressee to believe what she was told, the advisee can assess this act, as better or worse, on the basis of what recommends it. Accordingly, the proposal that (when addressed to another) assertions are, among other things, *advisings* to believe does not require us to model the conversational pressure of a telling on the strength of the asserter's *practical* authority. What is more, we might think that one who offers advice is owed some further sort of acknowledgement, as having done something that manifestly purports to be in the addressee's interest. Thus, this proposal can address CONTENT by saying that the speaker's expectation of proper treatment is an expectation to be recognized as having offered the advice that the addressee believe what he has been told. What is more, to be recognized in this way is to be recognized as having done something that can be assessed as good or bad, according to whether it really *is* in the addressee's interests to do as advised. So a speaker might then expect that her speech contribution will be assessed by the addressee as good or bad, according to whether it really is in her interests to do as advised (and so to believe what was said). And we might think that in this way Ridge's proposal can address INTERPERSONAL DEMAND too: the addressee harms the speaker when he fails to assess the advice as he was called upon to do. This is an interpersonal harm akin to improperly rejecting someone's free offer of something when they make it clear to you that they think that it is in your interest to accept the item being offered.

So far, so good. Or so it might seem.

My worry about Ridge's view is that it does not, after all, capture the proper form for the addressee's acknowledgement to take—with the result that it cannot adequately address ENTITLEMENT, or indeed any of the other constraints (appearances to the contrary notwithstanding). Here I have three related worries.

First, the advising proposal fails to capture what the audience owes to a speaker who tells him that p. In particular, representing the speaker S who tells A that p as *advising* A to believe that p would appear to represent S as making too meagre a claim on A.[3] Confronted with another's advice, you can take or leave it (as it were)—and even if you summarily decide to leave it,

---

[3] Interestingly, in this respect Gibbard's *demand* proposal might come close to the strength of the normative pressure on an audience. See below.

and so don't accept the say-so, it is unclear how grave a wrong you have committed. (After all, it's no skin off your adviser's back.) In fact—and contrary to what was suggested above—it's not even clear that the adviser would have grounds for feeling insulted or wronged. Perhaps she would have such grounds if she had a personal relationship with you, or if you had asked her for advice, or if you were jointly engaged on a communal project whose success turns on your acceptance, or... But recall that we are trying to model the speaker's entitlement to expect proper treatment as it obtains in *any* case in which the speaker tells the addressee something, and clearly there are many cases of tellings that do not involve any prior relationship with the addressee, just as there are many cases of tellings that were not made in response to any queries.

Secondly, representing the speaker S who tells A that p as *advising* that A believe that p would appear to represent S as making the wrong kind of claim on A. One offers advice for practical reasons: I advise you to φ when I think it is best for you, all things considered, to φ. My advice is good advice if it is indeed best for you, all things considered, to φ. But this is not the right sort of basis to rationalize your acceptance of what I asserted. For I might well regard it as best for you to believe that p, all things considered, for reasons that have nothing to do with the truth of p. (Your life will go much better if you believe what I tell you.) This would not appear to be the sort of pressure I put on you when I tell you that p. This might be rectified if the sort of advising one does in asserting is restricted to the aim of *getting at the truth*. But then we want to know why there is this restriction in the sort of advice one offers in a telling. That this is not a trivial matter is clear once it is recognized that a speaker might regard it as in the overall interest of an addressee to believe something, even when the speaker recognizes the falsity of the proposition in question.

These first two worries are related to my third and most serious worry regarding Ridge's account. It is far from clear that one who advises another to φ is owed anything in connection with her status as an epistemic authority on the matter at hand. Consider that our reaction to *unsolicited* advice is largely dismissive. When I advise you to do such-and-such, and I do so without any prior background with you, you might well respond by thanking me; but it is far from clear that you *owe* it to me to assess the goodness of my advice. To be sure, you might owe it to me to do so if I were entitled to expect you to recognize me as a good adviser; but given that we have no previous relationship to speak of, it is unclear what might entitle me to expect this, merely in virtue of the fact that I have advised you. Might there be something in the nature of advising another person, that the adviser is entitled to expect to be *presumed* to be good at advising? (Perhaps the presumption would be defeasible, with defeat requiring reasons for doubt.) If so, the adviser would be entitled to expect the advisee not simply to dismiss the advice (with a 'thank you'), but instead to assess the goodness of the advice. But without this presumption—and I don't think the mere act of advising carries any such presumption—it is hard to see how an unsolicited piece of advice requires the addressee to assess its goodness, and so, if the conversational pressure on an addressee is modelled on the act of advising him to believe what he was told, it is correspondingly hard to see how there is much pressure at all on him to assess the goodness of this advice.

Interestingly, on this score Gibbard's demand model would appear to do a bit better than Ridge's advising model. When a speaker tells her addressee that such-and-such, it does seem that there is a kind of demand on the addressee. As I noted above, I think Gibbard misstates the content of the demand: I don't think that the demand is a demand to be believed. (At the very least, this is not the sort of thing that a speaker is *entitled* to expect.) And I continue to worry that insofar as the authority required to make a legitimate demand is a *practical* authority, the model is off on the wrong foot. But still there would appear to be something like a demand on the addressee. What is wanted, it seems, is a demand that comes, not from one's status as a practical authority who can legitimately make (practical) demands on one, but from one's status as an *epistemic* authority whose status as such imposes *epistemic* demands on one. If we had an account that made all of this clear, we might be able to see our way to satisfying all of the constraints above.

In sections 3–5 I will look at three authors who purport to do just this. While I will find grounds to criticize all of them, they will point us in a better direction.

3

I want to begin my discussion of the alternative accounts by noting one thing that they all have in common with Gibbard's and Ridge's accounts. With Gibbard and Ridge, the accounts I am going to consider in sections 3–5 all regard the speaker's entitlement to expect proper treatment as generated by the performance of the speech act in question. But going beyond Gibbard and Ridge, they conceive of the performance of this sort of speech act in distinctly epistemological terms. In this respect they are advances over Gibbard and Ridge. Disagreement arises between them when we consider the *type* of speech act that is in question (tellings vs. assertions more broadly), as well as the *features* of that speech act which account for the entitlement to expect proper treatment. What is the relevant sort of speech act, and what features of that act are responsible for generating the speaker's entitlement to expect proper treatment?

In my opinion, the most detailed of the attempts to answer these questions is owed to Ted Hinchman (2005). He regards the type of act in question as a telling, and he conceives of tellings as 'invitations to trust'. It is worthwhile beginning with an extended quote from Hinchman himself. He writes,

> Imagine [audience] A manifestly looks as if he needs to learn the time, so [speaker] S tells him it's noon, but A doesn't regard himself as having thereby acquired any entitlement to believe it's noon. Imagine not that A regards himself as having acquired an entitlement to believe it's noon that gets defeated by such background knowledge as that S's watch tends to run fast, but that A regards himself as not having acquired any entitlement, not even a (now defeated) prima facie entitlement, to believe it's noon.... [Here,] A is failing to acknowledge S—he is, as we say, 'slighting' S.... [T]he explanation of S's sense of having been slighted... [is that] she has tendered an invitation to A to trust her and has explicitly been rebuffed.
> (Hinchman 2005: 565)

Glossing this, Hinchman goes on to provide an account of the nature of the 'abuse' involved in this sort of case:

> In telling A that p, S offers him something, an entitlement to believe that p, which she conceives as his for the taking. In recognizing her intention to tell him that p, A satisfies that intention, and S thereby counts as telling him that p. But in refusing to acknowledge the entitlement, he refuses the offer she makes in telling him that p.... [W]hat's at stake for S when she tells A that p is his recognition of her as worthy of his trust.
> (Hinchman 2005: 568)

In what follows I want to explore how this sort of view might try to address all of the remaining adequacy constraints.

To see how Hinchman's proposal addresses CONTENT, consider his claim that 'what's at stake for S when she tells A that p is his *recognition of her as worthy of his trust.*' Now Hinchman recognizes that an audience might have reasons for rejecting the speaker's statement—reasons that 'defeat' the 'prima facie entitlement' that the speaker offered. So we should interpret Hinchman as construing the expectation of proper treatment as an expectation of being recognized as 'worthy of [the audience's] trust', where this amounts to the following: speaker S is entitled to expect that her audience (A) *presume* her (S) to be trustworthy, where this presumption is defeated if A has sufficiently strong reasons for doubt. (In what follows, when I speak of the presumption of trustworthiness, I will assume that this presumption is defeasible in this way.)

Next, consider ENTITLEMENT. How does S's performing the act of telling, conceived as extending an invitation to trust, entitle S to expect to be presumed trustworthy (thereby putting pressure on A to so regard S)? Well, according to Hinchman, S's telling A that p involves S's tendering an invitation to A to trust S. This invitation is made in virtue of the facts that the act is one in which (i) S addresses A, (ii) S presents as true the proposition that p, (iii) intending thereby to be addressing A's need to know whether p, and (iv) intending as well to have the previous intention recognized by A. So our question is: how can the act of telling, so characterized, entitle S to expect A to presume her (S) trustworthy?

My answer is that it is not obvious that it does, since it is not obvious that it explains why the audience *owes it* to the speaker to presume her trustworthy. To bring out my doubts on this score, I want to consider a case in which what is offered is not a piece of information, but something else. Consider the following case:

The Chocolate Offer
Kimchi is aware that Juanita loves high-quality chocolate (and only high-quality chocolate). Kimchi is also aware that Juanita currently has no such chocolate to speak of, and that she manifestly looks as if she would love some. Kimchi then offers Juanita what she (Kimchi) regards as high-quality chocolate with the intention of addressing that lack, and she does so with the intention that Juanita recognize that this is her intention. Juanita recognizes these intentions.

I submit that, by themselves, the facts of this case do not entitle Kimchi to expect that Juanita will presume her (Kimchi) trustworthy in her chocolate-discernment. In particular, these facts do not underwrite the claim that Juanita would *wrong* Kimchi if she *didn't* presume her trustworthy in this regard. To be sure, Juanita's knowledge of the act that Kimchi performed gives Juanita a reason to believe that Kimchi regards the chocolate she offered Juanita as high-quality.[4] As a result, *if* Juanita has a reason to regard Kimchi's judgement on this score as good, this would give Juanita a reason to believe that the chocolate *is* high-quality. But it is hard to see why, in advance of having reasons bearing on Kimchi's chocolate-discernment, Juanita *owes it* to Kimchi to *presume* Kimchi's competence on this score.

Now insofar as Hinchman is committed to construing the expectation of proper treatment as an expectation to be presumed trustworthy, he is committed to thinking that tellings differ from offers of chocolate in this regard. But why is the presumption of trust owed in response to an act of telling, when it isn't owed in response to an act of proffered chocolate? After all, both cases involve scenarios in which something taken to be high-quality is offered in the commonly known intention of meeting the recipient's perceived need for high-quality things of that kind. So it cannot be any of *these* features that generate the entitlement to expect to be presumed trustworthy. And yet these are the only features Hinchman discusses in connection with the act of telling, conceived as an invitation to trust. It would seem, then, that Hinchman's analysis cannot satisfy ENTITLEMENT given his answer to CONTENT.

In fairness to Hinchman, he describes the act of telling, conceived as an invitation to trust, as an act in which the speaker intends the hearer to 'gain an entitlement to believe' what she is told through recognizing the speaker's intention (2005: 567). It might seem that he can appeal to this feature of the act of telling to address ENTITLEMENT. S's telling A that p makes available (to A) an entitlement to believe that p, in which case, absent stronger reasons for doubt, A should believe that p. S's expectation of being presumed trustworthy, then, can be represented as grounded in her expectation of being recognized as having offered her audience such an entitlement. Insofar as her speech intentions were mutually manifest, she would be entitled to this expectation.

The foregoing attempt to save Hinchman's account assumes that the mere performance of a certain type of speech act—the act of telling someone that p—provides a suitable epistemic basis to entitle the audience to accept what he was told (at least in the absence of reasons for doubt). How is this supposed to work? Although Hinchman (2005) is perhaps less than fully

---

[4] That is, she has such a reason so long as she has no reason to doubt Kimchi's sincerity in making the offer.

explicit, he might appeal to an idea presented by Richard Holton in connection with acts that invite others' trust. Here is Holton:

> ... I might think it appropriate to trust you to do a certain thing only if you invite me to do so; and it might be *that very invitation* that *leads me to think you reliable, since it signals a readiness to take on the responsibilities that my trust would bring.* (Holton 1994: 72; italics added)

While Holton is speaking of trust in general, Hinchman might apply Holton's point to the trust involved in cases in which one tells someone something. Such a construal of Hinchman's view is charitable. Not only does Hinchman employ Holton's language of 'invitation to trust' in describing the act of telling; what is more, construing him in this way appears to give his account what it needs to explain ENTITLEMENT. In particular, we can use Holton's mechanism to get at the distinctive kind of reason that (according to Hinchman) is generated by the act of telling: in telling you that p, and so inviting you to trust me, I give you a reason to think me reliable, since my invitation 'signals [my] readiness to take on the responsibilities that [your] trust would bring'. I am signalling this to *you* as my addressee; this readiness is not something I am offering to those whom I am not addressing. This would explain why Hinchman thinks overhearers do not get the same reasons for belief that are made available to the audience addressed (Hinchman 2005: 569).

In sum, Hinchman's revised approach to ENTITLEMENT, as reconstructed here, is this. S's act of telling A that p is an act in which S intends to make available to A an entitlement to believe that p. When S's intention itself is manifest to A, this gives A a reason to believe that S is reliable, since 'it signals [S's] readiness to take on the responsibilities that [A's] trust would bring'. When A has such a reason, A has a reason to believe that p, and so is entitled to believe that p unless A has stronger reasons for doubt. Putting all of this together, when S's intention in telling A that p is manifest to A, A ought to regard S as presumptively trustworthy with respect to p.

Unfortunately, this proposal is guilty of an illicit conflation. Since this conflation is at the heart of much theorizing about the sort of conversational pressure we are under when we encounter another's say-so, it behooves us to take care in bringing it out. I submit that the proposal above conflates

(i) entitling another—or giving another a reason—*to hold one responsible* in a certain way (a practical matter) and

(ii) entitling another—or giving another a reason—*to believe that one is responsible* in that way (an epistemic matter).

Let us grant (i): a speaker who invites an addressee's trust entitles the addressee to hold her responsible in the relevant way. In the case of a telling, this would presumably involve holding the speaker responsible for having sufficient evidence to provide an adequate epistemic basis for belief in the attested proposition (e.g. were the addressee to believe through accepting that telling). Even so, (ii) does not follow: even given (i), it does not follow that a speaker who invites an addressee's trust entitles the addressee to *believe* that the speaker *will* be responsible in the relevant way—that is, to believe that she *does* have such evidence. And it is clear that the two entitlements can come apart. Consider the teenager who tells his parents that he will be home by midnight. If the teen is not back by midnight, the parents will hold the teen responsible—'But you told us you'd be home by midnight!'—and they will do so whatever doubts they might have had when he originally told them of his plans. Or, for another example, consider the person with a known track record for lying. If he tells you that p, you are wary, and you probably don't regard yourself as having been given an entitlement to believe that p; but you will still hold him responsible if and when it is discovered that this statement, too, was a lie. The conflation between (i) and (ii) is thus illicit.

In response, it will be said that these are both examples in which the audience has grounds that defeat the entitlement to believe. Though correct, this point does not establish what Hinchman's defence requires. Hinchman contends that the very act of inviting to trust generates for the audience an entitlement to believe. The examples above suggest that we should distinguish between entitling an addressee to hold the speaker responsible (in connection with her trustworthiness), and entitling an addressee to believe that the speaker *will be* trustworthy. Once we make this distinction, it seems that invitations to trust generate only the former (practical) entitlement. Absent further argument, Hinchman's claim (that extending an invitation to trust generates an entitlement to believe) is groundless. And if this claim is groundless, we must conclude that our attempt at a charitable reconstruction of Hinchman's account of ENTITLEMENT fails to yield an adequate account: we have been given no explanation for how the speech act of telling entitles the speaker to expect to be *presumed* trustworthy.

We can draw a general lesson from this. Once the speaker's expectation for proper treatment is construed as an expectation to be presumed trustworthy, the plausible assumption that the speaker's entitlement to this expectation is generated by the act of telling itself will then commit us to regarding the very performance of the speech act itself as epistemically significant. The trouble is that Hinchman's account of the act of telling does not ascribe to that act features that would warrant regarding the act itself as epistemically significant in the required way. I conclude, then, that given how Hinchman's account answers CONTENT, it cannot simultaneously provide a plausible answer to ENTITLEMENT. If our goal is to understand the nature of the conversational pressure one is under when one is told that p, Hinchman's (2005) account fails to give us what we want.

4

Hinchman thought of tellings as invitations to trust; but perhaps we do better to construe tellings on the model of promising. This, I think, is close to the conception of telling that Richard Moran (2006) defends. He writes,

> ...the speaker, in presenting his utterance as an *assertion*, one with the force of *telling* the audience something, presents himself as *accountable* for the truth of what he says, and *in doing so he offers a kind of guarantee for this truth*. (Moran 2006: 283; italics in last phrase added)

Although Moran does not mention promises here, he does mention guarantees, and it is plausible to think of a guarantee as a kind of promise. Can this feature of telling—the implicit promise or guarantee that is made in the act of telling—allow us to address ENTITLEMENT, and so characterize what entitles a speaker to expect to be presumed trustworthy?

It might seem so. To see why, consider the act of promising itself. It can seem that if you promise me something, this gives me an epistemic reason to believe that your promise (guarantee) will be fulfilled. Thus Thomas Scanlon, remarking on the sort of trust one generates in the making of a promise, writes the following:

> ...[W]hen I say 'I promise to help you if you help me,' the reason I suggest to you that I will have for helping is just my awareness of the fact that not to return your help would, under the circumstances, be wrong: not just

forbidden by some social practice, but morally wrong....When I say 'I promise to be there at ten o'clock to help you,' the effect is the same as if I had said 'I will be there at ten o'clock to help you. Trust me.' In either of these utterances I do several things. I claim to have a certain intention. I make this claim with the clear aim of getting you to believe that I have this intention, and I do this in circumstances in which it is clear that if you do believe it then the truth of this belief will matter to you (perhaps, but not necessarily, because you may rely upon it in deciding what to do). Finally, I indicate to you that I believe and take seriously the fact that, once I have declared this intention under the circumstances, and have reason to believe that you are convinced by it, it would be wrong of me not to show up (in the absence of some truly compelling reason for failing to appear). The function of the expression 'I promise' need not be to invoke a social practice with its own special rules, but rather, like that of 'Trust me,' to indicate my awareness of the nature of the situation and my regard for the general moral fact that it would be wrong for me to behave in a certain way. (I call this a 'general' moral fact because it is not a fact peculiar to promising.)   (Scanlon 1990: 211)

For present purposes, Scanlon's basic point would appear to be this: if I promise you that I will φ, then I indicate to you that I recognize that I am under a moral obligation (to you) to φ—that I would wrong you were I not to φ. What is more, if you appreciate this, you can then treat my indication (of recognizing this moral duty) as an epistemic reason to believe that I *will* fulfil my moral duty. If that is so, then the act of promising generates for the addressee an epistemic reason to believe that the promise will be fulfilled.

In light of this, suppose that we think of the act of telling on the model of a promise. And suppose that we think that the promise that S makes in the act of telling A that p is the promise to A that S has the relevant evidence to warrant A's belief that p.[5] Such a view then appears to be well suited to avoid the objection I raised against Hinchman's account. In particular, the promising model of telling incorporates all that Hinchman's 'invitation to trust' model embraced, and more besides. It incorporates all that Hinchman's view

---

[5] Acts of tellings, unlike promises, have contents whose truth is typically not a matter over which the speaker has control. Consequently, since promises standardly concern states of affairs it is within the speaker's control to bring about, the implicit promise or guarantee in a telling must be construed as indirectly related to the truth of the telling. The proposal above is the most plausible version I can think of.

embraced, since (with Hinchman) the promising model holds that for S to tell A that p is for S to perform an act in which (a) S commits herself to the truth of p, and (b) S indicates to A that she stands ready to take on the relevant responsibilities. (Here again we can assume that the relevant responsibilities include those of having the relevant evidence and being able to provide this evidence as appropriate.) But the promising model incorporates more than this, since it also includes this: (c) S indicates her recognition that it would be morally wrong of her to fail in connection with the responsibilities in (b). According to the theory on offer, this condition, (c), is what generates for A epistemic reasons to believe that the responsibilities associated with the telling's promise will be fulfilled.

Consider now how the proponent of the promising model of telling might approach ENTITLEMENT. In telling A that p, S commits herself to the truth of p, and issues a guarantee as to her being relevantly responsible—thereby generating for A an epistemic reason to believe that S fulfils the evidential responsibilities associated with telling. Insofar as A recognizes that she has been offered such a reason, A ought to recognize that she has been given a reason to believe that p—namely, that S has (promised that she has) adequate evidence supporting p. So unless A has reasons for doubt, A ought to believe that p. But this is just to say that A's recognition that S has offered her such a reason is tantamount to A's recognition that S is to be believed regarding p unless A has reasons to the contrary—which in turn is tantamount to presuming S trustworthy with respect to p. It would thus seem that if S is entitled to expect A to recognize S's communicative intentions, S is thereby entitled to expect A to presume S trustworthy. Or so Moran and the promising/guaranteeing model might have it.

But I believe that, despite appearances, the foregoing account of ENTITLEMENT is susceptible to the very same objection I levelled against Hinchman's account: the appeal to promising adds nothing. It is one thing for a speaker S to do something that generates for her audience a reason to think that (S herself recognizes that) it would be immoral for S not to be trustworthy. When she does this, S gives her audience the right to *hold her responsible* for being trustworthy. This is precisely what a promise does;[6] and it is precisely what an act of telling, construed on the model of promising, does. But it is another thing for S to do something that generates for A a

---

[6] Compare Gary Watson, who writes, 'If you make a promise to me, you thereby authorize me to hold you responsible in certain ways; you undertake certain responsibilities' (Watson 1996: 237).

reason *to believe* that S *is* responsible. And it is the latter sort of reason that S would need to generate if she is to be entitled to expect A to presume her trustworthy. For if S's telling did not make it epistemically reasonable for A to believe that S has adequate evidence backing her (S's) telling, then A would be doing nothing wrong, *epistemically* speaking, in remaining agnostic regarding S's trustworthiness—in which case S's telling did nothing to 'earn S the right' to be presumed trustworthy. Nothing has been gained by the appeal to promising or guaranteeing.[7]

Moran himself comes very close to appreciating this point. He worries about how an act of telling, construed as involving a guarantee, can 'confer' on that act the sort of epistemic significance he needs it to have—that is, as an act that generates an epistemic reason for the audience to believe what they have been told. Moran's response to this worry is telling:

> ...for both parties this conferral [of epistemic significance on the act of telling] is by its nature an overt assumption of specific responsibilities on the part of the speaker. This is no more (or less) mysterious than how *an explicit agreement or contract alters one's responsibilities.*
>
> (Moran 2006: 288–9; italics added)

To my mind, this response only reinforces the objection above. The point of a contract or an explicit agreement, after all, is precisely to authorize or entitle the other party to *hold one responsible* for doing as the agreement or contract specifies. By contrast, one's *belief* that the contract *will* be fulfilled is justified, when it is justified, by one's evidence.[8] It is easy to lose sight of this since people typically don't enter into contracts unless they *already* have some evidence that their partner is reliable/trustworthy, and/or that the enforcement mechanisms are working properly. But of course this is not the picture the promising model offers us: that model has it that it is the very act of telling, construed as involving a promise, that generates one's epistemic reason for believing the teller/promissor to be trustworthy. It remains mysterious how this can be. In sum, we still lack an account of the sources and nature of the conversational pressure one is under when one is told that p.

---

[7] What is more, it would seem that the promising model of assertion is independently objectionable; see Owens (2006).

[8] Does saying this commit me to regarding testimony as merely a form of evidence from which the audience draws inferences? It doesn't; see section 6, where I address EPISTEMOLOGY from the perspective of my own account.

5

I turn now to the final extant proposal I want consider in this chapter, that of Miranda Fricker. I consider this now, both because my own view (to be presented in Chapter 5) is motivated in large part by hers, but also because of the prominence of her work. (She has been the most influential of those who have recently addressed the speaker's expectation of proper treatment.) To be sure, she has not explicitly addressed ENTITLEMENT. But her focus (in Fricker 2007) on INTERPERSONAL DEMAND and EPISTEMOLOGY, and her account of the justice and ethical dimensions of the speech act of testifying, constitute a novel way to approach ENTITLEMENT. It is true, of course, that the sort of wrong that Fricker has described under the label 'testimonial injustice' constitutes a special case of improper treatment of a speaker: it is the type that arises when 'prejudice causes a hearer to give a deflated level of credibility to a speaker's word' (Fricker 2007: 1). Even so, Fricker's reflections on the nature of this wrong suggest a more general way to think about the speaker's expectation of proper treatment.

Precisely what sort of wrong is involved when a speaker is the victim of testimonial injustice? Fricker notes that in such cases

> a hearer wrongs a speaker *in his capacity as a giver of knowledge, as an informant*....[T]he primary harm one incurs in being wronged in this way is an intrinsic injustice. (Fricker 2007: 5; italics added)

I submit that Fricker has put her finger on the source of the speaker's entitlement to expect proper treatment: when a speaker testifies to the truth of a proposition, certain dismissive reactions on the audience's part harm her in her 'capacity as a giver of knowledge, as an informant'. This suggests that the wrong in question is the failure to treat the speaker in the way that is due to a 'giver of knowledge' or 'an informant'. If this is correct, the speaker's entitlement to expect proper treatment reflects her entitlement to (expect to) be treated in a way befitting one who enjoys this status, when this status is manifested in the act of testifying.

Unfortunately, it is no straightforward matter to say what it is to be (and to be recognized as) a 'giver of knowledge', nor is it easy to discern what treatment is due to one who manifests this status in an act of testifying. In these respects Fricker's own reflections can leave us wanting more. To get at the status itself, she appeals to the distinction (owed to Craig (1999)[9]) between being an informant and being a mere source of information, where this is roughly the difference between explicitly and intentionally representing something as being the case and merely providing evidence that it is. While I think that this is on the right track, what we want explained in connection with ENTITLEMENT is how the very act by which one manifests one's status as an informant or a 'giver of knowledge' generates an entitlement to expect proper treatment. Unfortunately, on this matter, Fricker's account appears little better than the 'assurance' views of Hinchman and Moran. Fricker recognizes that speakers sometimes testify despite not having knowledge. In such cases, Fricker notes, it can be appropriate (= epistemically permissible) for a properly situated hearer to reject what S has to say, *without* wronging S as a 'giver of knowledge'. So the demand to recognize the speaker as a giver of knowledge cannot require regarding the speaker as *having* knowledge on every occasion on which she testifies. Nor will it help to understand this demand in terms of the speaker's entitlement to be *presumed* knowledgeable, for in that way lie objections analogous to the ones I raised against Hinchman and Moran. Unfortunately, Fricker appears to invite just such objections: when discussing the sort of treatment that is owed to one who testifies, she defends the claim that testimony is owed a 'default of credibility' (Fricker 2007: 60-9, 103-4, 136). Nor are we offered anything further with which to respond to the objections presented against Hinchman's and Moran's accounts.

In short, while Fricker's approach to the speaker's expectation of proper treatment starts off in a promising direction by locating the source of the entitlement in the speaker's status as a 'giver of knowledge', ultimately her own account does not withstand scrutiny. Still, I think we can take Fricker's promising start and do better. This will be my aim in Chapter 5.

---

[9] Grice (1957) had an earlier version of this distinction.

5
How to Treat a Testifier

1

In Chapters 3 and 4 I have been pursuing the idea that the sort of conversational pressure one is under when one observes another speaker's testimony can be understood in terms of the speaker's expectations of proper treatment, where a speaker is entitled to the expectation of proper treatment in virtue of having performed the speech act she did. In line with this I argued (in Chapter 3) that any adequate account of the conversational pressure in these types of case must satisfy five distinct constraints. It must

> identify the domain of claimings in which the speaker will have, and is entitled to have, an expectation of proper treatment, where this expectation is the sort that is in play in the four other constraints [the SCOPE constraint];
>
> identify what generates the speaker's entitlement to expect proper treatment (when she advances a claim) [the ENTITLEMENT constraint];
>
> characterize the content of the expectation of proper treatment [the CONTENT constraint];
>
> specify the nature of the wrong that is done when an audience violates this expectation [the INTERPERSONAL DEMAND constraint];
>
> show how the speaker's expectation of proper treatment coheres with an acceptable account of the epistemology of testimony [the EPISTEMOLOGY requirement].

And I argued (in Chapter 4) that no single account of these matters has succeeded to date.

Since the positive view I will be developing in this chapter emerges from the criticisms I levelled against the accounts from Chapter 4, it will be helpful to start with a brief recap of those criticisms. The structure of my critical remarks in Chapter 4 was this: if the speaker's expectation of proper treatment is an expectation to be presumed trustworthy, and if a speaker is entitled to this expectation by performing the act of telling (or some other act of advancing a claim), then we are owed an explanation for how the act of telling (claiming) generates that entitlement—and no account offered to date has provided this. All of the views considered in Chapter 4—the 'indirect speech act' views of Gibbard and Ridge, the 'Assurance' views of testimony of Hinchman and Moran, and the testimonial-injustice-based view of Miranda Fricker—fail insofar as the features they attribute to the act of telling or asserting do not underwrite an expectation to be presumed trustworthy. To be sure, Fricker's account appears to start off in a better direction, focusing on our status as 'informants' or 'givers of knowledge'. Still, her attempt offers nothing further with which to connect the act of telling to the speaker's entitlement to expect to be presumed trustworthy.

My aim in this chapter is to follow Fricker's lead in seeing the conversational pressure associated with testimony as deriving from a speaker's status as an 'informant' or a 'giver of knowledge', while rejecting the way Fricker connects this status to the speaker's expectation of proper treatment. With the authors I discussed in Chapter 4, I will continue to assume that a speaker's entitlement to expect proper treatment reflects the nature of the act she has performed when she testifies. However, I reject the claim that the expectation of proper treatment is an expectation *to be presumed trustworthy*. That is, I reject the answer that Hinchman, Moran, and Fricker all appear to give to CONTENT. At the same time, while I am rejecting Fricker's answer to CONTENT, I endorse her answer to INTERPERSONAL DEMAND, according to which a speaker who is not treated properly in connection with a claim she made is wronged (disrespected) in her capacity as a 'giver of knowledge'. The trick is to show how all of this emerges from the speaker's act of testifying itself. This is the trick I will aim to perform in this chapter.

2

It should be uncontroversial that a giver of knowledge is one who has the capacity to provide knowledge to others through performing a speech act in which she purports to do just that. Suppose that there are such speech acts— for now let's call this type of act the act of *testifying*—and suppose further that the purport of these acts can be discerned by one's audience. (I will return to this matter below.) Then we would be in a position to approach

CONTENT as follows: in testifying one is entitled to expect to be recognized as performing the sort of act through which one purports to make a piece of knowledge available to one's audience.

We can appreciate the precise content of the expectation to which the speaker is entitled on this score, as well as what sort of normative pressure this places on an audience, when we appreciate the nature of the job the testifier purports to be performing. Here is a job description for the relevant sort of speech act:

JOB DESCRIPTION
Present a content as true in such a way that, were the audience to accept it on the basis of accepting the speaker's speech contribution, the resulting belief would be a candidate[1] for knowledge.

A speaker succeeds in performing the job characterized in JOB DESCRIPTION only if she satisfies certain epistemic conditions (more on which in a moment). But independent of whether a speaker succeeds in performing the job, we are interested in the speech act in which she *purports* to do so. To a rough first approximation, it is this—purporting to perform the job in JOB DESCRIPTION—that is designated by the English verb 'to testify.'[2] (When the speaker succeeds in doing the job which she purports to be doing, we describe her as *informing* her audience.[3])

If what we are interested in is the nature of the conversational pressure exerted by the relevant (sub)class of testimony-constituting acts, we should focus our attention on this job—the job we purport to do when we testify. In particular, I want to argue, first, that a speaker's purporting to perform an act of the JOB DESCRIPTION sort *entitles* her to expect to be recognized as

---

[1] I say '*candidate* for knowledge' rather than 'knowledge', since things not pertaining to the speech act itself might prevent the audience's belief from attaining that status. For example, the audience might not have been entitled to accept the speech contribution. Here, of course, is the core issue in the epistemology of testimony. As I noted in Chapter 3, some epistemologists—'reductionists'—think that in order for an audience to be entitled to accept another's say-so, the audience must have suitable reasons for regarding the say-so as reliable; other epistemologists—'anti-reductionists'—think that it suffices that the audience has no reasons for doubting the reliability of the say-so. Happily, I don't have to settle this here.
[2] Compare E. Fricker (2017), where the speech act of telling is construed as purporting to take a certain kind of responsibility for the truth of what was told. Her view is an interesting mixture of a purport-based view and a promising model of telling.
[3] With thanks to Martin Smith.

having done so, and second, that it is by appeal to the nature of such acts that we can address the five core requirements from Chapter 3.[4]

The first step in our attempt to provide the account in question is to make clear the common knowledge that is generated when a speaker performs a speech act in which she purports to do what JOB DESCRIPTION says.[5] Here I assume—what I will be arguing in section 5 below—that there are straightforward and recognizable ways for a speaker to make manifest that she is performing an act of this kind. (These are ways that she would be entitled to assume are recognized by her audience.) If I am right about this, then when a speaker *has* performed an act of this kind, it should be a matter of common knowledge that she has done so. What is more, the purport of her act will (or should) be common knowledge as well. After all, if it is common knowledge that she has performed an act *of this kind*, then it is common knowledge which kind of act she has performed—where the kind of act in question is an act with the characteristic purport provided for in JOB DESCRIPTION. And since it is trivial—something anyone should know—that acts with a purport are successful as the kinds of act they are only when they *achieve* their purport (and unsuccessful otherwise), it will (or should) be common knowledge that the act the speaker performed was successful if and only if the speaker presented information as true in such a way that if her audience were to accept that information through accepting the speech contribution, the resulting belief would be a candidate for knowledge.

The second step is to make clear, as something that can also be assumed to be common knowledge, that if an act of this kind is to be successful, the speaker's speech contribution must satisfy certain distinctly epistemic standards. The reason for this should be obvious. The presentation of information as true in a speech act will be 'successful' in the sense required by JOB DESCRIPTION only if the belief that results when the audience accepts that speech contribution is a candidate for knowledge. But an audience's resulting belief *won't* be a candidate for knowledge unless the speech contribution itself has certain epistemic properties. To wit: you can't come to know what time it is if the speaker, in presenting a certain time as correct, just happened to guess the correct time, since in that case the truth of your resulting belief would be too lucky to count as a candidate for knowledge. Now, what is

---

[4] They are: SCOPE, ENTITLEMENT, CONTENT, INTERPERSONAL DEMAND, and EPISTEMOLOGY.

[5] At any rate, the common knowledge that the speaker is entitled to expect is generated.

involved in a speech contribution's having the right epistemic characteristics on this score—what is involved in it's being *epistemically well-off*, as I will call it—is a matter of some dispute. Some think that a speech contribution is epistemically well-off (and so is suitable for the knowledge-communicating role of testimony) only if the speaker has the knowledge that she is purporting to communicate;[6] others require that the speaker *express* that very knowledge in the speech act itself;[7] still others hold that it suffices for the speech contribution to be sufficiently reliable;[8] and there may be other possibilities still.[9] For my purposes the key point is simply this: when a speaker performs a speech act of this kind, it will be common knowledge that an audience who observes and comprehends the act will recognize that the act in question is successful only if the speaker's speech contribution is epistemically well-off.

The third step is to put all of this together. The nature of the act of testifying is that of performing a speech act in which one purports to fulfill JOB DESCRIPTION. Given a speaker S who testifies that p to an audience A, it will be common knowledge that S performed an act that is successful only if her (S's) speech contribution was epistemically well-off. What is more, someone who purports to do something whose success conditions are common knowledge can be taken to be presenting herself as purporting to satisfy those conditions.[10] (This is what it is for one's act to have the purport it has, when that purport is common knowledge.) But then insofar as those standards are epistemic standards that require that S occupy a certain epistemic standing with respect to the propositional content of her speech act, we get the result that, in testifying that p, S conveys that *she has the requisite standing*—which is to say, the relevant epistemic authority—for performing this act successfully. What S is entitled to expect of her audience A, then, is that S be recognized as having done precisely this (= conveyed that she has the requisite authority). What is more, in conveying that she has this authority, *S exerts normative pressure on her audience*: she is to be treated with the respect that is due to one who conveys having the relevant epistemic authority on the question whether p. And herein we have our account of CONTENT: the content of the expectation of proper treatment (when one testifies that p) is the expectation (i) to be recognized as someone who conveys that she is relevantly epistemically authoritative with respect to

---

[6] See e.g. Burge (1993), Audi (1997), Elizabeth Fricker (2006, 2012), among many others.
[7] See Turri (2011).   [8] See Lackey (1999, 2008).
[9] See e.g. Garcia-Carpintero (2004), Goldberg (2010).   [10] Compare Ross (1986: 77–8).

the truth of the proposition that p, and (ii) to be treated accordingly. To have your say-so summarily dismissed or dismissed improperly is to be disrespected in connection with the epistemic authority you have conveyed having had.

3

Before I go on to characterize what sort of treatment is due to one who conveys having such authority, it is necessary first to highlight the manner in which the foregoing enables us to give an account of ENTITLEMENT. The key contention is this:

Interpersonal Pressure
One who conveys that she herself has the relevant epistemic authority vis-à-vis the truth of a proposition she presented-as-true places her audience under Interpersonal (normative) Pressure to treat her with the sort of respect due to one who conveys having this authority.[11]

Interpersonal Pressure is what underwrites the idea that the audience 'owes it' to the speaker to treat her properly, where proper treatment is a matter of treatment appropriate to one who conveys having this authority. But what can be said in defence of **Interpersonal Pressure**? While a full answer is beyond the scope of this chapter, here I can outline the sort of answer I think ought to be given. It involves two claims, one about epistemic reasons, and the other about epistemic subjects:

EPISTEMIC REASONS
Necessarily, epistemic reasons are considerations that warrant (or contribute to the warrant of) doxastic attitudes in those who have such reasons.

EPISTEMIC SUBJECTS
Necessarily, people deserve respect partly in virtue of the fact that they are epistemic subjects, that is, subjects who are responsive to the epistemic reasons they have.

---

[11] I thank Alessandra Tanesini for emphasizing (in conversation) the importance of making the points in this paragraph explicit.

I do not intend either REASONS or SUBJECTS to be controversial. REASONS appears to be common ground among most philosophers, since it is the idea behind such widely acknowledged doctrines as that we ought to adjust our beliefs to our evidence, we ought to believe only what we have adequate (epistemic) reason to believe, and so forth. (And while I don't have space to defend this here, I suspect that there is a version of REASONS that refers, not to epistemic *reasons*, but to epistemic considerations more generally, of which epistemic reasons are a special case.) And, for its part, SUBJECTS appears to be common ground among theorists whose work aims to characterize the basis of respect for persons. We might think of SUBJECTS as the epistemic version of a more general thesis pertaining to subjects generally, to the effect that persons deserve respect partly in virtue of the fact that they are the sort of entity that is responsive to the total (practical and epistemic) reasons they have.

Suppose we combine REASONS and SUBJECTS with the three-step account developed above. The resulting picture is the basis for **Interpersonal Pressure**. Epistemic reasons warrant doxastic attitudes in those who have such reasons. One who testifies that p purports to be performing a job whose successful performance would require that she have (epistemically adequate) reasons in support of [p]. As a result, one who testifies that p conveys that she has such reasons. If she *does* have the reasons she purports to have, she has something that warrants a certain doxastic reaction—namely, belief in the very content of her act of telling. Insofar as she *conveys* that she has such reasons, she communicates to others that she has something that warrants a certain doxastic attitude on *their* part. To have her testimony summarily rejected, then, is to be disrespected in connection with her status as an epistemic subject—in particular, it is to be disrespected as a subject who conveys having the epistemic authority to settle the question at issue. In effect, to have one's testimony responded to in this way is to have one's capacity to discern the epistemic import of one's reasons questioned.[12] Since this capacity is at the heart of one's status as an epistemic subject, being called into question in this way cuts deeply; if the audience's basis for doing this is improper, this amounts to a fundamental form of disrespect. As speakers we are entitled to expect not to be disrespected like this.

---

[12] At least this is so when one's sincerity is not at issue.

But what, precisely, is owed to the speaker in this regard? In the typical case of testimony, others do not have access to a speaker's reasons, nor do they have access to her deliberations about those reasons (if indeed she did deliberate). So it would be too much if, on the basis of the injunction to respect other subjects, the interpersonal pressure on an audience were pressure to accept what a speaker says whenever *in fact* her say-so is backed by proper epistemic authority.[13] Rather, what a speaker's audience 'owes' her is to acknowledge the speaker's conveyed claim of relevant authority, and to factor this appropriately into their doxastic response to her testimony. More explicitly, I submit that proper treatment comes to this: *the audience should adjust their doxastic reaction to a proper (epistemic) assessment of the speaker's epistemic authority*,[14] since in doing so they are adjusting their doxastic reaction to a proper (epistemic) assessment of the act in which she conveyed having such authority. Audiences are thus under normative pressure to assess the speaker's act *epistemically*. **Interpersonal Pressure** is vindicated—and with it, my proposed answer to ENTITLEMENT.

4

The foregoing account of the act of testifying can be used to diagnose the error in 'assurance view' accounts of proper treatment (discussed in Chapter 4).

My claim on this score is that both Hinchman's and Moran's versions of the assurance view are guilty of running together the purport of trustworthiness with its presumption. On the one hand, it is true that the acts of testifying and telling are acts that *purport* to be trustworthy. On the other, it does not follow (and I have argued that neither Hinchman nor Moran have given us a reason to think) that these acts are acts that are to be *presumed* trustworthy. So while both Hinchman and Moran are correct that the speaker's entitlement to expect proper treatment derives from the nature of the sort of speech act wherein one 'assures' an audience of the truth of a proposition, they err in (being committed to) thinking that this correct point, which pertains to what we might call the interpersonal and pragmatic significance of testifying, can do double-duty as an account of the epistemic significance of the act of testifying. Both make this mistake, it seems, because

---

[13] As noted in Chapter 4, Miranda Fricker herself would appear to agree.
[14] In effect, this constitutes my answer to CONTENT.

both endorse a faulty assumption: that the (interpersonal) normative pressure a testifier puts on an audience, to be treated with the sort of respect due to one who conveys having relevant epistemic authority, is at the same time epistemically significant, generating a defeasible reason which (in the absence of reasons for doubt) rationalizes or entitles the audience's acceptance of that testimony.

While I agree with Hinchman and Moran that to have one's word summarily dismissed (or dismissed on inadequate evidence) is to be disrespected, I disagree that this shows that one's word is to be treated as presumptively trustworthy. Simply put, the features that generate a speaker's entitlement to expect a certain kind of respect from her audience—the speaker's purport to be doing a certain job, and (correspondingly) her conveying that she has the relevant epistemic authority to do so—do not themselves generate the sort of (defeasible) reason that would rationalize the audience's accepting what was attested to. Indeed, it would be most curious if such features *did* generate (defeasible) reasons that rationalized acceptance: presumably reasons for acceptance are epistemic reasons, and these don't come into existence merely because a speaker purports to be performing a certain job. Interestingly, both Hinchman and Moran appear to recognize this.[15] But they fail to see that as a result, if testimony *is* to be accorded some sort of default epistemic standing (as they and other anti-reductionists in the epistemology of testimony maintain), this must be on grounds *other than* the sort of respect one is owed as a speaker who testified that p.

This diagnosis puts me in a position in which to address EPISTEMOLOGY, i.e. to see how the (interpersonal) normative pressure on an audience (to react in an interpersonally proper way to observed testimony) relates to the epistemic task of accepting testimony only when it is epistemically proper to do so. When S testifies to A that p, this places (interpersonal) normative pressure on A to give S the respect that is deserved by one who conveys having the relevant authority regarding the truth of p. In effect, A 'owes it' to S to tailor her doxastic reaction to S's testimony so as to reflect a proper estimate of S's epistemic authority on the matter. What counts as a 'proper estimate' will depend on the correct view in

---

[15] See e.g. Moran (2006: 289) and Hinchman (2014). For his part, Moran recognized that in order for the speech act to succeed in having this sort of import, 'the appropriate abilities and other background conditions must be assumed to be in place for it to amount to anything' (289). These conditions require 'that the speaker does indeed satisfy the right conditions for such an act (e.g., that he possesses the relevant knowledge, trustworthiness, and reliability)' (289).

the epistemology of testimony: it might be a matter of having positive reasons with which to confirm (or disconfirm) S's epistemic authority (reductionism),[16] or alternatively it might suffice that the audience lack reasons to doubt S's epistemic authority (anti-reductionism).[17] But whichever of these theories is correct, the overall picture is this: in testifying that p, S puts interpersonal pressure on her audience A to adjust her (A's) doxastic reaction to reflect a proper (epistemically justified) estimate of the epistemic credentials of the testimony. If this is correct, we can recognize that in testifying a speaker puts one's audience under *interpersonal* normative pressure to regard her as purporting to be trustworthy, even as we continue to insist on the traditional epistemological view that nothing but a testimony's *epistemic* credentials (and the audience's epistemic perspective on this) rationalize its acceptance.

5

This leaves us with one final matter to be addressed: how is it that there can be a speech act that amounts to testifying? How can there be a speech act through the performance of which one purports to do what JOB DESCRIPTION provides for, such that one's purport is itself common knowledge among speaker and audience alike?

Happily, recent theorizing about the speech act of assertion is helpful here.[18] In particular, in order to explain how the act of testifying is performed, we can appeal to a popular view according to which assertion is governed by a constitutive rule requiring knowledge. The 'Knowledge Rule of Assertion' (henceforth 'KRA') is the view according to which assertion is the unique speech act that is governed by the following rule:

One must: [perform that act in connection with the proposition that p], only if one knows that p.[19]

---

[16] See e.g. E. Fricker (1987, 1994, 1995).
[17] See e.g. Coady (1992), Burge (1993), Goldberg (2014).
[18] In what follows I am borrowing heavily from previous work I've done on assertion, above all in Goldberg (2015b).
[19] Rob Stainton (in conversation) has noted that the uniqueness claim (about assertion being the *unique* speech act governed by KRA) is falsified on the plausible assumption that (pragmatic) presupposition, too, is an act which is governed by a knowledge norm—as in: don't presuppose that p (in the course of performing some speech act) unless you know that p. If this is so, we might try to fix the uniqueness claim by restricting it so that it bears on speech acts

I will not be arguing for KRA here.[20] Instead, I will briefly characterize how, if true, this view can be used to explain the mechanism by which a speaker can perform a speech act through the performance of which she purports to do the testifying job of JOB DESCRIPTION, such that this purport is itself common knowledge among speaker and audience alike.

Suppose that KRA is true and is implicitly known by all pragmatically competent speakers.[21] Then when S asserts that p to A, it will be common knowledge that what S has done is proper only if S knows that p. Since S performed the act under conditions in which it was common knowledge that her act would have such conditions of propriety, S can be held accountable for fulfilling those conditions. And insofar as all of this was easily foreseeable, S can thereby be seen as having conveyed through her act that she does, in fact, fulfil those conditions. (One who performs what is commonly known to be a rule-governed act thereby conveys to those who observe her that she followed the rules.[22]) Since those conditions require that she know that p, S can thereby be seen as having conveyed that she knows that p. But now consider what is true of one who, in performing the speech act that she did, presents p as true under conditions in which she conveys that she knows that p. Such a person can correctly be described as purporting to be

> presenting a content as true in such a way that, were the audience to accept it on the basis of accepting the speech contribution, the resulting belief would be a candidate for knowledge.

We can summarize this by saying that in performing the speech act she did, the speaker *is conveying that she is trustworthy with respect to whether p*. This is precisely the source of assertion's purported trustworthiness. It is also the source of assertion's suitability for the act of testifying or telling. Such, then, is one possible model of the mechanism by which an act of this sort is possible.

---

whose *at-issue* content is that p. (I thank Rob for insisting on the need to address this.) For relevant discussion, see Stainton (2016).

[20] See Williamson (1996, 2000), among many others.
[21] The assumption that KRA is implicitly known by competent speakers is motivated by the idea that such knowledge is part of what characterizes pragmatic competence in the production and comprehension of the speech act of assertion; this assumption earns its keep in enabling us to explain a variety of familiar features of our assertion practices. See Goldberg (2015b).
[22] A point in this vicinity is made in connection with assertion in Ross (1986: 77–8).

Of course, it still remains to be seen how an audience *recognizes* that an assertion has been made. On this score, many authors rest content with saying that a speaker's speech intentions are usually discernible in her speech acts. Armed with KRA, we can go a bit further. Suppose that S utters a declarative sentence from the common language which (interpreted in context) means that p. A question for the audience arises: why did S perform that act? Now suppose that the speech context is one in which it would be reasonable to assume that knowing whether p would be of some value to the someone in the audience. Insofar as the best explanation of why S uttered what she did is that she aimed to provide the audience with the knowledge she anticipated would be valuable to them, the audience then has a reason to believe that the act was one purporting to provide that knowledge. And when this explanation is better than the alternatives, the audience would then have a strong reason to suppose that the speaker aimed to be conforming to the rule which makes such acts (of knowledge transmission) available. If this is correct, then there is a straightforward and recognizable way to make manifest that one is performing an act of this sort: utter a declarative sentence from the public language, under conditions in which (it is reasonable to anticipate that) the best explanation for one's doing so is that one purported to be making that knowledge available to others. Notice, though, that since it is generally true that knowledge is useful or valuable to have, this sort of explanation will typically have something going for it. This might explain why *assertion will be the default construal of the force of an utterance of a declarative sentence.*

One implication of an assertion-based view of the expectation of proper treatment is worth underscoring. If this view is correct, then the domain of the expectation of proper treatment is the domain of assertion itself.[23] This casts the net quite a bit wider (as an answer to SCOPE) than 'assurance' views would have it, as they restrict their account to cases in which the speaker addresses herself to an audience and performs the act of *telling* (a special case of asserting). This disagreement over the scope of the phenomenon is at the same time a disagreement over the nature of the wrong that is done to a speaker when the expectation of proper treatment is violated. Since this will enable me to present my account of INTERPERSONAL DEMAND, it is worth developing the point a bit further.

---

[23] Here it is worth noting that many authors think that the domain of testifying just is the domain of asserting. See e.g. E. Fricker (1987), Sosa (1994), and Lackey (2008).

Consider that if asserting is sufficient for testifying, then the speaker need not *address herself* to an audience member in order to put (interpersonal) normative pressure on the audience member. Indeed, once this point is made, it can seem not merely true but obviously so. Recall Miranda Fricker's notion of an epistemic injustice. It seems strange to think that epistemic injustices can be perpetrated *only by those whom the speaker addressed*. Suppose Janice writes a report addressed exclusively to her boss. If the claims in her report are summarily dismissed by someone else out of misogyny, would we say that Janice is not the victim of an epistemic injustice since, after all, that reader wasn't the addressed audience? Or suppose that Joanne (an African-American woman) is speaking before a crowd of a dozen people, but is addressing only one of them, and tells him that p. If the other eleven people summarily dismiss her claim owing to a mixture of racism and misogyny, do we really want to say that she is not the victim of an epistemic injustice since, after all, none of these eleven was being addressed by her? Presumably not. But then it seems that whatever the interpersonal significance of second-personal address is—and I have no doubt that it has such significance[24]—it can't be what demarcates the domain of the speaker's expectation of proper treatment. It counts in favour of the assertoric model developed above that it yields the right predictions here.

[24] I discussed part of this significance in Chapter 2.

6
Anti-Reductionism and Expected Trust

1

In Chapter 5, I gave my positive account of what the audience owes to a speaker when she testifies that p. According to the account I defended there, the interpersonal normative pressure a speaker exerts on an audience derives from her entitled expectation of proper treatment, where this is tantamount to the expectation that the audience base his doxastic response to her testimony on a proper assessment of her epistemic authority on [p]. In this way, my account separates the *interpersonal* normative pressure generated by an act of testimony from the *epistemological* normative pressure generated by an act of testimony. What the latter amounts to, I argued, is not exclusively determined by the interpersonal demands one places on one's audience when one tells them something. Rather, it is determined by the correct account of the epistemology of testimony. And on that matter my own account was officially silent.

Still, it might be wondered whether the links between the interpersonal and epistemic dimensions of conversational pressure are more intimate than I have so far recognized. In this chapter I pursue one line of thought that purports to establish a more intimate connection between these two dimensions. However, whereas my claim in Chapter 5 was that no account of the interpersonal normative pressure on an audience, by itself, will determine the conditions under which it is *epistemically* proper to accept a piece of observed testimony, the line of thought I want to consider in this chapter aims to reverse the direction of the argument. More specifically, the line of thought I want to explore here is whether, on the assumption of a standard anti-reductionist approach to the epistemology of testimony, we can reach the Hinchman–Moran–Fricker contention that speakers are entitled to expect to be presumed trustworthy. While this is not the sort of argument

Revised from S. C. Goldberg (2019), 'Anti-Reductionism and Expected Trust', *Pacific Philosophical Quarterly*, 100: 952–70.

that Hinchman, Moran, and Fricker themselves pursue, this line of argument itself is broadly in keeping with the spirit of their positions, and in any case it is sufficiently interesting in its own right to be considered separately.

My summary conclusion is that if it is to be successful this line of argument will need to take on much heavier theoretical baggage than one might want, making it less attractive to those who might otherwise go in for it. Making out this point will enable me to explore further the interactions between the interpersonal and epistemic dimensions of conversational pressure.

2

Let *Anti-Reductionism* be the thesis that

AR   Audiences enjoy a default (but defeasible) epistemic entitlement to accept observed testimony.[1]

AR is a popular, though by no means universally accepted, thesis in the epistemology of testimony.[2] In this chapter I am asking whether this thesis can be used to support a claim regarding the interpersonal normativity involved in the act of testifying, pertaining to the expectation to be *presumed trustworthy*. The claim in question, which I will designate as *the Entitlement to Expect Epistemic Trust*, might be formulated as follows:

EEET   Speakers enjoy a default but defeasible entitlement to expect to be presumed trustworthy when they testify.[3]

EEET asserts that a speaker who testifies that p is entitled to expect the following: insofar as there are no relevant reasons for her audience to doubt

---

[1] When I speak of 'observed' testimony, I am assuming that it is observed *with comprehension*. I won't bother adding this each time; it should be understood.
[2] Classic defences include Ross (1986), Coady (1992), Burge (1993), and M. Fricker (2007). A more recent defence is in Perrine (2014).
[3] In what follows I will be speaking as if the entitlement is moral in nature. As I noted at the outset of this chapter, it is not clear whether those I cite in this connection regard the entitlement as moral, as distinct from some other sort of social or interpersonal entitlement. I don't think this affects the argument to be given here; the same points can be made, *mutatis mutandis*, regarding a social or interpersonal (but not distinctly moral) entitlement to expect trust. Still, for simplicity of exposition (and to allow the acronym of 'EEET') I will continue to speak as if the entitlement is a moral one.

her on this occasion, her testimony that p will be trusted (and so the speaker herself will be believed).[4] At the same time, EEET does not specify the nature of this entitlement, beyond noting that it is an interpersonal one. But whatever the nature of this entitlement, it is an entitlement to a distinctly *normative* expectation: the upshot is that an audience who fails in this regard, and so who does not trust a speaker's testimony despite the absence of reasons for doubt, does something (interpersonally) remiss—and so inflicts an interpersonal type of harm on the speaker. (The speaker is entitled to expect that this not happen.) In this chapter I am asking whether, and if so how, AR might be used to ground EEET. If it can, this would be an interesting example of a significant link between epistemic and interpersonal norms, and between epistemology and social normativity more generally.

At the outset, it can seem as though AR and EEET are made for each other.

In effect, AR asserts that audiences enjoy an epistemic permission to presume that a speaker's say-so is trustworthy, where this presumption is defeated only by determinate positive evidence to the contrary. This claim, which pertains to the epistemic dimension of the conversation pressure exerted by acts of testimony, reflects the idea that testimony itself is a *basic source of justification*: in the same way that we might think that one doesn't need reasons for thinking that one's perceptual experiences are a reliable guide to how things are prior to forming a justified belief through accepting the perceptual appearances, so too AR suggests that one doesn't require reasons for thinking that a piece of testimony is a reliable guide to how things are prior to forming a justified belief through accepting the testimony one observed. In both cases the source is (defeasibly) presumed to be reliable, where this presumption does not stand in need of justification itself.

This is why AR, a thesis in epistemology, can seem apt for motivating EEET, a thesis pertaining to the interpersonal dimension of the conversational pressure exerted by acts of testimony. Simply put, if testimony is (like perception) a basic source of justification, then it can seem that speakers who offer testimony to an audience are entitled to expect to be treated as

---

[4] This formulation may rankle some who think of trust in more robust terms, or as something directed at a person (and so not a piece of testimony). But it is common to speak of epistemic trust as the sort of trust that is relevant to testimonial exchanges; and when talking this way, it is common to speak of trusted testimony. I do not think that there is any untoward implication of speaking this way; if it were wanted, this talk could be accommodated within any more general theory of trust. I won't bother doing so here.

such. And this would appear to be tantamount to an expectation to be taken at one's word in any case in which one's audience has no reasons for doubt. On this sort of motivation, EEET captures the idea that there is an interpersonal affront in not having one's word be accorded the status that, according to AR, it has. These two doctrines seem made for one another.

As we saw in Chapter 4, the literature on testimony is full of theorists who support the marriage of AR and EEET. According to these theorists, audiences who do not accept what they are told despite lacking reasons for doubt are described as committing one or another offence against the speaker. Thus Ted Hinchman writes of a case in which a speaker S, noting that A is in need of the time, tells A that it is noon, where A lacks any reason for doubt. Hinchman notes that if A nonetheless rejects S's telling, regarding herself as having no reason to think that it is noon, this constitutes a 'slight' or an 'abuse' of the speaker (Hinchman 2005: 565, 568). Hinchman's point, of course, is that the audience does something impermissible when she rejects a speaker's say-so despite lacking any grounds for doubt. Others who join Hinchman in this sort of verdict include Richard Moran (2006: 301), who speaks of the 'offense' that is committed by hearers who do not react appropriately to tellings; Elizabeth Anscombe (1979: 9), who writes that 'It is an insult and may be an injury not to be believed'; Thomas Simpson (2012: 562), who echoes Anscombe's language when he writes that '[i]t is an insult to refuse to trust'; and, perhaps most familiarly, Miranda Fricker, who is well known for having drawn our attention to cases of 'testimonial injustice', in which 'prejudice on the hearer's part causes him to give the speaker less credibility than he would otherwise have given', thereby 'wrong[ing] a speaker in his capacity as a giver of knowledge, as an informant' (Fricker 2007: 4, 5). Not all of these authors focus on the epistemological dimension of testimony. But every one of them who does—all but Anscombe and Simpson—endorses something in the vicinity of AR.[5]

Stronger, there are clear grounds for thinking that the success of an argument for EEET—for the thesis that speakers who testify are entitled to expect to be presumed trustworthy—will presuppose the truth of AR. To see this, suppose AR is false. Then there is no default (defeasible) epistemic entitlement to accept what another says. Perhaps this is because another's say-so has no intrinsic epistemic significance to speak of;[6] or perhaps this is

---

[5] See Chapter 4 for details.
[6] This recalls the famous line from John Locke: 'The floating of other men's opinions in our brains, makes us not one jot the more knowing, though they happen to be true.'

because whatever epistemic significance another's say-so has ultimately derives from the auxiliary reasons the audience has to regard that say-so as credible. (Views in this vicinity are known in the epistemology of testimony as *reductionist* views.[7]) Whatever the correct epistemology of testimony is, so long as AR is false, the failure to accept another's testimony in the absence of reasons for doubt would appear *ethically innocuous* (or in any case innocuous from the perspective of interpersonal norms). To assume otherwise would be to assume that a speaker's interpersonal expectation of her audience can require the audience to believe something *for which he lacks epistemic entitlement*—as when he lacks reasons for doubt but also lacks positive reasons for trusting. It would be a strange mismatch indeed if the interpersonal norms of (epistemic) trust require a subject to accept a piece of testimony whenever he lacked reasons for doubt, while epistemology requires him to accept only when he has positive reasons for belief.[8] Thus it seems that those who hope to establish EEET will most likely have to do so *on the assumption that Anti-Reductionism is true*.

Might we argue for EEET by appeal to the interpersonal dimension of the conversational pressure exerted by the act of testifying itself, without having to proceed by way of an epistemic principle such as AR? While this is somewhat familiar terrain—I considered and rejected arguments of this sort in Chapter 4—it is worth a new look at this, as our current vantage point (afforded by my positive account in Chapter 5) provides me with a new angle on this topic.

How might we try to establish EEET by appeal to the interpersonal dimension of the conversational pressure exerted by the act of testifying itself, without having to proceed by way of an epistemic principle such as AR?[9] It is plausible to think that in the act of testifying to an audience, the speaker S assumes a responsibility to the audience A—a responsibility, for example, to treat A in a respectful fashion *qua* believer, or not to influence A haphazardly, etc. For this reason it might be argued that A *disrespects* S when A fails to recognize that S is discharging the responsibilities associated with testifying. And insofar as inappropriate rejection is tantamount to failing to recognize that a speaker is discharging this sort of responsibility, S is entitled to expect that she not be disrespected in this fashion. We might then think that an audience who (in the absence of reasons for doing so)

---

[7] See e.g. E. Fricker (1987, 1995).
[8] Below I will articulate my reasons for thinking that this mismatch is strange.
[9] I thank an anonymous referee for the suggestion that follows.

does not accept a speaker's testimony doubts the speaker's integrity and capability, and that this is an affront of sorts. Insofar as speakers are entitled not to be treated this way, we arrive at EEET. And if EEET can be motivated in this way, then there appears to be no need for the assumption of AR.

Unfortunately, the foregoing attempt to establish EEET without AR is problematic for a reason anticipated above. Let it be granted that the issue before us concerns the conditions under which an audience's non-acceptance of a speaker's testimony constitutes a form of disrespect of the speaker. If AR is false, then it can happen that an audience who lacks reasons for doubting the speaker's testimony nonetheless is *not epistemically entitled* to accept that testimony. Under such conditions, it seems patent that the audience's non-acceptance of that testimony should not be seen as a form of disrespect.[10] More generally, unless A is epistemically entitled to accept S's testimony, A's non-acceptance of that testimony is *epistemically proper*, and so appears not to be a form of disrespect. In this way we underscore a point I made above: if AR is false, so that an audience who lacks reasons for doubt is not thereby entitled to accept a speaker's testimony, then there is no basis for motivating the idea that such an audience disrespects the speaker by *not* accepting the testimony. In short, AR is the epistemological ideology informing EEET.

3

Granting then that the argument for the Entitlement to Expect Epistemic Trust (EEET) will presuppose the truth of AR, how might one try to argue *from* AR *to* EEET? Any such argument will need at least two additional premises (besides AR itself). These constitute what I will call two 'bridge principles' that are needed to link AR to EEET.[11] The need for these bridge principles is easily appreciated. AR is a claim asserting an *epistemic permission*; EEET is a claim asserting the speaker's right to a normative expectation of her audience, where (given the speaker's right to that expectation) the audience *ought* to do—is *obligated* to do—as the speaker expects her to do. For this reason, any theorist who hopes to argue from AR to EEET will need one bridge principle connecting AR's talk of *permissions* to EEET's talk of *obligations*—I will call this the *modal strength* bridge principle—and a

---

[10] I will be arguing for this in section 3.
[11] I thank an anonymous referee for suggesting this way of framing the issue.

second bridge principle to connect the *epistemic* modality in AR to the *non-epistemic* (ethical?) modality[12] in EEET—I will call this the *modal type* bridge principle. Only an argument that provides both kinds of bridge principle can get AR's claim, that an audience is (epistemically) permitted to accept what she is told (except when there are relevant defeaters present), to bear on EEET's claim, that speakers are entitled to expect to be trusted—that is, that speakers are entitled to expect that their testimony be accepted—by audiences who lack relevant defeaters.

In what follows I want to argue that if there is such an argument forthcoming it will need to take on heavier baggage than anything that has heretofore been acknowledged by those who endorse EEET. Stronger, I will be arguing that what appears to be the only plausible candidate for a modal *type* bridge principle will make it hard to find a plausible candidate for a modal *strength* bridge principle. If no such principle is forthcoming, the argument from AR to EEET would appear to be doomed.

I want to start my discussion, then, by focusing on what can be offered as the modal type bridge principle. Why should we think that an *epistemic* claim (pertaining to when audiences are epistemically permitted to believe a speaker) can be used to underwrite the sort of interpersonal demand set forth in EEET, where this is a claim pertaining to what speakers are entitled to expect of their audience? We have already hinted at a possible answer above, which in any case will already be salient to readers of Chapters 4 and 5: there are certain ways of responding to acts of testimony in which the audience *disrespects* the speaker, and speakers are entitled to expect not to be disrespected in these ways.[13]

If this natural thought is correct, we might hope to link AR's epistemic entitlement to EEET's non-epistemic entitlement by articulating what a speaker is entitled to expect of her audience when the speaker testifies to the truth of a proposition. One promising strategy for doing so—the strategy pursued by the authors I discussed in Chapter 4 (and below I will argue that it is unclear whether there are any other strategies available)—would be to conceive of *the act of testifying itself* as both epistemically and interpersonally significant, such that this very act manifests a link between epistemic and interpersonal normativity. Following this strategy, we might say that the

---

[12] Or, more generally, to the sort of modality corresponding to the type of normativity that is at issue.
[13] A version of this point has been stressed, most familiarly, by M. Fricker 2007, but versions are also present in the arguments of Hinchman 2005, Moran 2006, and McMyler 2011.

act of testifying is epistemically significant in the following sense: in testifying a speaker S provides a default epistemic entitlement to her audience A (to believe what S said). And we might say that the act of testifying is interpersonally significant in the following sense: A risks disrespecting S if A fails to respond properly to S's act of having provided a default epistemic entitlement.[14]

To arrive at an explicit candidate for the modal type bridge principle we might then reason as follows. To testify that p is to present oneself to one's audience as epistemically authoritative on the question whether p. If AR is true, S's testifying that p provides a default (but defeasible) epistemic entitlement for A to believe that p. Consequently, if A reacts to this by failing to accept this testimony even though there are no relevant reasons for doubt, A has thereby disrespected S *qua* epistemic authority. And testifiers are entitled to expect not to be disrespected in this way. But in that case, testifiers are entitled to expect audiences to accept what they say so long as there are no relevant defeaters present. This, then, gives us a (schematic) candidate modal type bridge principle: there are conditions under which a speaker is disrespected—and so in this sense wronged—as a testifier, in the very act whereby she provides the audience with a default *epistemic* entitlement to accept the testimony.

I just argued that we can link the epistemic normativity of AR with the non-epistemic normativity of EEET, and in this way can get a candidate modal type bridge principle, if we appeal to the kind of disrespect that an audience might exhibit towards a speaker whose testimony the audience improperly rejects (or fails to accept). This disrespect is a (normatively significant) failure to acknowledge the speaker's epistemic authority. In fact, it is unclear how *else* to link the epistemic normativity of AR with the non-epistemic normativity of EEET, save by appeal to this kind of disrespect. What *else* could entitle a speaker to expect to have her word be assigned a default credibility or trustworthiness, save that in the act of testifying she has done something that entitles her to expect to be respected for the epistemic authority she manifested (or purported to manifest) in that very act? It is thus no surprise that among proponents of EEET we find a good deal of discussion and analysis of the ways in which an audience disrespects a testifier.[15]

---

[14] In articulating this, I draw inspiration from Hinchman 2005, who comes very close to saying precisely this.
[15] This theme runs through Anscombe 1979, Hinchman 2005, Moran 2006, M. Fricker 2007, and McMyler 2011. See Chapters 4 and 5 for further discussion.

In what follows, then, I will be assuming that something like this modal type bridge principle is true: there are conditions under which a speaker is disrespected—and so in this sense is wronged—as a testifier, in the very act whereby she provides the audience with a default epistemic entitlement to accept the testimony. With such a principle in place we are part of the way to our conclusion asserting an Entitlement to Expect Epistemic Trust. But we are not there yet. For what is still needed is an account of *when* an audience exhibits this sort of disrespect.

As I see it, this is the central question facing those who aim to argue for EEET by way of AR: why should audiences who observe a speaker's testimony under conditions in which they lack reasons for doubt be regarded as *disrespecting* the speaker if they reject the speaker's say-so? One might have the impression that once we assume AR itself, the answer to this question is obvious. This impression, however, is faulty. Given AR, to affirm that there is disrespect in such cases is to make the following assumption: an audience who is (epistemically) permitted to accept testimony is such that she disrespects the speaker if she does not do so.[16] And it is far from clear why we should embrace this assumption. That an audience A is (epistemically) *permitted* to believe the speaker (= accept what she says) is one thing; that A is *obligated* to do so (on pain of wronging the speaker) is another. It is the latter claim that is needed by proponents of EEET.

Here, of course, we face the need for a candidate modal strength bridge principle—a principle with which to link the claim about (epistemic) permission to a claim about (interpersonal) requirement.[17] What sort of bridge principle might we propose?

Consider first a 'hybrid' principle, one which seeks to link epistemic entitlements to interpersonal requirements directly. The following is perhaps the simplest version of such a principle: if audience A is epistemically entitled (permitted) to accept S's testimony, then A is interpersonally required to accept S's testimony.[18] Unfortunately, this principle seems

---

[16] Recall that it was the allegation of disrespect that provided the linkage between the epistemic modality of AR and the moral modality of EEET. The key claim was that speakers are morally entitled not to be disrespected as testifiers.

[17] In what follows I will be speaking of *interpersonal* requirements. This is admittedly awkward language; it would be less awkward to speak of ethical requirements. However, I do not want to assume that the requirements in EEET are ethical; they may derive instead from social norms, or some other sort of norm of interpersonal behaviour, and theorists may not want to assume that these are ethical in nature. For this reason I stick with the admittedly more clunky language of 'interpersonal requirement'.

[18] One might wonder: if we are going to appeal to such a 'hybrid' claim for our modal strength bridge principle—one which directly links epistemic permissions to interpersonal

problematic on its face, in a way that indicates a problem facing any version of a 'hybrid' principle.

The difficulty facing the simple 'hybrid' principle can be brought out by noting that many entitlements or permissions have the following property: to be entitled or permitted to X is consistent with being entitled or permitted *not* to X. This property is obvious in connection with certain moral entitlements or permissions. For example, it is morally permissible for me to jump rope right now, and it is also morally permissible for me not to jump rope right now. When it comes to jumping rope right now, my hand isn't morally forced one way or the other. It is also true of (some) legal entitlements or permissions: it is legally permissible for us to enter into a contractual relationship, and it is legally permissible for us not to enter into a contractual relationship (our hands aren't forced, legally speaking). When this is so—when one's hand isn't forced by the relevant sort of normativity—I will describe the case as a 'fully permissive' one. (The question whether to jump rope now is fully morally permissive; the question whether to enter into a contractual relationship is fully legally permissive; and so forth.) Now AR is a claim about epistemic entitlements or permissions. Suppose then that the epistemic domain is like the moral and legal domains, in that there are fully permissive epistemic cases as well. And suppose further that we have such a case in a scenario involving a speaker S's testimony: it is true both that audience A is entitled to accept S's testimony that p, and that A is epistemically entitled *not* to accept S's testimony that p. (That is, A's hand is not forced from the epistemic point of view: A could, with epistemic permission, go either way.) In a fully permissive epistemic case involving S's testimony that p, A is epistemically entitled/permitted *not* to accept that testimony. Consequently, if we assume (for *reductio*) that A is (interpersonally) required to accept S's testimony so long as no relevant defeaters are present, we are committed to the (absurd) possibility of cases in which *what is (interpersonally) required forbids what is (epistemically) permitted*. Such an absurdity would materialize in cases in which, in addition to being epistemically permitted to accept S's testimony, A was also epistemically permitted not to accept A's testimony. It would seem, then, that if we are to avoid this

---

requirements—do we *also* have a need of the modal type bridge principle? Or can we make do with such a 'hybrid' principle alone? I think we still need the modal type bridge principle: to the extent that the 'hybrid' principle has any plausibility, it inherits this plausibility from a picture which ascribes to the act of testifying both interpersonal and epistemic properties. That is to say, whatever plausibility the 'hybrid' claim has, it inherits it from the modal type bridge principle I characterized above.

absurdity, we must insist that *there are no fully permissive epistemic cases*. That is, we must insist that in any case in which A is epistemically permitted to accept S's testimony, it is *not true* that A is epistemically permitted *not* to accept S's testimony. This, rather than the 'hybrid' principle mentioned above, is the sort of claim that appears to provide the modal strength bridge principle we need.

Still, defenders of the simple 'hybrid' modal strength bridge principle may not be impressed with the foregoing argument. They might respond by questioning whether it really is absurd to suppose that there are cases in which what one is interpersonally required to do comes apart from what is epistemically permitted. To bolster their case, they might think to highlight another domain in which such a 'strange disconnect' between interpersonal and epistemic normativity has been alleged to exist, at least by some theorists. I have in mind the domain of trust in friendship (a matter I discuss at length in Chapter 7). Various authors (e.g. Baker 1987, Keller 2004, Stroud 2006, and Hazlett 2013) have argued for a doctrine of *epistemic partiality in friendship*, according to which the normative demands of friendship can require beliefs that violate ordinary standards of epistemic rationality or justification. Perhaps it is not absurd after all, then, to suppose that the interpersonal demands arising from testimony may forbid something that epistemology regards as permissible.

Unfortunately, the appeal to the doctrine of epistemic partiality in friendship is no help on the present score, and so is of no help to those who would defend the 'hybrid' modal strength bridge principle. For one thing, the doctrine of partiality is a very controversial thesis even as restricted to the domain of beliefs about our friends,[19] and one would hope to avoid such costs in making a case for EEET from AR. What is worse, if the proponent of the argument from AR to EEET proposes to embrace this 'strange disconnect' by appeal to the doctrine of epistemic partiality in friendship, in effect she would be proposing to extend the application of (what even its proponents acknowledge is) a controversial thesis, from the limited domain of friendship, to *testimonies generally*. To wit: if it is strange to think that friendship can place demands on us that force us to violate epistemic requirements, it should be strange as well to think that *any testifier*

---

[19] For arguments against this doctrine, see Kawall (2013), Hawley (2014a), and Chapter 7 of this book.

whatsoever can put demands on us that forbid us from doing what epistemology would otherwise permit.[20] This should seem implausible even to the proponents of epistemic partiality in friendship.

In sum, the simple 'hybrid' modal strength bridge principle is not an option. What is more, the argument for this has nothing to do with the simplicity of the candidate principle I have considered. It has to do instead with the absurd implication of deriving interpersonal requirements directly from epistemic permissions. I conclude that any candidate 'hybrid' modal strength bridge principle will be equally objectionable.

Happily, there is another option. As noted, the problem we just encountered arises if we try to derive interpersonal requirements directly from epistemic permissions. That this won't do is seen in epistemically permissive cases, in which audience A's hand is not forced: it is epistemically permissible for A to accept S's testimony, but it is also epistemically permissible for A not to accept S's testimony. But suppose we simply deny that there are any epistemically permissible cases in this domain. That is, suppose we hold that in any case in which it is epistemically permissible for A to accept S's testimony, it is epistemically *impermissible* for A *not* to accept S's testimony. Then we might think that this very claim amounts to the modal strength bridge principle we need. On the assumption that there are ways in which an audience A disrespects a speaker S by responding inappropriately to S's testimony, the claim would then be that inappropriately responding to S's testimony is a matter of not accepting it when one has epistemic permission to do so—simply because when one has epistemic permission to do so, one lacks epistemic permission *not* to accept.

In effect, the candidate modal strength bridge principle we are considering is a particularly strong version of Anti-Reductionism. The standard version of Anti-Reductionism is the one I presented above:

AR   Audiences enjoy a default (but defeasible) epistemic entitlement to accept observed testimony.

By contrast, the version proposed here would amount to the claim that

---

[20] This way of putting the point can seem to raise the spectre of doxastic voluntarism. This appearance can be avoided if we think in terms, not of belief, but of acceptance. This would introduce other complications, but as these are irrelevant to the main point I am making here, I will ignore them.

AR_REQ[21] Audiences enjoy a defeasible epistemic permission to accept observed testimony, and in the absence of relevant defeaters they are epistemically *required* to accept observed testimony.[22]

This version, AR_REQ, would then constitute the modal strength bridge principle.

If it were otherwise plausible, AR_REQ, together with the assumed modal type bridge principle characterized above, would appear to give those who hope to argue for EEET precisely what they need. As noted, it would play the role of the modal strength bridge principle, since AR_REQ links epistemic permissions to epistemic requirements. In addition, AR_REQ is in keeping with the idea that if an audience A's rejection of a speaker S's testimony (under conditions of no defeaters) is to manifest disrespect for S, it must be the case that A is *required* to accept S's testimony (under these conditions of no defeaters). Simply put, if AR_REQ is true, then A *is* required—*epistemically* required—to accept S's testimony whenever A is epistemically entitled or permitted to do so. And we might think that if A is epistemically required to accept S's testimony, this is because of the epistemic authority S manifested in testifying as she did—in which case we might also think that A's rejection (or non-acceptance) of S's testimony manifests a kind of disrespect for S's authority. And we would have what we need.

Unfortunately, it is far from obvious that AR_REQ is true. On the contrary, AR_REQ appears to be (or to assume) a version of the very strong epistemic principle known as *Uniqueness*. Standard versions of Uniqueness are often formulated in terms of evidence, as follows:

UNIQ For any subject A, proposition p, and body of evidence E possessed by A, there is one uniquely rational doxastic attitude for A to have towards p.[23]

For my purposes here, however, I will need a variant formulation of the doctrine of Uniqueness itself. There are two reasons for this. First, whereas the present discussion is oriented around Anti-Reductionism, and so speaks of *entitlements*, UNIQ speaks of *rationality*. Second, whereas the present discussion is oriented around Anti-Reductionism, and so does not mention

---

[21] 'REQ' is shorthand for 'Requirement'.
[22] With thanks to an anonymous referee for suggesting that the point be framed in this way.
[23] Often UNIQ is put in terms of credences, but this degree of sophistication is not necessary for my argument so I will gloss over it.

evidence at all, UNIQ talks about evidence.[24] (This is important since many proponents of AR do not think of testimony in terms of evidence at all.) For these reasons I propose instead to recast the doctrine of Uniqueness in terms of (epistemic) entitlements rather than rationality, and to replace talk of A's evidence with talk of A's 'total epistemic system', where this is taken to include not only all of A's evidence, but also all of the 'inputs' into A's cognitive system—including testimonial inputs, whether these are conceived as evidence or not. To this end, I offer the following recast version of Uniqueness:

> $UNIQ_R$ For any proposition p and subject A whose total epistemic system is T, there is exactly one doxastic attitude which A would be epistemically entitled to have towards p.

My point above, to the effect that the argument from AR to EEET will depend on the doctrine of Uniqueness, can be framed in terms of two claims: first, that the version of Anti-Reductionism needed to argue for EEET is AR_{REQ} (as opposed to the more standard AR), and second, that AR_{REQ} amounts to (or assumes) a version of $UNIQ_R$. Perhaps this is obvious. After all, AR_{REQ} is based on the idea that, when it comes to our doxastic response to testimony, there are no epistemically permissive cases—no cases in which it is true, both that A is epistemically entitled to accept S's testimony, and that A is epistemically entitled not to accept S's testimony. And epistemic permissivism is precisely what $UNIQ_R$ denies.

4

My claim, then, is that those who aim to argue from AR to EEET will need to assume UNIQ (in the form of $UNIQ_R$). Below I will suggest why this result should worry proponents of EEET. Here, however, I want to revisit a suggestion I considered and rejected above: whether, on the assumption of AR, EEET can be established merely by appeal to the interpersonal dimension of the act of testifying itself.[25] If so, the proponent of the argument from AR to EEET can avoid having to assume Uniqueness after all. In this section I reinforce my scepticism regarding this option.

---

[24] I thank an anonymous referee for urging me to address both of these differences.
[25] I thank an anonymous referee for the suggestion to follow.

As I noted in section 2, it is plausible to think that in the act of testifying to an audience, the speaker S assumes a responsibility to the audience A—a responsibility in connection with the influence on A's beliefs that S aims at when she gives testimony to A. What is more, it would seem that S is discharging this responsibility when, in the act of testifying, she provides a default epistemic entitlement (permission) to A to accept what S has said. And if this is so, then we might anticipate that A disrespects S in a case of this sort when, lacking reasons for doubt, A nevertheless does not accept S's testimony. For this non-acceptance might be seen as a way in which A disrespects S: in not accepting S's say-so despite lacking reasons for doubt, A fails to acknowledge that S has discharged the responsibilities associated with the act of testifying. Since this argument appears to proceed without any need of the doctrine of Uniqueness in any of its forms, we appear to be able to argue from AR to EEET without the need for UNIQ or $UNIQ_R$.

I am now in a position to diagnose a faulty assumption to which this line of argument is committed. The assumption in question is this:

ACKNOWLEDGEMENT Given a case in which (i) S testifies that p and (ii) A lacks reasons to doubt S's trustworthiness in this connection, the *only* way for A to acknowledge that S has discharged her responsibilities *qua* testifier on this occasion involves accepting S's testimony that p.

To appreciate why the line of argument above is committed to ACKNOWLEDGEMENT, suppose that ACKNOWLEDGEMENT is false, so that there is some *other* way for A to acknowledge that S has discharged her responsibilities *qua* testifer, without A herself having to accept S's testimony. If A hasn't failed to acknowledge S's having discharged her responsibilities *qua* testifier, then A hasn't disrespected S *qua* testifier. And since the argument for an entitlement to expect epistemic trust appeals to a premise asserting the expectation not to be disrespected *qua* testifier, the result is that the argument above would fail in its attempt to establish EEET.

But if the line of argument above must assume ACKNOWLEDGEMENT, the faultiness of this assumption itself can be brought out by example as well as by argument.

There are various examples that can be used to falsify ACKNOWLEDGEMENT. Each of these illustrates how an audience who does not accept a speaker's testimony on an occasion (despite lacking reasons for doubting the speaker's trustworthiness) might nevertheless acknowledge that the speaker has discharged her relevant responsibilities *qua* testifier on that occasion.

Perhaps the most obvious examples are high stakes cases. S, unaware of what is at issue for A regarding whether p, testifies to p on what are objectively good grounds; A has no reason to doubt that S has good grounds for her testimony; but since A has a good deal at stake regarding whether p, A does not accept S's testimony, and explains herself by way of the stakes. (A to S: 'I have no reason to doubt that you are perfectly responsible in what you say, but given what is riding on it for me I can't just take your word. I hope you understand.')

Next, consider examples in which A has a personal, vested interest in finding out for herself whether p. S testifies to p on what are objectively good grounds; A has no reason to doubt that S has such grounds; but since A has a personal, vested interest in finding out for herself, she does not accept the testimony. (A to S: 'I have no reason to doubt that you are perfectly responsible in what you say, it's just that I need to see for myself; it's nothing against you, I hope you understand.')

Finally, consider cases involving an audience whose epistemic standards are (consistent and) unusually demanding.[26] S testifies to p on what are objectively good grounds; A has no grounds for doubting that S's testimony would provide what by ordinary standards would warrant the testimonial belief that p; but since A's epistemic standards are unusually demanding, she accepts nothing (in any circumstance) unless she is warranted in being nearly (epistemically) certain regarding its truth, and so does not accept S's testimony. (A to S: 'I have no reason to doubt that you are perfectly responsible in what you say, but—nothing against you!—it is my long-standing policy not to accept anything that is not virtually certain. I hope you understand.') In getting such an explanation from A, S may feel a lingering sense of hurt from A's implicit repudiation of S's (ordinary) epistemic standards.[27] Still, insofar as A is employing standards that are themselves within the range of acceptable epistemic standards, S's hurt in this regard would not reflect an interpersonal infraction on A's part. It would be akin to the sort of hurt one can feel when one offers something one takes another person to want or need, where in fact the other person

---

[26] It must be borne in mind that at this point in the dialectic my opponent is trying to avoid the need to assume Uniqueness, and so must allow for the possibility of permissive cases. In such cases, subjects with unusually high epistemic standards are permitted *not* to believe what ordinary standards would permit them to believe.

[27] I thank an anonymous referee for making this point. The referee noted that the response, 'I know you said so and I could believe you but my tolerance for risk is low,' sounds pretty insulting. I grant this but deny that the nature of the insult tells against my analysis. See above.

does have the relevant want or need, yet where even so one's offer is rebuffed with a polite 'No, thank you.'[28]

I now want to offer an argument to supplement the point I am making with these three examples. Like these examples, the argument will take aim at the assumption of ACKNOWLEDGEMENT—the claim that the *only* way for an audience A to acknowledge that a speaker S has discharged her responsibilities *qua* testifier on a given occasion (on which A lacks reasons to doubt S's trustworthiness) involves accepting S's testimony on that occasion. To this end, consider domains in which one's response to another's overture is governed by *permissive norms*. These are domains in which, when one is offered some good G, the relevant norms permit acceptance of G, but they also permit non-acceptance of G. I submit that the following claims capture two perfectly general features of our engagements with one another in such (permissive) domains: first, S's being responsible in the performance of act R (by which S offers A something S regards to be of value to A) does not establish any presumption that A ought to accept S's offer; and second, A can acknowledge S's responsibility in performing R without accepting what S offered. These two features are co-present in a variety of normative domains. Take the legal domain. S offers a contract to A, and is legally responsible in doing so: the offer is in good faith, S satisfies all of the legal preconditions for making the offer, and so forth. Even so, A can readily acknowledge S's behaviour as exhibiting S's strong sense of legal responsibility without there being any presumption that A ought (legally or ethically) to accept the contract. Next, take the social domain. S invites A to a party, and is socially responsible in doing so: S was authorized to make the invitation, it was made in good faith, S anticipated that A would love the activities, the food, and the crowd, and so forth. Even so, A can readily acknowledge S's invitation as exhibiting S's strong sense of social responsibility without there being any presumption that A ought (socially or ethically) to accept the invitation. (A polite 'no thank you' suffices.) For yet another alternative, take the domain encompassing the norms of friendship. S extends her friendship to A, and is ethically responsible in doing so: S is aware of the normative demands of friendship and is prepared to act accordingly, S's offer is in good faith, S genuinely values A's company, and so forth. Even so, A can readily acknowledge S's act of extending her friendship to A as exhibiting S's sense of ethical responsibility

---

[28] Compare CHOCOLATE OFFER from Chapter 4.

without there being any presumption that A ought to accept S's friendship. (Here, A may owe S more than a polite 'no thank you'—perhaps some explanation of the rebuff is in order, to enable S to 'save face'—but the point remains that there is no presumption that A ought to accept S's friendship.)

While these are only three cases, the fact that cases from three different normative domains pattern together suggests a generalization: when the norms governing A's reaction to an offer are *permissive* norms, a subject S's being relevantly responsible in her overtures to A does not, by itself, establish any presumption that A ought to accept what S offered; and, accordingly, A is not required to accept the offer in order to be in a position to acknowledge that S's overture was made in a responsible fashion. It stands to reason that the same goes for the act of testifying, where S extends her word to A and is (interpersonally and epistemically) responsible in doing so. Insofar as we allow that the domain governing our response to testimony is an epistemically permissive one, A can readily acknowledge the responsible way in which S gave her word without this acknowledgement generating any presumption that A ought to accept S's word. The burden is on those who would deny this: once we allow that the epistemic norms governing our reactions to testimony are themselves permissive, why should we think that a point that holds across *other* permissive domains *doesn't* hold with respect to testifying?

This completes my case for thinking that those who hope to argue from AR to EEET cannot do so merely by appeal to the interpersonal features of the act of testifying itself: simply put, if an audience's enjoyment of an epistemic permission to accept a speaker's say-so does not epistemically *oblige* her to accept that say-so, her failure to accept the say-so does not, by itself, constitute a way of disrespecting the speaker. Consequently, insofar as the proponent of EEET grounds the speaker's expectation of trust in an allegation to the effect that *anything less constitutes a form of disrespect of the speaker*, what is needed is a way of vindicating this allegation. We have now come full circle, as we have returned to my conclusion from above: the sought-after vindication will need to assume the doctrine of uniqueness ($UNIQ_R$).

5

Let us take stock. As I have been construing it here, the argument from Anti-Reductionism (AR) to the Entitlement to Expect Epistemic Trust (EEET) requires two additional premises. One is a claim linking the epistemic normativity of AR with the interpersonal normativity of EEET; I called this the modal type bridging principle. The other is a claim linking AR's talk of (epistemic) permissions to EEET's talk of (interpersonal) requirements; I called this the modal strength bridging principle. I suggested that the only plausible modal type bridging principle will focus on the conditions under which an audience A *disrespects* a speaker S by rejecting S's testimony inappropriately. But the notion of inappropriate rejection appears to require that the rejection be epistemically inappropriate; and the difficulty is that while AR itself alleges an epistemic permission to accept, it does not speak of any epistemic requirement to accept. The result is that we need a stronger version of Anti-Reductionism, AR_{REQ}, than what is in play in the debate in the epistemology of testimony. Insofar as AR_{REQ} denies the possibility of epistemically permissive testimony cases, it is a special case of the doctrine of Uniqueness. If this is correct, then the argument from AR to EEET must endorse the doctrine of Uniqueness (in something like the form of $UNIQ_R$).

This result should be of interest for several reasons.

First, the point is surprising: nowhere in the various discussions of EEET in the literature has there been any acknowledgement that the case for EEET depends on the doctrine of Uniqueness. Indeed, nowhere in the most prominent discussions of EEET is Uniqueness (or anything in the vicinity) so much as mentioned.[29] Hence this result amounts to a surprising, and heretofore unacknowledged, commitment of those who would argue for EEET.

Second, this result is not only surprising but potentially problematic for those who would embrace EEET. Whether in its traditional form, UNIQ, or the version I have formulated here, $UNIQ_R$, the doctrine of Uniqueness is a highly controversial doctrine. To be sure the traditional variant, UNIQ, is endorsed by various authors,[30] but it is doubted or rejected by at least as many as have endorsed or defended it.[31] Although here is not the place to debate the merits of the doctrine, the prevalence of the doubts should give proponents of EEET pause. In addition, the prevalence of these doubts indicates that the set of theorists who are in a position to see the attractions

---

[29] Here I have in mind Hinchman (2005), Moran (2006), M. Fricker (2007), and McMyler (2011).
[30] See e.g. White (2005), Matheson (2011), Dogramsci and Horowitz (2016), Schulthies (2017), and Greco and Heddon (forthcoming).
[31] See e.g. Rosen (2001), Douven (2009), Ballantyne and Coffman (2011), Brueckner and Bundy (2012), Kelly (2010, 2013a, 2013b), Schoenfield (2014, 2018), Kopec (2015), Podgorski (2016), Raleigh (2017), Sharadin (2017), Simpson (2017), and Titelbaum and Kopec (unpublished manuscript).

of EEET is somewhat limited: that set should not include anyone who doubts or rejects Uniqueness.

This last point is worth developing at greater length.

I begin with the motivation for so-called 'permissivist' views of epistemic normativity (= those that deny Uniqueness). Such views tend to be motivated by the idea that people can have all sorts of different values that can affect the conditions under which it is epistemically proper (permissible) to believe a proposition. For example, some people place a high value on having true beliefs and a comparatively lower value on avoiding false beliefs; such people might properly adopt a lower threshold for what is epistemically permissible to believe than those whose values are the reverse. Alternatively, some scientists place a comparatively high value on simplicity relative to other theoretical virtues; others place a comparatively high value on explanatory power; still others place a comparatively high value on empirical adequacy. And each will then have the epistemic standards corresponding to her value commitments. Since there are no Epistemic Gods who determine which values are the 'correct' values to have from an epistemic point of view (so the 'permissivist' line of argument runs), the result is that any—or at any rate more than one—of these perspectives is legitimate. What is more, even if someone endorses one set of values (and so endorses the epistemic standards corresponding to those values), nothing prevents her from moving to endorse a different set of values (and so moving to endorse the epistemic standards corresponding to those alternative values).

For those theorists who are attracted to 'permissivist' accounts of epistemic normativity on this sort of basis, there is a glaring problem with the case for an Entitlement to Expect Epistemic Trust. EEET itself is a universal claim: it does not differentiate between audience types, and so does not differentiate between audiences with different tolerance for risk, or who make different trade-offs regarding the value of true belief and the disvalue of false belief, or who vary according to the theoretical virtues they privilege. Those theorists who embrace a 'permissive' account of epistemic normativity will regard this lack of differentiation as curious. Such theorists will ask: is it really right to think that, *no matter the audience*, a speaker is entitled to expect to be believed so long as the audience lacks evidence to the contrary? This seems strange if we allow that some audiences are more risk-averse than others, and that this fact is reflected in the legitimate epistemic standards that govern their belief-forming practices. Theorists who endorse such 'permissive' accounts can readily allow that, in their reactions to testimonies, audiences ought to make differentiations only where epistemology permits this; but these theorists will deny that this is sufficient to establish anything as strong as EEET. On the contrary, a highly risk-averse audience who places a great deal of value on avoiding false belief may well refuse to accept any testimony except in cases in which she has excellent reasons for doing so. Even if it is assumed, with AR, that such an audience is nevertheless *entitled* to accept testimony whenever she lacks reasons for doubt,[32] even so she does not make use of this permission—and this reaction is itself epistemically permissible (assuming Uniqueness is false). In this way we see that anyone who endorses a 'permissive' account to epistemic normativity should not find EEET attractive.

I have just given two reasons for thinking that my result—that the case from AR to EEET requires a version of the doctrine of Uniqueness—is an interesting one. To these I add a third: the fact that any would-be argument from AR to EEET requires something like $UNIQ_R$ tells us something about the relationship between the two normative domains that are in play when one testifies: interpersonal normativity and the normativity of epistemology. In section 2 I developed the idea that, despite their operating with different kinds of normativity (epistemic and interpersonal), AR and EEET appear to be made for each other. AR alleges that audiences enjoy a default (but defeasible) epistemic entitlement to accept what they are told; and EEET alleges that speakers enjoy an entitlement to expect their testimonies to be ascribed a default (but defeasible) trustworthiness or credibility. In this way it can seem that EEET merely puts an interpersonal imprimatur on a speaker's expectation that her audience recognize the epistemic significance that, according to AR, her testimonies have. We now see that this isn't quite right, and that capturing the link between them will be significantly more involved than one might have initially supposed. The entitlement to have one's word ascribed a default credibility rests on the assumption that, in the absence of reasons for doubt, audiences are under some sort of obligation to accept what they are told. But this sort of obligation is nowhere near anything that Anti-Reductionism itself provides for. This might be rectified by employing a stronger version of Anti-Reductionism, according to which

---

[32] It might be wondered whether Permissivism—the denial of Uniqueness—is compatible with Anti-Reductionism. It is. To see this, we need only consider that Anti-Reductionism can be reconfigured in permissivist terms as the claim that *there is a legitimate epistemic standard on which* an audience is entitled to accept observed testimonies unless she has relevant reasons for doubt. If such a claim is a bit weaker than standard formulations of AR itself, it is nevertheless 'in the spirit' of the doctrine of Anti-Reductionism, insofar as it acknowledges that testimony *can* be a basic source of epistemically permitted belief.

in the absence of reasons for doubt, audiences are epistemically *required* to accept what they are told. But this is far stronger than anything for which one finds an argument in the epistemology of testimony literature.

I conclude, then, that the prospects of arguing from AR to EEET are, at present, dim. I should add that I draw this conclusion as someone who thinks—and who has gone to great pains in this book to argue—that there is a significant interpersonal normativity involved in the performance of speech acts (including testimony-constituting acts),[33] that the notion of epistemic injustice itself is of central importance to both ethics and epistemology, and that AR, or something like it, is true. Still, the lines connecting the dots are not as straightforward as one might have hoped.

---

[33] For a recent sustained reflection on the ethical dimension of this particular speech act, see Shiffrin (2013).

7
Does Friendship Exert Pressure on Belief?

1

In previous chapters I argued in passing against the postulation of what I called a 'strange disconnect' between the interpersonal and epistemic normativity associated with acts of telling or asserting. More specifically, I rejected the idea that telling someone something (or making a statement in their presence) can impose interpersonal demands that conflict with the demands of epistemology itself. While the postulation of this sort of 'strange disconnect' between the two normative domains might be tempting to some (i.e. when doing so enables them to preserve a cherished doctrine), I argued that we should reject this idea out of hand. In this chapter I address what I regard as the strongest argument offered *in defence of* the strange disconnect. According to this argument, the norms of friendship sometimes impose interpersonal demands which require one to violate the norms of epistemology. The contention here is that being a good friend sometimes requires being *epistemically partial* to what one is told concerning one's friend. If the 'strange disconnect' is to be motivated at all, it will most likely be motivated in this way. By the same token, if this sort of argument *fails*, this would support my repudiation of the 'strange disconnect' itself, and we would be left in a position in which to embrace the idea that the interpersonal norms involved in telling someone something do not conflict with the norms of epistemology—even in cases involving a friend. My aim in this chapter is to establish precisely this.

In this first section, however, I want to bring out why the phenomenon of friendship might be thought to support the idea that these normative domains—the interpersonal and the epistemic—can come into conflict.

Revised from S.C. Goldberg (2019), 'Against Epistemic Partiality in Friendship: Value-Reflecting Reasons', *Philosophical Studies* 176: 2221–42.

Conversational Pressure: Normativity in Speech Exchanges. Sanford C. Goldberg, Oxford University Press (2020).
© Sanford C. Goldberg.
DOI: 10.1093/oso/9780198856436.001.0001

To begin, being someone's friend or loved one affects how you interact with the person: we treat our intimates differently from how we treat strangers. This is seen even in the way we go about forming beliefs about our friends: in general, we tend to give them the benefit of the doubt in all sorts of ways. We do so when it comes to third-party reports we hear about our friends. As Sarah Stroud remarks, 'as a matter of general tendency we do react differently to reports... when these concern our friends' (Stroud 2006: 504). And the same holds when it comes to our friends' own testimony about themselves. This is especially clear when the friend repudiates an allegation against her, under conditions in which it is common knowledge that there is some evidence suggesting her guilt. In such cases we tend to be more willing to believe our friend—or at least to assign a higher credence to what she tells us—than we would in a case involving a stranger or other non-intimate.

The foregoing is simply a description of how we actually behave towards our friends. But it is no stretch to think that this is how we *ought* to treat our friends. After all, friendship not only inspires us to behave in certain ways, it also places demands on us. Not only do we give our friends the benefit of the doubt, we 'owe it' to them to do so. Only now it can begin to seem as though there is a conflict between the norms of friendship, taken to include whatever interpersonal demands friendship generates, and the norms of epistemology, taken to include the standards for epistemically proper (or justified) belief and responsible belief-formation. Those who embrace the appearances here[1] endorse the 'strange disconnect' recently mentioned: they endorse the idea that the interpersonal demands of friendship itself can require us to show epistemic partiality towards our friends, thereby violating the norms of epistemology.

The goal of this chapter is to argue that this case for the 'strange disconnect' fails: we can honour the demands of friendship without forming beliefs that epistemic standards would prohibit. If this is so, then the point for which I argued in previous chapters stands: the interpersonal demands that are imposed on one when one observes another's testimony do not conflict with the norms of epistemology. This remains the case even when the information concerns one's friend, and even in cases in which it is one's friend herself who is asking one to trust her.

---

[1] As noted above, these include Baker (1987), Keller (2004), Stroud (2006), and Hazlett (2013). Others acknowledge the appearances but aim to explain them away: two recent papers in this vein are Kawall (2013) and Hawley (2014b). I am in the latter camp.

2

My thesis, then, is that the interpersonal demands of being a good friend do not require epistemic partiality. The doctrine of epistemic partiality itself requires a bit of sharpening. Let us use 'doxastic response' to cover the various methods and practices one brings to bear in forming, revising, and sustaining belief in the face of new information, as well as the beliefs that result from the use of such methods and practices.[2] Then we can formulate the doctrine of Epistemic Partiality in Friendship as the claim that

> EPF There are cases in which one receives new information about a friend—about her character, behaviour, past, abilities, and so forth—where satisfying the demands of friendship requires a doxastic response that fails to satisfy ordinary epistemic standards of justified belief and/or responsible belief-formation.

Many philosophers endorse some version of EPF. Thus Sarah Stroud writes that

> Friendship places demands... on our *beliefs* and our methods of forming beliefs.... [T]his epistemic partiality is contrary to the standards of epistemic responsibility and justification held up by mainstream epistemological theories. (Stroud 2006: 499; italics in original)

And Simon Keller concurs: '... [E]pistemic norms sometimes conflict with the requirements of good friendship' (Keller 2004: 499).

As formulated, EPF is neutral as to where the information itself comes from—whether it is a report or it is non-testimonial evidence. And even where the information is testimonial, EPF is neutral as between whether the report comes from the friend herself or from a third party. But insofar as our interest is in the nature of conversational pressure, we have reason to give special attention to cases in which the information itself comes from the mouth of the friend herself. Such cases enable us to frame the allegation of the 'strange disconnect' in a particularly sharp way: does the fact that *a friend* told you something put an additional pressure on you to believe her

---

[2] This could be expanded to speak instead (or in addition) of credences, but as the literature to date has focused on belief, I will follow the literature.

even when doing so would violate the standards of epistemology? For this reason, I want to distinguish the allegation of epistemic partiality itself, as framed by EPF above, from the allegation of epistemic partiality in cases involving the say-so of a friend (where what is at issue is the epistemic trust we place in our friend's say-so itself). I frame the latter as follows (the subscript making clear that this is the sort of partiality involving Epistemic Trust of a friend):

EPF_{ET} There are cases in which a friend tells one something where one's satisfying the demands of friendship requires a doxastic response that fails to satisfy ordinary epistemic standards of justified belief and/or responsible belief-formation.

The doctrine of Epistemic Partiality, whether in its generic form EPF or its more specific form EPF_{ET}, is a controversial doctrine. Katherine Hawley aptly captures part of what is controversial in these views:

... [I]f Stroud and Keller are correct, ... friendship can give us reasons to believe our friends trustworthy, reasons which can go beyond whatever epistemic reasons we have to adopt this belief; these are reasons which do not apply to beliefs about the trustworthiness of nonfriends. (Hawley 2014b: 2034)

According to Hawley, what is controversial is the contention that friendship provides a decidedly non-epistemic reason for belief—in particular, for belief in a friend's trustworthiness. While I agree with Hawley's point—the contention she articulates on Stroud's and Keller's behalf is indeed controversial (in sections 6 and 7 I will be arguing that it is false)—I think that the controversial nature of the doctrine of Epistemic Partiality itself (= EPF) goes beyond this. For the case for EPF is based on the following general idea: there are ways of forming beliefs about one's friends that are both required by the demands of being a good friend and such that the resulting beliefs are (would be) epistemically unjustified. *One* of these ways of forming beliefs is through an inference from our belief in a friend's trustworthiness; this way is central to the sort of epistemic partiality in EPF_{ET}, where what is at issue is whether to believe a friend's say-so. But this is not the *only* way partiality is alleged to arise in beliefs regarding one's friends. If we are to vindicate the case against EPF (and by extension against EPF_{ET}), we must target all of the belief-forming practices thought to be implicated in the case for partiality.

This is what I shall try to do in what follows. My claim will be that, while it is indeed true that the norms of friendship place demands on us in how we go about forming beliefs regarding our friends—in particular, there are various practices we ought to engage in as we do so—none of these violates any ordinary epistemic standard of justified belief. Of course it is also true that we sometimes form *unjustified* beliefs out of friendship; but I submit that this is not forced on us by the standards of being a good friend.

3

I want to begin by enumerating the various practices we engage in as we form and sustain beliefs about our friends. On this score we cannot do better than to return to Stroud (2006), one of the seminal papers on epistemic partiality in friendship. Stroud describes four separate but interrelated practices of this sort. (While she is remarking about our doxastic reactions to reports *about* our friends, rather than testimonies *from* them, it is easy to appreciate that some versions of these apply to both.) First, we exhibit SERIOUS SCRUTINY of negative claims about our friends:

> ... [W]e tend to devote more energy to defeating or minimizing the impact of unfavorable data than we otherwise would.... [W]e are more liable to scrutinize and to question the evidence being presented than we otherwise would be.... [W]e will go to greater lengths in the case of a friend to construct and entertain alternative and less damning interpretation of the reported conduct than we would for a nonfriend.... (2006: 505–6)[3]

Second, we tend to draw DIFFERENT CONCLUSIONS about our friends:

> ... [W]e draw different conclusions and make different inferences than we otherwise would.... [W]e are simply less likely to conclude that our friend acted disreputably, or that he is a bad person, than we would be in the case of a nonfriend. (2006: 506)

Third, we extend INTERPRETATIVE CHARITY towards them:

---

[3] Notice that Stroud's own formulation here (and in what follows) is descriptive rather than normative—she is describing what we do, rather than what we 'owe'. But it is clear from her presentation that she thinks that we do as we ought to do.

What seems to be characteristic of the good friend is not a stubborn denial of obvious, incontrovertible facts about her friend but something more subtle.... It is a matter of extending more interpretative charity to your friends than you naturally would to strangers. (2006: 506–7)

And fourth, we treat the fact that they are our friend as a REASON relevant to our deliberation about what to believe about them:

... [T]he good friend's reason for adopting these differential epistemic practices seems to be simply that the person in question is her friend. But that someone is your friend is not itself a relevant epistemic reason ... to form different beliefs about him than you would about anyone else. (2006: 513)

With these points in hand, Stroud's argument proceeds to use two assumptions to make the case for Epistemic Partiality in Friendship (EPF). The two assumptions are these:

A1   The doxastic responses described by SERIOUS SCRUTINY, DIFFERENT CONCLUSIONS, INTERPRETATIVE CHARITY, and REASON all reflect the interpersonal demands of friendship itself, so that we *ought* to act so as to make them true (see Stroud 2006: 501–4)

A2   The result of our conforming to these demands is that we acquire beliefs that fail to satisfy ordinary epistemic standards (see Stroud 2006: 519–21)

Given A1 and A2, we arrive at the conclusion of EPF: there are cases in which the beliefs we form as we seek to fulfil our friendship-generated obligations do not satisfy ordinary epistemic standards of justified belief and/or responsible belief-formation.

4

So far I have been talking generically about the violation of 'ordinary epistemic standards of justified belief and/or responsible belief-formation'. In what follows it will be helpful to be a bit more explicit about such standards. In order to be as neutral as possible but also as general as possible (i.e. to ensure that any relevant standards are covered), I will speak of the epistemic standard according to which *one ought to believe in accordance with one's evidence.* (This construal should be acceptable to defenders of EPF, as they often frame their argument in these very terms.) In these terms, Stroud's basic idea—indeed, the basic idea behind the various arguments for the doctrine of Epistemic Partiality in Friendship—is that there are cases in which one 'owes it' to one's friends to react (doxastically) to information about them in ways that are not warranted by one's total evidence. As noted above, this sort of case for EPF rests on the twin assumptions of A1 and A2. In terms of our present construal of 'ordinary epistemic standards'. A2 will now read:

$A2_{Evid}$ Beliefs formed through some or all of the practices above fail to satisfy ordinary epistemological standards—fail to be warranted by one's total evidence.

In what follows I want to be as concessive as I can. Accordingly, I will grant that SERIOUS SCRUTINY, DIFFERENT CONCLUSIONS, INTERPRETATIVE CHARITY, and REASON capture our actual practices. And I will grant A1 as well: the interpersonal demands of friendship require that we participate in all of the practices described. What I deny is that anything epistemically untoward follows from these two concessions. To show this, I will need to argue that $A2_{Evid}$ (and hence A2) is false. I will do so by presenting a model on which A1 is true but $A2_{Evid}$ is false; and I will argue that this model offers a plausible account of all of the doxastic responses mentioned in A1.

The key notion I will be using, as I seek to establish that $A2_{Evid}$ is false (despite the assumed truth of A1), is that of *value-reflecting* reasons. Once we appreciate the value-reflecting reasons in play in friendships, we will appreciate that participation in the practices noted above, in the way that friendship demands, is epistemically innocuous.

The basic idea behind the notion of a value-reflecting reason is not new. Ethicists have employed the idea to capture the practical reasons we have in virtue of our values—deriving either from *the values themselves*, or from *our valuing* them.[4] In this chapter I will employ the version which speaks of our valuing, not of the values themselves—but nothing hangs on this choice. (A more objective notion of value-reflecting reasons can be developed by

---

[4] For various theories in this rough vicinity, see e.g. Lewis (1989), Kolodny (2003), Schroeder (2007), Chang (2013), and Sobel (2016).

focusing on the values themselves.) In any case, the version of value-reflecting reasons I will employ can be brought out in three steps.

The first step is to make clear what is involved in valuing something. Suppose that V is something one values. Part of what it is to value V, I submit, is to do what you can to preserve, promote, and/or protect V, and to avoid doing what would demote, undermine, or threaten V. Thus we can say that if you value V you have *practical* reasons to act so as to preserve V, or to protect V, or to promote V, and so as to avoid doing what would demote, undermine, or threaten V. These practical reasons are prima facie, of course: they can be outweighed by other practical reasons you have, they can be undermined by epistemic reasons to think that V ought not to be valued, and so forth. But they are prima facie practical reasons that derive from your valuing V. And since all of the foregoing claims derive from the nature of valuing something, they will be familiar to anyone who is moderately reflective. I will call them *V-generated, value-reflecting practical reasons*.

The second step is to make clear that these practical reasons come in degrees. The more S values V, the stronger her V-generated, value-reflecting practical reasons—that is, her reasons to do what she can to preserve or promote or protect V, and to avoid doing what would demote or undermine or threaten V—and so the weightier other practical reasons would have to be to outweigh her V-generated, value-reflecting practical reasons. The limiting case is a case in which S regards V as inviolable—say, because S regards V as a moral value, and so regards V as something that cannot be sacrificed for any non-moral good—in which case S is committed to there not being any other (non-moral) practical reasons that outweigh her V-generated, value-reflecting practical reasons. To be sure, even if S at present regards V as inviolable, it still may happen that she acquires *epistemic* reasons to doubt this; but insofar as she at present regards V as inviolable, she is committed to thinking that no other (non-moral) practical reason can outweigh her V-generated value-reflecting reasons.[5]

The third step is to make clear that one can have *epistemic* reasons to think that some person S values V. Part of what it is to have such reasons is to have epistemic reasons to think that S has (and recognizes having[6]) prima

---

[5] Here I disregard for the sake of simplicity the question whether moral values themselves can be in conflict with one another, giving rise to the need to distinguish prima facie moral duties with *ultima facie* moral duties. The picture could easily be modified to accommodate this point, but I won't bother doing so here.

[6] This assumes that S is moderately reflective.

facie practical reasons to do what she can to preserve or promote or protect V, and to avoid doing what would demote or undermine or threaten V. What is more, insofar as one has epistemic reasons to believe that S's valuing of V is strong, one's epistemic reasons support one in thinking that S's V-generated, value-reflecting practical reasons are correspondingly strong. Epistemic reasons of this kind I call *value-reflecting epistemic reasons*.

I now want to suggest that the temptation we as theorists might feel towards embracing Epistemic Partiality in Friendship—the pressure deriving from the thought that SERIOUS SCRUTINY, DIFFERENT CONCLUSIONS, INTERPRETATIVE CHARITY, and REASON will force a subject to violate ordinary epistemic standards on justified belief and/or responsible belief-formation—can be explained away as an understandable, but ultimately wrongheaded, attempt to come to grips with a phenomenon that is best explained in terms of value-reflecting reasons (epistemic and practical).

5

Suppose, with A1, that we 'owe it' to our friends to react to new relevant information about them—whether from their own mouth, or from some other source—in the ways captured by SERIOUS SCRUTINY, DIFFERENT CONCLUSIONS, INTERPRETATIVE CHARITY, and REASON. How can this be if we are to continue to form and sustain epistemically justified, responsibly formed beliefs about our friends? To answer this, we need to appreciate the value-reflecting reasons that are generated by a mutually valued friendship. In what follows I will be focusing primarily on the case in which the information comes from the friend's own mouth. This is in keeping with the book's main focus on the kinds of conversational pressure that a speaker brings to bear on her audience in speech exchanges, and it will enable us to bring out how friendship is supposed to present the best case for the 'strange disconnect' that is my target. Even so, what I have to say about these cases, where the information comes from the friend's own say-so, can be generalized to cover the case where the information comes from a third party, or even from a non-testimonial source of evidence—and below I will be suggesting how the account generalizes in this way.

Suppose that both S and A mutually recognize that they value their friendship with one another. In that case, both have practical reasons to do what they can to preserve and/or enhance the friendship and to avoid doing what will jeopardize or undermine the friendship, and they know this of one another. Now take a case in which S tells A that she (S) is not guilty of having committed some terrible deed of which she has been accused, where, prior to S's say-so, A had a good deal of evidence to think that S had done so. What we want to know is how it is that A can respond in the manner described above—that is, in keeping with SERIOUS SCRUTINY, DIFFERENT CONCLUSIONS, INTERPRETATIVE CHARITY, and REASON—and yet still have a justified, responsibly formed belief regarding S's guilt or innocence. The key lies in appreciating the relevant set of value-reflecting reasons in play. We will need to identify the value-reflecting *epistemic* reasons that A has, as well as those that S has; but we will also need to identify the value-reflecting *practical* reasons that A has, as well as those that S has.

Consider first the value-reflecting *practical* reasons that each has to do what they can to preserve or enhance the friendship and to avoid doing what they can to harm or jeopardize the friendship.

Let us start with speaker S herself. In those cases in which S tells A that p, S is in effect inviting A to trust her,[7] in which case S enhances the friendship if she is worthy of A's trust on this occasion (i.e. she is telling the truth out of competence and the desire to do so), and S risks harming the friendship if she is *not* worthy of A's trust on this occasion (i.e. she is lying or else is speaking unwarrantedly). From this we surmise that S has (friendship-generated, value-reflecting) practical reasons to tell the truth, and (friendship-generated, value-reflecting) practical reasons to avoid lying or speaking unwarrantedly.[8] In general, these reasons will be stronger in accordance with the degree to which S values the friendship. We can think of this as a source of practical normative pressure (deriving from the friendship) to tell the truth, where this normative pressure goes beyond whatever practical (ethical) pressure there is on any speaker to tell the truth.

For his part, audience A also has (friendship-generated, value-reflecting) practical reasons to behave in certain ways, and to refrain from behaving in

---

[7] See e.g. Holton 1994 and Hinchman 2006. While I do not endorse Hinchman's account of the epistemology of testimony emerging from the idea of telling as 'inviting to trust' (for which see Chapter 4 as well as Goldberg 2015b), for present purposes I regard this as an apt description of an aspect of the interpersonal nature of the act of telling.

[8] The idea that a speaker might have affective reasons for truth-telling is itself a point that has been made by many others, from many different points of view. See e.g. Baier (1986), Baker (1987), Jones (1996, 2004), and Hawley (2014b).

certain ways. Consider again that in telling A that p, S is in effect inviting A to trust her. So A risks jeopardizing the friendship if A responds inappropriately to this request for trust. More specifically still, A risks jeopardizing the friendship in any case in which it is true *both* that S is worthy of A's trust *and* that A fails to trust S. (The case in which S is not worthy of A's trust but A trusts anyway is not one in which A damages the friendship; it is one in which S does so.) So A has (friendship-generated, value-reflecting) practical reasons to do what he can to avoid risking this sort of damage to the friendship. To be sure, this does *not* mean A has practical reasons to believe S; rather, A's practical reasons are reasons to do what he can to avoid the case in which S is deserving of trust but A fails to extend it. (Precisely what these reasons require of A is a matter to which I will return in a moment.)

Notice that even in cases in which A receives a report about S that comes from someone other than S, value-reflecting reasons may be in play. To see this, suppose that A hears a third-party report to the effect that S has behaved very badly. In such a case, the danger to the friendship A has with S comes when either A disbelieves something good about S or believes something bad about S, where A's (dis)belief in question does not match the facts. In cases of third-party reports, A has practical value-reflecting reasons to do what he can to avoid the cases in which he falsely believes something bad of S or else fails to acquire a true belief of something good about S. But, whether the case is one in which the information comes from the friend's say-so or from a third party, in both cases there is practical (normative) pressure bearing on the audience's reaction to the observed speech. (What this comes to is a matter to which I will return shortly.)

Now consider that ordinarily friends are aware that they each value the friendship. What is more, in ordinary friendships each tends to act on the (friendship-generated) practical reasons (s)he has, at least when those reasons are not outweighed or defeated by other reasons. For if it weren't usually the case that the friend acted on these friendship-generated practical reasons, the friendship itself would probably not last. And in ordinary cases friends will be mutually aware of this. This bears on the sort of normative pressure exerted on an audience who observes a report about a friend.

Start with the case in which S and A are good friends, where S tells A that p, where this is some proposition concerning S herself (her behaviour, her character, etc.). In this case, we get the result that both S and A will be aware of the (friendship-generated, value-reflecting) practical reasons that each of them has on those occasions when S tells A that p, and both will have *epistemic* reasons to think that each of them will act on their (friendship-generated, value-reflecting) practical reasons, at least when those reasons are not outweighed or defeated by other reasons. So: A has epistemic reasons to think that, when it comes to S's telling A that p, S has (friendship-generated, value-reflecting) practical reasons to speak truly and avoid lies and unwarranted speech,[9] and that S is likely to act on them at least when there are no sufficiently strong competing reasons in play;[10] and for her part S has epistemic reasons to think that, when it comes to A's reaction to S's telling him that p, A has (friendship-generated, value-reflecting) practical reasons to do what he can to avoid the situation in which A disbelieves S despite S's having deserved A's trust. This means that (it is mutual knowledge between S and A that) A should be careful before *dis*believing S—lest A risk disbelieving S when S deserved A's trust, thereby damaging the friendship itself.[11]

I submit that this practical pressure *just is* the felt pressure that leads people to think that the demands of friendship can require epistemic partiality. To distrust a friend is to risk damaging the friendship,[12] where the friendship *is* damaged when one does not give one's friend what is her due. In cases in which S tells her friend A something, it is S's due as a friend to be recognized by A as speaking under conditions in which (1) in addition to all of the ordinary moral and practical reasons to be a truth-teller, S has

---

[9] It is to be noted that these practical reasons go beyond what an ordinary speaker has in making assertions. This is why A might think to herself, 'Surely S wouldn't lie *to me*.' Interestingly, if a third party, T, knew that S and A were good friends and that S just addressed her assertion that p to A, T herself could reason analogously: 'Surely S wouldn't lie *to A*.' (With thanks to Katherine Hawley for noting this third-person analogue, in discussion.) Of course, there is one possibility A is in a position to rule out that overhearer T is not: the possibility that S and A are *conspiring* to get someone to reason in the precise way described above, thereby getting any overhearer who knows of S's and A's friendship to believe that p with great confidence. (For a discussion of the normative pressure deriving simply from the nature of assertion, as opposed to friendship, see Goldberg (2015b).)

[10] If there are other practical reasons that S acts on, this must be because those reasons outweigh her value-reflecting practical reasons of friendship, in which case her valuing those other things is so great she is willing to risk serious damage to the friendship itself to preserve them—and S should anticipate that A would be able to work this out.

[11] This is why, though it is 'bruising' whenever one is not believed (Anscombe 1979), it is *particularly* bruising not to be believed by one's friends, since in effect this makes clear that the friend is confident enough in the falsity of what one says that he is willing to risk damaging the friendship (where the damage would arise in the case in which one was, after all, trustworthy on this occasion).

[12] The idea that there are potential costs associated with forming negative beliefs about friends is a fairly common one. The claim that these costs might be used *as part of an argument against Epistemic Partiality*, as I am trying to do here, has been explicitly made only by a select few. For a particularly clear statement of this, see e.g. Kawall (2013: 364–5) and McHugh (2013: 1124). My own view is closer to Kawall's, as McHugh's version appears to rely on the denial of Uniqueness. See section 6.

strong practical reasons not to risk harming the friendship by lying or speaking unwarrantedly, and (2) S has a claim of friendship on A's reaction to her speech. An audience A who recognizes (1) and who also knows that her friend S typically acts so as to promote or preserve the friendship has *additional epistemic reasons* to believe S—that is, epistemic reasons that go beyond the sorts of reasons A might have to believe a stranger whom A recognizes to be similarly epistemically placed; and an audience A who recognizes (2) will recognize that he (A) himself is under normative pressure (deriving from the friendship) to do what he can to ensure that the 'harmful' scenario of disbelieving a friend's trustworthy testimony does not come to pass.

Notice that similar things can be said of the case in which A observes a third-party report that p, where this concerns some proposition concerning S herself (her behaviour, her character, etc.). Here the risk is that A will fail to believe something good, or will falsely believe something bad, of S, thereby damaging the friendship.[13] There is thus practical pressure on one who hears a third-party report regarding one's friend: there is pressure to avoid these outcomes. Again, we can think of this normative pressure in terms of value-reflecting reasons generated by the friendship itself: A has value-reflecting reasons to do what he can to avoid both of these outcomes. I submit, once again, that this *just is* an instance of the felt pressure that leads people to think that the demands of friendship can require epistemic partiality.

6

With this we reach the heart of the matter: what *can* an audience do to minimize the prospect of the 'harmful' scenarios, wherein A disbelieves his friend S under conditions in which, in fact, S was worthy of A's trust, or alternatively (in cases of third-party reporting or non-testimonial evidence) wherein A fails to believe something that is both true and reflects well on S, or believes something that is false but which reflects poorly on S? After addressing the former sort of case (in which the report comes from one's friend) first, I will then extend the proposed analysis to cases involving third-party reports and non-testimonial evidence.

---

[13] See n. 13.

In cases in which it is A's friend S herself who tells A that p, the 'harmful' scenario—the scenario which A has (practical, value-reflecting) reason to avoid—is one in which two conditions hold: S was worthy of A's trust, and yet A disbelieves S. Consequently, one thing A might do to ensure he avoids this scenario would be to *believe* S, since this will ensure that the second condition of the 'harmful' scenario does not hold. But this cannot be the solution to our puzzle. For one thing, whatever one thinks of trust being under one's control,[14] belief surely is not; so if the (non-testimonial) evidence is overwhelmingly stacked against S, A may not be able to believe her. For another, the proposal that S should avoid the 'harmful' scenario by believing S out of friendship is a recipe for partiality (EPF); whereas what I aim to show is that we can accommodate the (interpersonal) normative pressure on A to respond to S in terms of what he owes S as her friend, *without* endorsing EPF. Happily, there are other things A might do to minimize the prospect of the 'harmful' scenario. A might seek more evidence, trying to see whether there are other (exculpating) considerations of which she was not previously aware; A might double- and triple-check to make sure his total evidence does in fact support the (friendship-risking) conclusion; and/or A might think hard about whether there are other (epistemically permissible) glosses of the evidence he already has, perhaps reflecting alternatives he had neglected to consider, consistent with belief in S's innocence. In fact, I submit that A has value-reflecting practical reasons to do each of these things, deriving from the friendship itself.

This claim—that A has (friendship-generated, value-reflecting) practical reasons to get more evidence, to double- and triple-check his route from the evidence to the (friendship-risking) conclusion, and to consider whether there are alternative (epistemically permissible) construals of the evidence itself—enjoys independent motivation. The sorts of practical reason at issue are quite common, and can be seen in cases having nothing to do with friendship.

First, we sometimes find ourselves at a given time t with practical reasons to collect more evidence, and then (after doing so, at t_1) to readjust our beliefs/credences to fit our new total evidence (including the newly acquired evidence)—*even if* the evidence we currently have at t would ordinarily justify belief. This occurs when we have practical reasons at t to reopen

---

[14] See e.g. Holton (1994) for a defence of the thesis that we can decide to trust.

inquiry. This point should not be controversial; in any case, it involves no violation of any ordinary epistemic standard. I offer three illustrations.

One can have practical reasons to reopen inquiry because this is demanded by the standards of one's profession. Suppose Mary is a paediatrician specializing in asthma. As a trained physician, she already has a substantial body of belief regarding the treatment of asthma. Even so, if Mary has not followed the literature on recent trends in asthma treatment in quite some time, then when she encounters a patient with an unusual case of asthma, she 'owes it' to her patient not to reach a verdict about the best course of treatment (even if she has had a belief about this) until *after* she has read whatever new research has been published since she last checked. Here, her 'owing it' to her patient to get more evidence is a matter of her living up to the professional standards set by the American Academy of Pediatrics.

Alternatively, one can have practical reasons to reopen inquiry because of a promise one has made. Suppose Juan and Leandro are conversing about the current state of the labour dispute. Juan offers various reasons for his confidence that there have been no recent developments. If Leandro (wanting a higher degree of warranted confidence than these reasons provide) remains unsatisfied, and if in response Juan promises Leandro to find out more, then Juan 'owes it' to Leandro to find out more. In that case, even if (before collecting the evidence he has promised Leandro to collect) Juan currently believes with justification that there have been no recent developments in the labour dispute, he should revisit the matter *after* acquiring the new evidence.[15] Here, his 'owing it' to Leandro to get more evidence merely reflects his promise to do so; and his having to revisit the question (concerning developments in the labour dispute) after getting this additional evidence is driven by the ordinary epistemic requirement to conform one's belief to one's (current) evidence. Again, there is nothing strange about this; it involves no violation of any epistemic standard.

Finally, one can have practical reasons to reopen inquiry in cases involving high stakes. When a good deal hangs on the outcome of one's choices and actions, it can behoove one to refrain from judging on the evidence one currently has, even if one's current evidence would be sufficient for judgement in low-stakes cases. Several recent epistemologists have used cases of

---

[15] An alternative analysis is possible: perhaps Juan should suspend until he collects new evidence. For an excellent discussion of the epistemological dimensions of suspension, see Friedman (2017).

this sort to argue that practical considerations (e.g. stakes) can affect the standards for justified belief and knowledge; this is the view known as 'pragmatic encroachment' in epistemology (Hawthorne (2004); Stanley (2005); Fantl and McGrath (2009)). But one need not endorse the doctrine of pragmatic encroachment—a controversial thesis to be sure—to appreciate how high stakes can generate practical reasons to reopen inquiry. For an alternative interpretation is that what shifts in these cases is *not* the standards on justified belief or knowledge (they remain invariant), but rather the standards on justified action: sometimes one shouldn't act until one has a degree of certainty that goes beyond the minimum required by justified belief and knowledge.[16]

I submit that friendship itself is another instance of this same general phenomenon whereby we can have practical reasons to reopen inquiry. Suppose that S tells A something important about herself that goes against A's current evidence. In some cases, where the friendship between S and A is strong enough and A's evidence to the contrary is not particularly weighty, the value-reflecting reasons in play can tip the balance of reasons in favour of A's accepting this say-so. This merely reflects the fact that A is aware (and has epistemic reasons to believe) that S has friendship-generated value-reflecting practical reasons not to lie or speak unwarrantedly to A. (This is why it can be epistemically kosher to react differently to testimony from a friend than from a non-intimate, as we don't standardly have such reasons in cases involving non-intimates.[17]) But now suppose the other reasons A has for *dis*believing S's testimony *are* weighty, *more* weighty in fact than the value-reflecting epistemic reasons A has for thinking that S wouldn't jeopardize the friendship by lying or speaking unwarrantedly. In that case, I submit that A owes it to S to get more evidence, and in particular to make sure A has explored all of the places that are most likely to deliver further significant evidence (including evidence vindicating S's say-so). This is no more impermissible from an epistemic point of view than is Mary's consulting with the *Journal of Pediatrics* or the *Journal of Asthma* etc., or a subject's looking for more evidence in cases involving particularly high stakes. These cases merely make manifest that we sometimes have practical reasons to reopen inquiry.

---

[16] See e.g. Brown (2008) and Reed (2010, 2012). Indeed, I would speculate that value-reflecting practical reasons can be used to resist the argument for pragmatic encroachment; this is a matter to which I hope to return in the near future.

[17] This point has been made by Hawley (2014b: 2037). I will discuss differences between our accounts in section 7.

There is a second way in which the practices by which we form beliefs regarding our friends instantiate a more general (ordinary, epistemically innocuous) practice: we sometimes have practical reasons to see whether or not there are alternative (epistemically permissible) construals of our evidence. This claim can seem relatively uncontroversial if we assume that for any single body of evidence, there is always more than one set of beliefs that are rendered rational by that evidence. Given this assumption, subjects would be free to search for and to endorse *the most friendly of all the epistemically permissible construals of the evidence*—in which case it is easy to see friendship as something that generates practical reasons to consider alternative construals. However, the assumption that makes all of this seem uncontroversial is itself controversial, as it amounts to the doctrine we encountered in Chapter 6 under the name 'permissivism'. As we saw there, permissivism is the denial of Uniqueness, which I repeat here:

UNIQ   For any body of evidence E (possessed by subject S) and proposition p, there is a uniquely rational doxastic attitude S should have in p.

While some writers have endorsed permissivism (= rejected UNIQ) as a way to avoid having to endorse Epistemic Partiality in Friendship (EPF),[18] I would prefer not to take this route. For one thing, as I noted in Chapter 6, permissivism itself (like UNIQ) is a controversial doctrine, and it would be best to avoid having to take a stand on this matter if we can do so. For another, this move is unnecessary for present purposes: even if we *endorse* UNIQ, the point remains that there can be cases in which subjects have practical reasons to see whether there are alternative construals of their evidence.

To see this, suppose UNIQ is true. This is a thesis about what is uniquely rational for a subject A to believe—what distribution of credences is uniquely rational for A—given her evidence. Of course, this need not match *A's own view* as to what she ought to believe (or how she ought to apportion her credences), given her evidence. After all, our judgements regarding what our evidence supports are fallible.[19] One way to take the

---

[18] See e.g. Hawley (2014b), where this is defended at length, McHugh (2013: 1124), and Kawall (2013: 366-7), where a version of this sort of strategy is presented as one of various points that can be made against EPF.

[19] The idea that one might be wrong about what one's own evidence supports is a theme of much recent 'externalist' literature in epistemology. See e.g. Williamson (2000, 2014) and Lasonen-Aarnio (2010, 2014).

present idea—that we 'owe it' to our friend to see whether there is any construal of the evidence consistent with belief in her innocence—is to treat it as an injunction to double- and triple-check, and to call as many helpful alternatives to mind as we can to see whether our evidence rules them all out. This is perfectly compatible with the doctrine of UNIQ; the injunction to double- and triple-check, and to call as many helpful alternatives to mind as we can, merely reflects our imaginative limitations and our fallibility at determining what our evidence supports (and what it rules out). So even if UNIQ is true, we can still have friendship-generated, value-reflecting practical reasons to double- and triple-check, and we can have friendship-generated, value-reflecting practical reasons to see if there are alternative construals of our evidence consistent with belief in our friend's innocence. Again, there is nothing epistemically untoward about any of this; behaving in this way violates no ordinary epistemic standards of justified belief and/or responsible belief-formation. If anything, it reflects a special motivation to try to *live up to* those standards.[20] Notice that this is as true whether the report comes from one's friend, or it comes from a third party: one has practical reasons to do things that will minimize the risk of damaging the friendship, and having done these things, one then can fix one's belief in the ways demanded by the norms of epistemology itself.

In sum, it is commonplace that we sometimes have value-reflecting practical reasons to get more evidence before reaching a verdict, as well as value-reflecting practical reasons to see whether there is any more favourable construal of our current evidence. There is nothing untoward about any of this; it has nothing specifically to do with friendship. What friendship does, I submit, is to provide us with value-reflecting practical reasons that reflect *our valuing the friendship itself*. In this way we can account for 'the peculiar ways in which trustors are required by their trust [of a friend] to approach the evidence' (Wanderer and Townsend 2013: 9). Once we see this, I submit, the felt pressure to endorse the doctrine of Epistemic Partiality in Friendship evaporates.

---

[20] Perhaps it will be said that this reflects badly on cases not involving friends, where we don't have this extra motivation. So be it; the point is that we don't owe it to strangers to double- and triple-check.

7

Although the account I am proposing employs the notion of value-reflecting reasons, and in this way differs from existing attempts to resist the case for EPF, still it may be wondered how different it actually is. After all, several of the most prominent claims I am making have been made by others (above all, by Kawall 2013 and Hawley 2014b), and this can prompt one to question the need for the appeal to value-reflecting reasons.[21] (Perhaps the sort of 'conversational pressure' that obtains in cases in which we consider say-so regarding our friends is handled better in some other way.) In this section I address this concern, arguing that the work that is done by value-reflecting reasons—above all, by value-reflecting *practical* reasons—makes the present proposal superior to alternative ways to model the sort of conversational pressure at issue. The overriding virtue of the present proposal is to make clear that various disparate phenomena cited by others in their case against EPF can all be understood in terms of one underlying mechanism—that of value-reflecting reasons—which is independently motivated and which enables us to eschew the substantial epistemological assumptions other responses embrace. (This is particularly virtuous in the present context, in which we are trying to understand the nature of the pressure exerted by friendship on belief.)

To begin, I am not the first to note (in connection with the attempt to resist EPF) that speakers are often more trustworthy when speaking to their friends than when speaking to strangers. Hawley (2014b) makes precisely this point when she writes that

> it is often more reasonable to believe your friends will prove trustworthy to you than to believe this of strangers, since your friends are objectively more likely to fulfil your trust, however they behave to others. (2014b: 2037)

Analysing this point as reflecting the value-reflecting reasons in play (as I have) yields an important insight that is missed by Hawley's analysis: *the very same mechanism* that generates the increased (interpersonal) normative pressure on speakers to be trustworthy when their audience is a friend, also generates the (interpersonal) normative pressure on *audiences* to do more than they ordinarily would do to minimize the friendship-damaging risks

---

[21] I thank an anonymous referee for indicating the need to take this up more explicitly.

involved when they are forming beliefs about their friends.[22] This is important, since without this it is unclear how to address cases in which the information about one's friend comes, not from the friend's own testimony, but in some other way. While Hawley (2014b) is silent about these cases,[23] my analysis applies to them as well, and so can be used to show that even in situations in which the information comes, for instance, from non-testimonial evidence or from a third party, the case for EPF can be resisted.

Nor am I the first to respond to the argument for EPF by appeal to the *negative (practical) effects of believing bad things about your friends*. Indeed, both McHugh and Kawall appreciate the point that, when it comes to forming beliefs about your friend, the potential negative effects of believing bad things about them give you reasons to collect more evidence, to double-check, and so forth.[24] However, both of them accommodate this point by endorsing pragmatic encroachment. Their reasoning on this is implicit but instructive. I might offer the following rational reconstruction: (1) before fixing on a belief that would threaten the friendship, the good friend should, for example, collect more evidence; (2) this first point, (1), appears to be a form of partiality which threatens ordinary standards of epistemology; but (3) these appearances can be explained away by appeal to the assumption that the standards for justification can be raised and lowered by pragmatic factors.[25] This reasoning captures the core strategy shared by McHugh and Kawall, which is to acknowledge (1) but explain away the impression of partiality by endorsing pragmatic encroachment.

On this score Kawall's more extended discussion of these matters is instructive. He appears to hold an even stronger view: not only *can* one explain away the appearances of partiality in (2) by appeal to pragmatic

---

[22] Above I pointed to two risks: that of failing to trust a friend who is worthy of one's trust (as in cases in which it is the friend who tells one something); and that of acquiring false beliefs of something untoward about one's friend (as in cases in which the information comes from a third party).

[23] As noted in the introduction, she discusses only the special case in which EPF$_{ET}$ is at issue.

[24] See McHugh (2013: 1124–5) and Kawall (2013: 365–7).

[25] Here is what Kawall says: 'given the serious harms that could result from believing a negative claim about a friend, an agent would require significant justification in order for it to be rational for her to act as if the claim were true. In turn, *this means that the level of epistemic justification that would be required for the agent to know that p would also be especially high in such a case*. It is epistemically required that the good friend seek greater evidence, treat a wider range of possibilities as relevant, and so on in order to know. As such, there would be no conflict between epistemic norms and any belief-forming behaviour that is required (or merely permissible) by the standards of friendship.' (Kawall 2013: 366–7; italics added) For McHugh's part, see (McHugh 2013: 1133 n. 24).

encroachment, this is the *least costly* way to do so. My basis for this attribution is as follows. Kawall explicitly recognizes the costliness of the appeal to pragmatic encroachment (these costs prompt him to offer a second ('more conservative' (2013: 367)) response to EPR). Given these costs, it is reasonable to think he would have preferred another (less costly) way to explain away the appearances of partiality in (1). Yet he only offers a pragmatic encroachment model for doing so. Hence my impression that he must think this is the *least costly* way to accommodate (1) without conceding EPF. As I say, Kawall does not rest his case against EPF on his appeal to pragmatic encroachment; but it is important to recognize that without the appeal to pragmatic encroachment Kawall has no way to explain away the appearances in (2), and so no way to accommodate (1). (Below I will argue that the result of failing to accommodate (1) would render his account inadequate.)

Happily, my account of the conversational pressure on audiences (when they encounter say-so regarding a friend) makes clear that appealing to pragmatic encroachment is *not* the least costly way to accommodate (1) while resisting the appearances of partiality in (2). We can do so by construing the interpersonal (normative) pressure in these cases as reflecting the value-reflecting practical reasons that are generated by the friendship itself. Such an account is less costly, as it eschews the need for encroachment. In addition, such an account is also independently motivated: it makes do with a point that needs to be acknowledged anyway, independent of considerations of friendship. Simply put, there can be practical reasons to acquire more evidence *even in cases in which there can be no question of any shift in the standards for justified belief and knowledge.* This is the point of the case of Juan's promise to Leandro. Everyone should allow that Juan's promise to Leandro to get more evidence generates a practical reason for Juan to get more evidence. But here the practical reason is generated by the promise, and so has *nothing whatsoever* to do with stakes or anything else pragmatic encroachers typically cite to motivate pragmatic encroachment. Here, a pragmatic encroachment analysis would be entirely out of place: the mere fact that Juan promised Leandro to get more evidence does not raise the stakes for Juan (and we can suppose that Leandro wants greater certainty even though nothing much hangs on this for him either). Consequently, we have clear independent reason to acknowledge that there can be practical reasons to collect more evidence, where the subject's possession of such reasons does not affect the standards for justified belief in any way. But once we see that we will need to acknowledge such reasons anyway, it would be best (and would result in a simpler, more satisfying account of the conversational pressure in play) to see if we can treat friendship, too, in terms of its role in giving us practical reasons to get more evidence, without thereby raising the standards for justified belief. This is precisely what is accomplished by the analysis I favour, in terms of value-reflecting practical reasons.

Of course, as I noted above there is another way that Kawall and others have thought to accommodate the effects of friendship on belief-formation (short of embracing EPF): they embrace epistemic permissivism (= the denial of UNIQ). Kawall endorses this as 'a second, more conservative position concerning epistemic norms that would also treat any distinctive belief-forming behaviours (and resultant beliefs) of good friends as epistemically permissible' (Kawall 2013: 367). And for her part, too, Katherine Hawley has permissivism play a central role in how she resists the case for EPF (Hawley 2014b: 2039–40).

But this is not a good way to resist the case for EPF: the embrace of permissivism is costly, inadequate, and unnecessary. It is costly in that permissivism, like pragmatic encroachment, is a highly contentious doctrine in epistemology, and all else equal it would be best to avoid taking on such heavy commitments if one can. It is inadequate since a model that represents the normative pressure that friendship brings to bear on belief-formation *only* in terms of permissivism does not explain how friendship gives us reasons to acquire additional evidence and to double- and triple-check. After all, permissivism is a thesis regarding what one is epistemically permitted to believe *given one's evidence*, whereas what is wanted is an understanding of how friendship can give one reasons to (among other things) *collect additional evidence* and to double- and triple-check. Finally, the appeal to permissivism is unnecessary, because one can explain all that needs explaining in terms of the independently motivated notion of value-reflecting pragmatic reasons, as these arise in contexts of friendship.

At this point, a defender of Kawall's position might object to the charge of inadequacy as follows.[26] While permissivism itself does not predict that (or explain why) someone who hears something negative about a friend should go out and collect more evidence before settling on belief, permissivism is *compatible* with this claim. Consequently, it seems that permissivism, together with a recognition of the existence of ethical or otherwise practical

---

[26] I thank an anonymous referee for indicating the possibility of this response.

reasons to collect more evidence on the matter, gives us what we want: an account that shows why satisfying the norms of friendship does not require violating the standards of epistemology. What more could be wanted?

In response, I submit that this defence of Kawall's position faces a dilemma, according to whether it accepts or rejects the following claim:

VRR   In the cases at issue, the practical reasons to get more evidence are themselves value-reflecting reasons (deriving from the friendship itself).

Suppose that the defender of Kawall's position rejects VRR. This position would then leave us with a mystery: why should we think that there *are* such practical reasons in play, given that they do not derive from the value that the person places on the friendship itself? To be sure, one answer to this question is to see the potential risk to the friendship itself as an instance of *particularly high stakes*, and to treat higher stakes as raising the standards of justified belief. (These higher standards would then require the possession of additional evidence for those beliefs that risk harming the friendship.) But this is just to endorse pragmatic encroachment all over again, whereas Kawall himself had advertised the appeal to permissivism as a move that enabled him to *avoid* having to endorse pragmatic encroachment. It would seem, then, that the defender of Kawall's position would do better to respond to the dilemma by embracing VRR. But if so Kawall's defender has in effect come to endorse the very thesis I have been defending; and in that case, since I have argued that value-reflecting reasons *alone* suffice to account for all that needs accounting for, it seems that the appeal to permissivism is unnecessary. In short, it seems that even if it is true that the appeal to permissivism is *compatible* with the claim that a subject can have practical reasons to collect more evidence before fixing on belief, this compatibility does not advance the case for Kawall's position (in comparison with a position which resists epistemic partiality by appeal to value-reflecting reasons).

In sum, in comparison with other recent attempts to resist EPF, the proposed analysis in terms of value-reflecting practical reasons has several significant virtues. For one thing, it allows us to unify various otherwise disparate phenomena as all reflecting the pressure of practical reasons to act in certain ways, whether these bear on the speaker—she has value-reflecting practical reasons to be especially worthy of trust when speaking to a good friend—or on an audience whose evidence appears to support an unhappy hypothesis regarding a friend—he has value-reflecting practical reasons to collect more evidence, to double- and triple-check that his verdict is supported by the evidence, and to generate as many alternatives as he can. For another, the appeal to value-reflecting reasons allows us to say all of this without need for the additional heavy-duty baggage that would come with having to endorse either pragmatic encroachment or epistemic permissivism. Finally, it does so in terms of a notion—that of value-reflecting practical reasons itself—that enjoys independent motivation.

8

In this chapter I have been addressing what I regard as the strongest case for the sort of 'strange disconnect' I targeted in previous chapters. This case centres on the allegation that friendship sometimes mandates epistemic partiality—that when we encounter information regarding a friend we sometimes are under a kind of interpersonal (normative) pressure to respond in ways that would violate the norms of epistemology. While this allegation does not focus specifically on information gained through speech, the case involving a friend's say-so is nevertheless of particular interest here insofar as it highlights the distinctive sort of conversational pressure that obtains when a friend asks us to trust her. In response I have argued that the case for epistemic partiality fails. My main contention has been that what appears to be a friendship-induced pressure to violate epistemic standards in one's doxastic response to information regarding a friend is actually better understood as a familiar kind of pressure arising from the practical reasons generated by the value we place on our friendship itself. While these practical reasons do give us reason to do such things as gather more evidence, scrutinize the evidence we have, and double- and triple-check our reasoning from the evidence, none of this violates any epistemic standards. If I am right about this, then considerations of friendship, including the trust friends ask us to have in their say-so, do not undermine my case against the 'strange disconnect'. We remain free to endorse my conclusion from previous chapters: the interpersonal demands that arise when a speaker tells one someone something (or makes a statement in one's presence) do not conflict with the epistemic requirement to believe according to the evidence.

PART III
UPTAKE OF UPTAKE

8
Conversational Silence

Qui tacet consentire videtur, ubi loqui debuit ac potuit
(He who is silent, when he ought to have spoken and was able to, is taken to agree)
—*Latin proverb*

1

A good deal of recent attention has been paid to the normative dimension of our practice of assertion. In addition to the many discussions of the ethical and social norms pertaining to speech in general,[1] there has also been a good deal of more narrowly tailored work on the normative dimension of the act of assertion itself. In this respect I highlight recent discussions concerning the norm(s) of assertion (the standards for warranted assertion),[2] as well as the discussion of the norms governing the uptake of assertion (i.e. the epistemology of testimony literature).[3] It is curious that, to date, no similar attention has been paid to the normative dimension of *the uptake of uptake*—the norms and assumptions which inform our verdicts about whether an assertion was accepted in cases in which the audience did not explicitly indicate doing so. After all, it would seem that in the same way that a speaker can do (practical and epistemic) harm to an audience by asserting

---

[1] A good deal has been written on this topic. For some recent work, see Kukla and Lance (2009), Lance and Kukla (2013), Kukla (2014), Cuneo (2014), and Shiffrin (2014). Relevant here, too, is the literature on illocutionary silencing; see Langton (1993), Langton and Hornsby (1998), Bird (2002), Maitra (2009), McGowen et al. (2011), and McGowen (2019).
[2] In addition to two recent volumes dedicated to the topic (Brown and Cappellen 2010; Goldberg 2020) and several book-length treatments (Goldberg 2015a; McKinnon 2015), the topic has been popular in the journals as well. For an overview of recent work, see Goldberg (2015b).
[3] In addition to a recent volume dedicated to the topic (Lackey and Sosa 2006) and several book-length treatments (Coady 1992, Goldberg 2007 and 2010, Lackey 2008, Gelfert 2014, Shieber 2015), see also Proust (2012). For a helpful overview of the various positions, see also Lackey (2010, 2011).

unwarrantedly (thereby generating, or risking the generation of, false belief), and an audience can do (practical and epistemic) harm to a speaker by rejecting an assertion unwarrantedly (including cases of epistemic injustice),[4] so too an audience can do (practical and epistemic) harm to other participants in the conversation by allowing or even leading them to operate on false assumptions regarding the audience's own attitude towards the asserted content—and so too an observer can do (practical and epistemic) harm to an audience by *misconstruing* the audience's response to the mutually observed assertion. It is high time, then, to consider the normative dimension of the uptake of uptake. This is the topic of this and the next three chapters (through Chapter 11). In them I will be arguing that this topic—the uptake of uptake—presents us with yet another form of conversational pressure.

In this chapter I will focus in particular on the reaction in which an audience is *silent* in the face of another's assertion. I will be arguing that insofar as we are entitled to expect cooperation in conversation, we are entitled to expect that silent audiences have not rejected the assertion. (As we will see, this is not quite enough to warrant the further expectation that the audience has *assented* to it, but it is enough to warrant the further expectation that she has *accepted* it in Stalnaker's sense of 'accept'.[5]) On the view I will be developing, the entitlement to expect no silent rejection is one that derives from our entitlement to expect cooperation in conversation. Such is the nature of our conversational practices, I will argue, that participants in conversations *have a generic reason to regard silent rejection of a publicly observed assertion as uncooperative*. Insofar as one is entitled to expect conversational partners to be cooperative, then, one is entitled to expect that one's partners will not remain silent in rejection. However, since this generic reason (to regard silent rejection as unhelpful) springs from the presumption of cooperativity in conversation, any reason to question or doubt that cooperativity will be a reason to question or doubt the presumption that an audience is not silent in rejection; and in this way we see that the entitlement to expect no silent rejection is itself *defeasible*.

---

[4] See my discussion in Chapter 5.
[5] Stalnaker writes that the 'essential effect' of an assertion is 'to change the presuppositions of the participants in the conversation by adding the content of what is asserted to what is presupposed.' (Stalnaker 1999: 86) His sense of 'accept' captures this; one 'accepts' an assertion in this sense so long as one allows the assertion to have its essential effect. One can do this only for the purpose of the present conversation, and so without believing what was said. (I thank Tom Dougherty for encouraging me, in conversation, to make this point explicit.)

The entitlement just described is one we enjoy as observers of other participants in a conversation. But insofar as we ourselves are being observed by others in turn, we too can be held accountable for our participation in the practice. Thus, corresponding to the (defeasible) entitlement that participants in a conversation have for expecting that an audience is not silent in rejection, any audience who is known to have observed an assertion and who rejects, or who otherwise has doubts regarding, the observed assertion has a generic *pro tanto* conversation-generated practical reason to give some public indication of this. This, in effect, is the core notion of conversational pressure at play in this chapter: as audience to others' claims made in public settings, we are under 'normative pressure' to signal our doubts or disagreement when we have them. This, I argue, is a special case of a more general, and more familiar, phenomenon: we are under normative pressure not to engage in behaviours that *recklessly or negligently risk harming others*. In the case of silence in the face of another's public assertion, the paradigmatic sort of harm is an epistemic harm: under certain conditions to be made clear below, the audience who fails to indicate publicly his rejection of the mutually observed assertion recklessly or negligently risks misleading other participants into forming false beliefs—in particular, as to his own reaction to the assertion, but also, as a possible consequence, as to the truth-value of the asserted proposition itself.

2

I will be developing the idea that there is an important connection between silence and non-rejection—that is, between remaining silent in the face of another's assertion in the context of a conversation, on the one hand, and not rejecting the claim, on the other. Given what Stalnaker calls the 'essential effect' of an assertion and the weakness of the notion of 'acceptance' (both of which I discuss below), non-rejection is effectively the same as acceptance (if only in the context of the conversation); so the connection I will be defending can be described as that between silence and acceptance. Before moving on to my argument, however, I first want to discuss an interesting argument in this vicinity that was developed by Philip Pettit.[6] His argument is a bit more general than mine: where I am focused more narrowly on silence in

---

[6] Another, more recent argument on the conversational significances of silence is in Swanson (2017), who models the phenomenon as one involving what he calls 'omissive implicatures'.

the face of an observed public statement, he is addressing silence in the face of observations of others' actions more generally. But his conclusion is very similar: he aims to establish a connection between silence and *approval* of what one observes. While I believe that his argument is ultimately unsuccessful, its failure is instructive.

Pettit (1994) defends the proposed connection between silence and approval in the context of a novel defense of the right to free speech.[7] In a nutshell, Pettit's core claim is that under conditions of free speech,

> the silent observer gets as close as makes no difference to the position of meaning or communicating by her silence that she approves of what she observes... [S]ilence in the presence of freedom of speech is itself capable of becoming a form of meaning and communication... [S]ilence is enfranchised. (Pettit 1994: 49)

Pettit's ideas here are two. First, when one is free to speak out—when one lives under a well-functioning political regime which includes robust free speech protections—one's silence is a choice that 'speaks' for itself. Second, what this silence 'says' in such circumstances is (in Pettit's words) 'that she approves of what she observes'. That this is the default interpretation of silence reflects a further assumption Pettit appears to be making, to the effect that insofar as one is free to express disapproval, failure to do so indicates approval.[8] This is all presented in defence of the right of free speech itself: Pettit's claim is that from the perspective of our participation in political life it is a good thing that silence is 'enfranchised' in this way, as it empowers citizens to participate in the discussions of the day (even in their silence), it is a crucial mechanism in the generation of consensus (which itself is central to our social identities), and it helps us 'police' (53) one another's behaviour through making it easy and cost-free to manifest our attitudes to one another.

It is important to be clear how strong Pettit's conclusion is.[9] His view is that, under such conditions, to remain silent in the face of another's action is in effect *to perform a speech act* in which one communicates one's approval.[10] More specifically, his claim is that under conditions of free

---

[7] The following discussion of Pettit's views has been deeply influenced by a discussion of these matters with Tom Dougherty. (It should go without saying that he bears no responsibility for the flaws of my discussion.)

[8] Here I follow Langton 2007 in ascribing this assumption to Pettit.

[9] My reading of Pettit here is heavily indebted to Langton (2007).

[10] Compare the 'omissive implicature' account of Swanson (2017).

speech one's remaining silent constitutes an act exhibiting all of the features that Grice associated with communicative acts (= those acts having non-natural meaning). Indeed, this was the point Pettit makes immediately before the quote above:

> The core requirement for meaning or communication, by the sort of theory associated with Paul Grice, is that the following conditions hold, and hold as a matter of common belief: that the speaker intends her audience to form a certain belief (or related state); that she intends that they recognize that intention; and that she intends that their recognition of this intention help to lead them to fulfil it, help to get them to form the relevant belief.... It will be clear, then, that under our account of silence—silence in the presence of freedom of speech—the silent observer gets *as close as makes no difference to the position of meaning or communicating* by her silence that she approves of what she observes.
>
> (Pettit 1994: 49; italics added for emphasis)

On this view silence is not merely *evidence for* approval, or something that *gives others the right to regard one* as approving; it actually *constitutes* that very approval. According to Pettit, what one *means* (in Grice's sense) in remaining silent is that one approves of what one has observed.

I think Pettit's view on this score is far too strong.

First, as an empirical matter, the conditions Pettit lays out above—the conditions on an act's being meaningful in Grice's sense—would not appear to obtain in most cases of silence in the face of another's public act. Pettit rightly notes that for Grice an act is meaningful only when it exhibits a kind of reflexive[11] intentionality: one performs an act *intending* one's audience to recognize one's communicative intention, partly on the basis of their recognition of this very intention.[12] I submit that, as a matter of empirical fact, this reflexivity is often, perhaps even usually, absent in cases of silent reaction. This is certainly so when one's silence is a reaction to another's *non-linguistic* action. But I would say that it is also true when one's silence is a reaction to another's speech act. To be sure, at least under many ordinary conditions in which a speech exchange is a conversation, an audience who

---

[11] I borrow 'reflexive' in characterizing Gricean intentions from Bach; see Bach and Harnish (1979).

[12] For an interesting discussion of the nature of this sort of reflexive intention, see Bach (1987). (This paper is responding to worries raised by Recanati (1986).)

remains silent in the face of another's statement should expect it to be highly likely that she will induce a certain uptake in those who observe her silence: she should anticipate that they are likely to take her to have accepted the claim that was made. But in this respect the situation is akin to cases Grice regarded as *falling short* of meaning and communication, than it is to cases involving Gricean (non-natural) meaning. Recall for example the case of the thief who, wanting to frame Jones for the crime, surreptitiously leaves Jones's handkerchief by the crime scene, anticipating that the detectives will regard this as evidence of Jones's guilt (so long as they don't discover the thief's role in planting this evidence). Or recall the case of the parent who leaves the broken glass on the floor for her partner to see, in the manifest intention to get her partner to recognize that their child has broken the vase. Grice denied that either of these was a case of meaning anything: in the former case the relevant intention was not manifest (and so was not reflexive either), whereas in the case of the broken vase the intention was manifest but not reflexive. So too, I submit, most cases of silent responses to assertions are cases that would be more correctly described as ones in which the audience's silence *leads* observers to believe the audience has approved (perhaps even deliberately so), albeit without *meaning* this in Grice's sense. The type of case Pettit envisages is much less common: it doesn't happen very often that a silent audience member intends observers to regard her silence as produced with the intention that they regard her as having approved of the observed (non-linguistic or speech) act, partly on the basis of their recognition of this very intention.

In addition to these empirical doubts, I share Rae Langton's (2007) worry that, even under conditions of robust free speech protections, there are all sorts of factors whose presence should make it manifest that an audience's silence is not to be regarded as expressing her approval. As Langton herself makes plain, publicly expressing one's disapproval can be personally or professionally costly. Indeed, in section 6 I will survey a wide variety of contexts in which it would be wrong to regard an audience's silence as implying anything like approval or assent or acceptance (or even non-rejection).

But I have a third reason for doubting the success of Pettit's argument: I believe that this argument is guilty of overkill. While I hold (with Pettit) that there is a wide class of speech contexts in which there is a significant connection between silence and something in the neighbourhood of approval, I also think that we don't *need* to say anything as strong as Pettit has said in order to formulate and defend the relevant connection. Here it will be helpful to have in mind a much-neglected distinction, first developed by Simmons (1976), between acts that are (in Simmons's words) 'signs of consent' and acts that 'imply consent'. (While he speaks of consent, it will be clear how to apply this distinction to the type of circumstance in which the relevant attitude is rather approval or acceptance.) Simmons spells out the difference as follows:

> In calling an act a 'sign of consent,' I mean that because of the context in which the act was performed, including the appropriate conventions (linguistic or otherwise), the act *counts as an expression of the actor's intention to consent*; thus, all genuine consensual acts are the givings of 'signs of consent.' But in saying that an act 'implies consent,' we mean neither that the actor intended to consent nor that the act would normally be taken as an attempt to consent. (1976: 286)

Simmons goes on to say that an act can be taken to 'imply consent' in one of three ways: it 'may be such that it leads us to conclude that the actor was in an appropriate frame of mind to, or had attitudes which would lead him to, consent if suitable conditions arose'; it 'may be such that it "commits" the actor to consenting'; or alternatively it 'may be such that it binds the actor morally to the same performance to which he would be bound if he had in fact consented' (1976: 286).

While Pettit's view appears to be that silence in the face of an observed act is a 'sign' of one's approval, my sense is that it is much more plausible to regard silence as something that (at best[13]) 'implies' one's approval. My own view won't quite amount to this, but it will be in the neighbourhood. In any case Simmons's notion of 'implied consent' (as distinct from 'signaled consent'), as applied to cases in which the relevant attitude is approval or acceptance, is very important for my purposes. For if an observer is to recover the significance of an act in which consent is merely implied rather than signalled, the observer will need to make inferences from the subject's behaviour in the context, and these inferences may themselves involve considerations pertaining to the cooperativity of the exchange itself. This approach, I submit, will give us the leeway we need to arrive at a more plausible characterization of the relation between silence and (something like) approval. For one thing, it gives us room to allow for a kind of

---

[13] See section 6, where I talk about the constraints on an observer who aims to rely on the hypothesis that an audience's silence implies consent.

defeasibility in the process by which an observer arrives at the hypothesis that the silent audience has approved. For another, it enables us to ask about the nature of this inference, and in particular how cooperativity considerations bear. My claim will be that they bear centrally: when it comes to silence in the face of another's public assertion, the inference, *from* the claim that the audience is silent in reaction, *to* the claim that the audience has accepted the assertion, is itself backed by participants' entitlement to regard other conversational participants as cooperative. For it is the presumption of conversational cooperativity, together with the norms of our assertoric practices, which mark silent rejection as uncooperative. This can seem surprising: it might have seemed that the inference from an audience's silence to his approval is backed by (for instance) construing his silence as particularly strong *evidence* of his approval. But I think this natural thought is guilty of misconstruing what in the first instance is a non-epistemic entitlement (reflecting our expectation of cooperativity in conversation) for an epistemic entitlement. All of this will need unpacking.

3

My thesis, then, is that when it is manifest that an audience has observed another's public assertion, the audience is under normative pressure to avoid silent rejection or silent doubt. I am not the first person to have held views in this vicinity. In addition to Pettit's account just discussed, views on which we are under some normative pressure to speak out if we dissent are familiar in ethics and in political philosophy. Such views are especially prevalent in connection with our duties to resist oppressive practices and institutions: our duty to speak out appears grounded on the idea that to fail to do so is to acquiesce in the perpetration of harms and injustices.[14] In this chapter I want to suggest that this normative pressure obtains in situations that are far removed from contexts of ethical remonstration and political dissent: such pressure is present whenever we are engaged in speech exchanges that are conversations in Grice's sense.

In Chapters 4–6, I have developed the idea that a speaker who asserts exerts a kind of normative pressure on her audience, where the pressure in

---

[14] See section 6; and see also Maitra (2012: 16) for the idea that there are cases in which to remain silent in the face of certain speech is to be 'complicit' in the harms brought about by that speech.

question involves both an interpersonal[15] and an epistemic dimension. The contribution I aim to make in this chapter is to link this pressure, together with the possible downstream (epistemic and practical) harms that can arise in the course of our reaction to a public assertion, to generate normative expectations concerning *the uptake of uptake*.[16]

The structure of the remainder of the chapter is organized around its core claim, which is that there is a defeasible entitlement to expect No Silent Rejection:

NSR In speech exchanges which are conversations in Grice's sense, all competent language users enjoy a default (albeit defeasible) entitlement to expect that an audience who was manifestly silent in the face of a publicly made assertion has not rejected that assertion.

The sort of entitlement I have in mind is of the same type as our entitlement to expect cooperativity in those speech exchanges that are Gricean conversations. In order to develop and defend NSR, I will need to defend several claims about the broad practice of assertion. The first is a normative claim: under conditions of cooperation, silent rejection is normatively marked— with the result that conversational participants enjoy a (defeasible) entitlement to expect that audiences *not* be silent in rejection of a mutually observed assertion. I argue for this claim in this section, by appeal to the normative dimensions of the practice of assertion. The second is an empirical claim: it is a familiar fact that people will often regard a hearer's silence as indicating (not just non-rejection but) acceptance. I argue for this empirical claim in section 5. The result of these two claims is the sort of conversational pressure that lies at the heart of this chapter: participants in conversations have a generic *pro tanto* conversation-generated practical reason to give a public indication when they reject or harbour doubts about an assertion (at least when it is mutually manifest that they observed the assertion). I will go on to argue that the normative pressure exerted by such a conversation-generated practical reason evaporates when the

---

[15] As in Chapters 3–7, I will speak of normative pressure as 'interpersonal' when it is the kind(s) of normative pressure that reflects what is owed to other people—whether because the act in question is ethically required, or it is mandated by social norms or by the norms of some legitimate practice in which we are participants, or it is demanded by norms of yet some other kind(s) (such as the norms of friendship).

[16] Here I will sometimes speak of our entitlement to expect certain things of other participants in a conversation, while at other times I will speak of the practical reasons that those participants have (to do as we properly expect them to do).

observer's presumptive entitlement to expect no silent rejection is defeated. I provide an account of such defeat in the last sections of this chapter.

My argument for thinking that conversational participants are entitled to expect no silent rejection depends on two claims. The first is Grice's claim that conversations are cooperative, rational activities. The second is my claim from Chapters 4 and 5, to the effect that a speaker who asserts that p puts her audience under some rational/epistemic pressure to accept that p. My strategy is to use these two claims to argue that silent rejection of a public assertion made in conversation can be presumed uncooperative.[17] As a result, *modulo* some caveats to be spelled out below, subjects who are entitled to regard a speech exchange as a conversation are thereby entitled to expect that participants who are silent in the face of a mutually observed assertion have not rejected that assertion; and (again *modulo* caveats) audiences who observe an assertion made in the course of a conversation have a *pro tanto*, conversation-generated practical reason to signal their rejection or their doubts. Having argued for this, I will go on in the next section to strengthen my conclusion: the expectation of non-rejection itself is tantamount to an expectation of *acceptance* (in Stalnaker's sense of 'accept'); and the expectation of acceptance can be strengthened to an expectation of *endorsement* or *belief* in contexts in which it is reasonable to assume that the point of the conversation is, or includes, the exchange of reliable information.

I begin with a claim concerning the cooperative nature of conversations. The point that conversations are rational, cooperative activities is familiar, of course, from Grice (1968/1989). Grice himself was clear about the sense in which he thought conversations are cooperative activities:

> I would like to be able to think of the standard type of conversational practice not merely as something that all or most do *in fact* follow but as something that it is *reasonable* for us to follow, that we *should not* abandon.... (Grice 1968/1989: 29)

And he goes on to spell out the relevant sense of 'reasonable' as follows:

> anyone who cares about the goals that are central to conversation/communication (such as giving and receiving information, influencing and

---

[17] In section 6 I will argue that this presumption is defeasible.

being influence by others) must be expected to have an interest, given suitable circumstances, in participation in talk exchanges that will be profitable only on the assumption that they are conducted in general accordance with the Cooperative Principle and the maxims.

(Grice 1968/1989: 30)[18]

I take the 'suitable circumstances' to be those that are free of coercion, in which people are engaged with one another of their own free will. Under such conditions, the claim that conversations are cooperative is not—or at least is not merely—an empirical description of how we actually proceed in our speech exchanges, but how we *ought* to proceed in them. It is clear that Grice's point characterizes the normative dimension of conversational practice.

Next, I move on to my second claim: a speaker who makes an assertion puts her audience under some rational/epistemic pressure to accept what was asserted. I argued for a version of this claim in Chapters 4 and 5. Here it will be helpful to recall the line of argument from those chapters. The challenge I was addressing was to understand how two apparently disparate kinds of normative pressure can simultaneously bear on those who observe an assertion: how it is that an audience can *wrong* a speaker by responding to her assertion in ways that are improper or unjust, while at the same time the audience's doxastic response to the speaker's assertion is exclusively answerable to epistemic norms. After arguing that the various extant accounts are inadequate (Chapter 4), I offered an alternative account (Chapter 5) according to which the act of asserting that p is one in which it is (or should be) mutually manifest that the speaker has conveyed having the relevant epistemic authority on the matter of whether p—with the result that she is owed a certain kind of respect in virtue of this. The 'rational/epistemic pressure' to accept an observed assertion, then, ultimately derives from the conveyed epistemic authority that is part of the act of assertion itself. Since a speaker who asserts that p conveys being relevantly epistemically authoritative, a colingual who attends to the assertion[19] ought to base his doxastic

---

[18] The Cooperative Principle is the principle that enjoins speakers to 'make your conversational contribution such as is required, at the stage at which it occurs, by the accepted purpose of direction of the talk exchange in which you are engaged'. And the four maxims are those of Quantity, Quality, Relation, and Manner (Grice 1968/1989: 26).

[19] Does this mean that we are free to ignore assertions made in our midst? No. At a minimum, if they are addressed to us, the very act of address generates a (defeasible) claim on our attention (see Chapter 2).

reaction on an epistemically proper evaluation of her (conveyed) authority. Insofar as the audience has a doxastic response that is not based on (or informed by) an epistemically proper assessment of the speaker's conveyed authority, the audience is failing (not merely epistemically, but also) interpersonally.[20]

By itself, this point—that a speaker who asserts that p places her audience under some rational/epistemic pressure to accept that p—bears only on how the audience reacts doxastically, not on how they react publicly. However, we can discern the relevance of the foregoing to the *publicness* of the reaction by noting the generic interest parties have in tracking the doxastic reactions of the various participants in a speech exchange. This is seen in ordinary cases of conversation, as each participant must track the other participants' (non-)acceptance of the assertions that are made in the course of the conversation itself—if only to remain apprised of the state of the context at any given point in the conversation. What is more, a speaker who asserts can ordinarily be presumed to have the perlocutionary intention to induce in her audience the acceptance of what she asserted. (Not all assertions are informed by this intention, of course, but this perlocutionary intention may be *presumed* in the absence of reasons to think otherwise.[21]) Now, if an asserter can be presumed to have this perlocutionary intention, then insofar as this presumption holds it is reasonable to suppose further that the speaker will disprefer the reaction of rejection. This is for the simple reason that when her assertion is rejected it is not successful in its (presumed) perlocutionary aim.

The preceding points enable us to argue for a conclusion of some independent interest: *it is ipso facto uncooperative to remain silent in one's rejection of another's assertion*. Suppose that it is (or should be) mutually manifest that making an assertion puts one's audience under rational/epistemic pressure to accept. This makes rejection the dispreferred reaction; we might register this by saying that rejection is *marked*.[22] Given the

---

[20] What Miranda Fricker labels 'testimonial injustice' is the special case in which the audience's reaction is based on an epistemically improper downgrade in the speaker's authority, where this is owed to identity prejudice.
[21] See Goldberg (2015b: chapter 3) where I discuss at length the basis of the presumption of this perlocutionary intention in assertion.
[22] I borrow this use of 'marked' from Farkas and Bruce (2009), who go so far as to say that rejection of an assertion in a conversation creates a 'conversational crisis' in need of resolution. (They draw our attention to the difference between an utterance of 'No he isn't' in response to the assertion that John is home, as against the question whether John is home.) See Farkas and Bruce (2009: 83–4).

manifest interest everyone has in tracking the doxastic reactions of each of the participants to the public assertion, the audience is aware, or should be aware, of the generic interest others (including the speaker) will have in determining whether the rational/epistemic pressure to accept was acceded to. Now insofar as an audience's reaction is the non-marked (preferred) one of acceptance, things can proceed without further ado. (There is no need to expend the energy or take the time required to indicate that one is allowing assertion to attain what Stalnaker[23] calls it 'essential effect'—that of updating the common ground to include what was asserted.[24]) Another way to put this point is in terms of cooperativity: it is not uncooperative to remain silent in one's acceptance of another's assertion. After all, in the joint action of the conversation, to accept an assertion (even silently) is to be aligned with the speaker and the other parties to the conversation on how to proceed: all are agreed on allowing the assertion to have its essential effect. It is only when one's reaction is the *dis*preferred one of rejection that one has a practical reason to make this manifest. For in this case one is *not* aligned on how to proceed: one must interrupt matters to ensure that assertion doesn't have its essential effect. In effect, one has created a 'conversational crisis' in need of resolution (Farkas and Bruce 2009: 83). To fail to indicate this, under conditions when (i) other participants have a standing interest to discern one's reaction and (ii) one's reaction is the marked (dispreferred) one of rejection, is *ipso facto* uncooperative in connection with the joint action of (Gricean) conversation.[25] Since what underwrite this result are familiar aspects of the practice of assertion itself—aspects which will be, or at any rate should be, familiar to all competent speakers—the result is that the uncooperative nature of silent rejection will be, or at any rate should be, familiar to all competent speakers.

I am now in a position to defend NSR, as deriving from these familiar features of the practice of assertion itself. Anyone who is entitled to regard a

---

[23] See section 4 for an argument defending my appeal to Stalnaker at this point in the argument.

[24] 'To make an assertion is to reduce the context set in a particular way, provided that there are no objections from the other participants in the conversation.... [T]he essential effect of an assertion is to change the presuppositions of the participants in the conversation by adding the content of what is asserted to what is presupposed. This effect is avoided *only if the assertion is rejected*.' (reprinted in Stalnaker 1999: 86; italics added) See also Stalnaker (2014: 51 and 98) for more recent statements. The idea that assertions are proposals to add to the common ground is a theme emphasized by Clark and Schaefer (1989), Clark (1996), and Ginzburg (1996, 2012).

[25] Below I will reinforce the claim that silent rejection is uncooperative, by appeal to the familiar practice of regarding silence as implying assent. At this point in my argument, however, I have no need to appeal to this aspect of our practice.

speech exchange as a conversation—which is to say anyone who is participating in a conversation of the sort that is covered by Grice's Cooperative Principle—is *ipso facto* entitled to presume that the participants are cooperative. Since silent rejection is uncooperative, participants to a conversation are entitled to expect that, absent positive reasons to think otherwise,[26] an audience who is silent in the face of an assertion *has not rejected the assertion*.[27] And this is simply to say that there is a (defeasible) entitlement, deriving from the features of the practice of assertion (and available to any competent speaker who is entitled to regard their speech exchange as a conversation), to expect that the silent audience has not rejected the public assertion. In short, NSR holds. The flip side of this, of course, is that *audiences* in a conversation have a *pro tanto* conversation-generated reason, when they reject another's assertion, to indicate this publicly—as to fail to do so is to be uncooperative. This is a kind of conversational pressure that is exerted on audience members when they have been observed by other audience members as having themselves observed a publicly made assertion.[28]

---

[26] See sections 6 and 7 below.
[27] Compare Maitra (2012: 113), where silence in the face of another's speech act (under conditions in which the audience could have spoken up) 'licenses, and so grants authority to, the speakers', where the authority in question is the sort that 'puts speakers in a position to perform their intended acts'. Maitra's view is importantly different from mine, as she is interested in the act of subordination that occurs in hate speech; her thesis is that 'in staying silent, [those who observe an act of hate speech] are, to some extent, *complicit* in what the hate speaker does' (116). But it is clear that Maitra endorses the view, which I aim to develop here, that silence in the face of another's speech entitles others to interpret that silence in a certain way—this, after all, is what renders those who are silent 'to some extent *complicit*'. My claim is that insofar as the interpretation is unwanted, this generates a reason for the audiences to speak out in disagreement. Maitra seems to concur at least in the case of observed hate speech: she holds that those who observe such speech 'have some moral obligation to speak up' (116). See also Hay (2013) for a defence of the duty to speak up against oppressive acts (whether these are speech acts or non-linguistic acts).
[28] An interesting issue, raised by an anonymous referee, concerns the uptake of not-at-issue content—presuppositions, for example. Is there any entitlement to expect audiences with doubts to speak out against an update triggered by a speaker's *presupposing* that p? In general I think that there will be no systematic answer to this, in part because I think that the category of not-at-issue content is a bit of a grab-bag: it includes not only presuppositions but also implicatures and insinuations, and it is not clear to me that all of these phenomena call for a unified treatment. It is an interesting question to consider why this is. Presuppositions are very interesting in this regard: as Lewis (1979) notes, there would appear to be some sort of pressure to accommodate presupposed propositions when they are not already part of the context set, and it is unclear how this pressure to accommodate bears on any alleged pressure to speak up if one disagrees. Langton (2018) discusses this phenomenon in some detail. Limitations of space, however, prevent me from considering this and related topics here, though I hope to return to these matters at a future time.

4

The argument above appeals to Stalnaker's model of conversational dynamics on which the 'essential effect' of an assertion is 'to change the presuppositions of the participants in the conversation by adding the content of what is asserted to what is presupposed'. In defence of this appeal to Stalnaker's model, I note that Stalnaker's claim—that this is assertion's 'essential effect'—is a very weak one. After all, acceptance of an assertion, according to this model, is simply acquiescence in its having this effect, at least for the purpose (and in the context) of the conversation. As Stalnaker himself makes clear, one's acceptance need not extend beyond the conversation; and one's move to accept need not be rationalized on epistemic grounds (one might be willing to go along with the asserter in this context merely not to make a fuss, or to see where it leads). Hence what Stalnaker characterizes as assertion's 'essential effect' is something that, because of what is involved in the notion of 'acceptance' will be present in any context in which an assertion is made, *whatever* the perlocutionary ends the speaker might have in asserting. This will allow us to capture conversational dynamics even in situations in which it is manifest that the speaker has no (perlocutionary) intention of getting the audience to *believe* what she asserts.

Two features of this model are worth highlighting.

First, in effect, the expectation of no silent rejection in NSR is tantamount to an expectation of *acceptance*. This is because for any assertion, either it is accepted (= allowed to have its essential effect) or it is not (= not allowed to have its essential effect). For this reason we can simply *define* rejection as non-acceptance. That is, any case in which the audience does not allow the assertion to have its essential effect—whether because the audience explicitly repudiates it, or because the audience has practical reasons for resisting the update, or because the audience remains agnostic and does not want to allow the update associated with the assertion (and these are not exhaustive)—is a case of rejection. Since this is so we can reformulate NSR to read as follows:

> NSR= In all speech exchanges which are Gricean conversations, all competent language users enjoy a default (albeit defeasible) entitlement to expect that an audience who was manifestly silent in the face of a publicly made assertion has accepted that assertion.

Although I will continue using NSR in what follows, I will sometimes speak of our entitlement to expect acceptance (rather than no silent rejection). In any case it is to be borne in mind that these are effectively equivalent expectations.

But there is a related, second point to be made of NSR: precisely because the status of acceptance just is the status of allowing an assertion to have its essential effect, both NSR and NSR= are relatively weak principles. The expectation that they permit or authorize is a weak one: when one is in a conversation one is permitted to expect that, when an assertion is publicly made, participants to the conversation allow the relevant update to the common ground unless there is some public indication otherwise (by one or more of the participants). Neither NSR nor NSR= entitles us to expect that participants *believe* what was asserted, or that they recognize that *there are good reasons to believe* what was asserted; only that the other participants allowed the update.

We can strengthen the norm in contexts in which it is reasonable to assume that the aim of the conversation is, or includes, the serious exchange of reliable information (in the mutual attempt to determine what is the case). For when this is the conversational aim, any move to update the common ground is warranted only when there are adequate epistemic grounds for doing so. And this means that acceptance is warranted only when it is *epistemically* warranted, that is, only when there are adequate grounds for believing what was asserted. I will call such contexts 'epistemically sober' contexts.

There would appear to be good reasons to suppose that epistemically sober contexts are the default. This is a theme running throughout Seana Shiffrin's extended reflections on the ethical and legal dimensions of speech (Shiffrin 2014). She argues that having a reliable and efficient medium for discerning one another's propositional attitudes is central to our moral and social lives, and that as such we are morally entitled to the 'default presumption' (11) that an arbitrary speech context is (what I would describe as) epistemically sober. Such contexts, she argues, contrast with 'epistemic suspended contexts,' in which

> ascertainable facts about the situation itself, or the actions or utterances of one or more participants, deprive the listener of the epistemic warrant to presume, in a predictive sense, that the speaker will tell the truth.
> (Shiffrin 2014: 16)

Much of Shiffrin (2014) deals with the justification and dynamics of the moves into and out of epistemically suspended contexts. But exits, on her view, are the exception to the rule. In this same spirit, the idea that epistemic sobriety is the default appears to be in the background of Tyler Burge's familiar (if controversial!) reflections on the Acceptance Principle, which asserts a *pro tanto* entitlement to accept an (apparently) intelligible presentation-as-true of a propositional content one comprehends (Burge 1993). Burge's idea is that the seeming intelligibility of a presentation-as-true indicates that its source is rational, and so, since rational sources constitutively aim at the truth, one is entitled to accept the presentation-as-true unless one has stronger reasons for doubt. But it is noteworthy that there are other grounds for regarding epistemically sober contexts as the default.

In sum, any context that is reasonably regarded as epistemically sober is a context in which we can strengthen NSR and NSR=, replacing 'no silent rejection' and 'acceptance' with 'assent' and 'believe'. The result would be the following:

NSR+ In all Gricean conversations in which the presumption of epistemic sobriety is reasonable, all competent language users enjoy a default (albeit defeasible) entitlement to expect that an audience who was manifestly silent in the face of a publicly made assertion has assented to that assertion (and so believes what was asserted).

This is perhaps the strongest of the norms governing silence in conversation. Insofar as a good many of our exchanges are in epistemically sober contexts, this norm is regularly in play. In what follows I will not bother to distinguish between non-rejection, acceptance, and assent, except where the failure to do so is likely to lead to confusion.

5

Let us use 'the practice of assertion' to designate the set of expectations, rules, and norms that pertain to the making of and reactions to assertions, where familiarity with this set partially characterizes pragmatic competence in the use of a language. My thesis so far is that NSR itself is part of the practice of assertion. As such NSR is in place whenever assertions are made. If this were true, we might expect some empirical evidence of this in our practice of assertion itself—evidence, in other words, that people regularly do interpret others' silence as indicating their acceptance. In this section I want to provide some (limited) empirical evidence to this effect. To this end, let the 'assent interpretation of silence' (or 'assent interpretation' for short) be the interpretation on which a hearer's silence in the face of an assertion is taken to indicate her assent.[29] The evidence I will provide here is evidence that the assent interpretation is an ordinary and recognizable part of our practice of assertion. This offers further support for my thesis so far; but it also highlights the kind of harm one can do to others if one remains silent in rejection.

I begin with a variety of different examples, from historical and contemporary sources, suggesting that it is a familiar part of our conversational practices that silence in the face of an observed assertion is (often; with some regularity) taken to indicate assent or acceptance.

An initial source of evidence can be found in the number of languages in which there is a familiar proverb to the effect that silence is tantamount to assent or acceptance. By my count there are at least ten such languages. These include Latin (*'Qui tacet consentire videtur, ubi loqui debuit ac potuit'*; 'He who is silent, when he ought to have spoken and was able to, is taken to agree'); Persian ('Silence is the sign of consent/agreement/acceptance');[30] Russian ('silence is a sign of consent/silence gives (means) consent');[31] Dutch ('Wie zwijgt, stemt toe' or, alternatively, 'Zwijgen is instemmen'; 'Whoever is silent, agrees');[32] Greek ('σιωπή καμιά φορά λέει βαριές κουβέντες'; 'Sometimes silence makes important statements');[33] Icelandic ('Þögn er sama og samþykki'; 'Silence is the same as acceptance');[34] Spanish (*'Quien se calla, otorga'*; 'Silence is consent'); French (*'Qui ne dit mot, consent'*; 'Who is silent, consents'); and Portuguese (*'Quem cala, consente'*; 'Who is silent, consents'). No doubt there are others. Indeed, the

---

[29] Here I am disregarding Simmons's (1976) distinction, mentioned in section 2, between giving *signs* of assent and *implying* assent. This distinction is important when characterizing the normative dimension of the practice and the status of the silence itself, whereas here I am simply giving evidence that people often regard another's silence as the basis for an ascription to them of the attitude of assent (without noting whether the former is seen as a sign of or as implying the latter).
[30] See Habibian (1995/2002: 136). (With thanks to Reza Hadisi for bringing this to my attention.)
[31] See Lubensky (1995/2013: 331). (With thanks to Reza Hadisi for bringing this to my attention.)
[32] With thanks to René van Woudenberg for bringing this to my attention.
[33] With thanks to Christos Kyriacou for bringing this to my attention. Kyriacou indicated to me that while this proverb speaks of silence as 'making important statemements' without characterizing what those statements are, the proverb is often used in contexts in which silence is taken as assent.
[34] With thanks to Finnur Dellsén for bringing this to my attention.

McGraw-Hill Dictionary of American Idioms and Phrasal Verbs[35] lists American English as such a language: among their list of proverbs they include 'If you do not object to what someone says or does, you can be assumed to agree with or condone it.' That there are so many languages in which there is a proverb to this effect indicates the status of the assent interpretation as something proverb-worthy, and hence (one might assume) ordinary and familiar.[36]

A second source of evidence that the assent interpretation is a familiar part of our conversational practice is in the number of quotations in ordinary circumstances in which people rely on the assent interpretation. There are many, and in many different time periods. In Plato's Cratylus dialogue,[37] Plato has Socrates tell Cratylus in an aside that 'I shall assume that your silence gives consent.' (Cratylus 435b) Cratylus is represented as silent in response. Presumably, Plato would not have had Socrates give expression to an interpretation of silence that would have been regarded by his readers as highly controversial or downright dubious, since to have done so would have been distracting. Consequently, from the fact that he had Socrates make this claim, and that he represented Cratylus as silent in response (as if the assumption expressed were familiar to him), we can infer that Plato regarded this assumption as one that was standard among those he anticipated as the readers of the dialogue.[38] Moving to the late nineteenth century we have the example of Mark Twain, who goes further still. In a private letter to his wife, Twain writes that '*Silence has given assent* in all ages of the world,' adding that this 'is a law of nature, not of ethics'.[39]

If we expand our focus to include silent reactions (not to assertions per se but rather) to others' actions more generally, we find pervasive historical evidence attesting to the prevalence of a generic attitude towards such silence. In particular, those who are silent (or who do not act) in the face of another's actions are typically taken to acquiesce in the performance of

---

[35] McGraw-Hill Dictionary of American Idioms and Phrasal Verbs (The McGraw-Hill Companies, Inc., 2002).
[36] The existence of the Latin proverb suggests that the practice goes back quite a bit.
[37] For the dialogue, see Reeve (1997).
[38] One might worry that the very fact that Plato's Socrates had to *say* this indicates that it *wasn't* a standard interpretation. But it seems to me that, given Cratylus' silent response, the text is better interpreted as Socrates' attempt to make explicit what was an implicit part of conversational practices in ancient Athens.
[39] Letter to Olivia Lewis Langdon, 3 December 1872; as cited in Powers 2006: 328. (Italics in original.)

the action (and to have no objections to its acceptability).[40] That we typically interpret such silence as indicating acceptance or at least acquiescence (or perhaps Pettit-style 'approval') explains the strong moral disapproval we typically feel towards those who are silent in the face of actions that are unjust or immoral.

Examples of speakers evincing this sort of disapprobation are easy to come by. In the late eighteenth century, then-Vice President Thomas Jefferson, helping the Kentucky and Virginia legislatures draft resolutions denouncing the Alien and Sedition Acts (which made it illegal for anyone to advocate secession from the union), denigrated 'silent acquiescence' to the Acts, proclaiming such silence to be 'highly criminal.'[41] In the mid-twentieth century, Rabbi Joachim Prinz was eloquent in speaking out against silence in the face of Nazism:

> When I was the rabbi of the Jewish community in Berlin under the Hitler regime, I learned many things. The most important thing that I learned under those tragic circumstances was that bigotry and hatred are not the most urgent problem. The most urgent, the most disgraceful, the most shameful and the most tragic problem is silence.[42]

Two decades later a similar attitude was expressed by various people in connection with silence and inaction during the civil rights movement. Thus at his civil rights sermon at the Ebenezer Baptist Church on 30 April 1967, Dr. Martin Luther King noted that 'There comes a time when silence is betrayal.'[43] Several years later, commenting on the civil disobedience that was then raging in the United States, Hannah Arendt (1970) wrote, 'Jemand, der weiß, daß er widersprechen kann, weiß auch, daß er gewissermaßen zustimmt, wenn er nicht widerspricht.' (Roughly: 'Someone who knows that he can object also knows that he agrees, in a fashion, if he does not

---

[40] There are important exceptions to this, of course, in which it would be improper and even criminal to assume that silence is tantamount to assent. This is especially true in legal settings, in which two parties are engaging one another contractually, or in settings where one party's acting without the consent of the other party would constitute a crime. (See especially sections 6 and 7 below, and especially footnote 65, where I offer an account of these cases, as principled exceptions to a more general rule.) However, I stress that at this point I am merely noting as a fact that silence is (often; standardly) taken as a form of assent; and here the fact that the law needs to make explicit exceptions to the permissibility of doing so would be some indication that the facts are as suggested.

[41] Kentucky Resolutions of 1799.

[42] Source: <http://www.haaretz.com/opinion/.premium-1.710489>, cited 22 March 2016.

[43] Source: <http://www.informationclearinghouse.info/article2564.htm>, cited 20 October 2015.

object.')[44] Finally, to bring matters up to date, we might cite Rabbi Bradley Artson who, commenting recently on the Jewish response to injustice and oppression, remarks that 'our silence and inaction in the face of contemporary injustice and oppression is akin to assenting to it'.[45] Alternatively, we might cite the philosopher Carol Hay, who during the 2016 presidential campaign wrote,

> We should hereby call on Trump and his supporters to denounce the violence and bigotry being committed in his name. Their silence on this issue will henceforth be presumed to indicate their approval.[46]

To be sure, Hay's use of 'henceforth' suggests that she is in effect *enacting* (or trying to enact) the norm authorizing us to regard silence as approval; and this suggests that the norm *wasn't* in place beforehand. But, while it might be thought that this is evidence *against* the prevalence of the assent interpretation, precisely the opposite is true: Hay's move to (try to) enact this norm is a very familiar one (we see it also in the statement often made in the wedding ceremony, 'Speak now or forever hold your peace')—and this suggests that (not just the act enacting it but also) the norm itself is a familiar one. Consider, for example, that one could *not* get away with saying something like the following: 'Those who do not scratch your noses right now will henceforth be taken to acknowledge your guilt of a felony crime.' The reason that Hay's comment passes in a way the nose-scratching comment wouldn't is that she is appealing to a norm that is already widely recognized as familiar and legitimate.

The foregoing statements express attitudes regarding silence in the face of *unjust acts*, rather than in the face of *an observed assertion*. But several points can help us connect these statements to the special case of silence in the face of another's speech act of assertion. As noted above, the attitude of disapprobation regarding silence in the face of injustice would appear to rest on the general assumption that silence implies acquiescence to the performed act.[47] Of course, assertions themselves are (speech) acts in their

---

[44] With thanks to Anne Burkhardt, University of Cologne, for this translation.
[45] Source: <http://www.myjewishlearning.com/article/no-neutrality-silence-is-assent/>, cited 20 October 2015.
[46] 'Silence on Hate Speech Construes Consent', *Philadelphia Inquirer*, 28 November 2016. Compare Maitra (2012: 113).
[47] It may rest on a weaker assumption, to the effect that many people will *assume* that silence implies acquiescence. This weaker assumption might be read into the quotes above. At a minimum, Jefferson, Prinz, King, Arendt, and Artson all appear to worry that *other people*

own right. And as I noted above, to acquiesce to this sort of act is to allow it to have its essential effect—that is, to allow the common ground to be updated by adding the asserted content to what is presupposed in context. If this is correct, the de facto popular linkage between silence and acceptance of another's assertion, as indicated by the various proverbs and quotations above, can be seen as a special case of our attitude towards silence (or inaction) in the face of others' actions more generally.

I move now to evidence for thinking that the assent interpretation is (not only psychologically but also) *socially* salient. We find something in the neighbourhood of the assent interpretation built into certain familiar social practices of group decision-making.[48] Consider the practice known as the 'tacit acceptance procedure' (also known as the 'silence procedure'), which is employed by committees charged with ratifying a report. This procedure involves the circulation of the draft document to the members of the committee, on the assumption that if no objections are made prior to the publicly expressed deadline, it is taken to be accepted by the members of the committee. Such a procedure is described in Berridge (2010):

> ...a proposal with strong support is deemed to have been agreed unless any member raises an objection to it before a precise deadline: silence signifies assent—or, at least, acquiescence.... Silence procedure is employed by NATO, the OSCE, in the framework of the Common Foreign and Security Policy of the European Union (EU) and, no doubt, in numerous other international bodies.[49]

Here we see a social practice that embeds something in the neighbourhood of the assent interpretation.

In sum, while there is a wide variety of distinct views in the foregoing linguistic, historical, and social sources—they differ over the precise

---

who observe the participants' silence will take this silence to indicate acceptance, thereby emboldening those who are perpetrating the injustices and enfeebling those who might otherwise try to resist (by making them think that the support for the injustice is much greater than in fact it was). This weaker assumption would suit my purposes here. Suppose that the assumption that silence implies acquiescence is only merely widely endorsed. In that case, I could say that the assent interpretation is a special case of a general attitude that many people have towards silence in the face of others' actions. This conclusion is in keeping with my hypotheses of the psychological and social salience of that interpretation.

[48] Indeed, this was a point on which Pettit (1994) relied in giving his argument regarding 'enfranchised silence'.
[49] G. R. Berridge (2010: 158).

significance of silence, and the conditions under which that significance is correctly ascribed to another's silence—I submit that these sources all point to the conclusion that the assent interpretation is both psychologically and socially salient.

I want to conclude this section by noting a second (albeit more speculative) kind of evidence attesting to the psychological salience of the assent interpretation. This is from the psychological work exploring the conditions under which we accept others' assertions.

In work on the psychological dimensions of the comprehension and assessment of others' say-so, the psychologist Daniel Gilbert and a team of researchers have argued that acceptance itself is the *psychological default*. In fact, their claim was stronger still: they argued that the evidence supports the hypothesis that comprehension of a spoken or written message 'includes an initial belief in the information comprehended' (Gilbert et al. 1999: 221) and that rejection itself (a) occurs only after this initial (if very brief) acceptance and (b) requires conscious effort on the part of the hearer. But whether or not this stronger claim regarding comprehension is true, there would appear to be ample evidence from cognitive psychology to think that acceptance is a psychological default.[50]

If this is true, then we have some reason to speculate that the assumption that silence implies acceptance, too, is a psychological default. While this speculation is answerable to relevant empirical results, I want to venture a hypothesis in advance of getting those results. Suppose Gilbert is correct that acceptance is a psychological default. Presumably this is nature's way of ensuring a certain kind of efficiency in our ability to pick up information from our conspecifics: we are hardwired to take on what they say, with rejection being something that requires more conscious effort. (As Thomas Reid noted in the eighteenth century, the effectiveness and reliability of this arrangement is aided by the fact, or what he argued was the fact, that we are also hardwired to speak truthfully, so that lying or other forms of deliberate deception require conscious—and hence potentially detectable—effort.) Assuming that this is the correct way to think of the psychological default of acceptance, then we might think that regarding others as accepting what was asserted is *also* a psychological default, and for the very same reason: this is nature's way of ensuring a certain kind of efficiency in our ability to pick up information from others. Only in this case the information

---

[50] For an extended discussion, see Evans et al. (2011) and the citations contained therein.

concerns, not what was said, but the acceptance by others of what was said. This 'collateral' information is typically very important: work in groups requires planning, which in turn often requires that we coordinate our beliefs. In this respect it makes sense that there should be a single default, both for the acceptance of others' sayings, and for the acceptance *of our fellows' acceptance* of others' sayings. This would aid our reliability and efficiency as we solve coordination problems that arise in the course of planning with others.[51]

I want to conclude this section by noting that if I am right that the assent interpretation is psychologically and socially salient, and that it is a common interpretation of silence, then we can reinforce NSR itself. For insofar as there is a widespread and familiar practice of regarding silence as indicating acceptance, the audience who silently rejects another's assertion thus runs the risk of harming the speaker in a way that is independent of the potential 'insult or injury'[52] of the rejection itself: namely, by allowing the speaker (and/or other participants) to presume that he (the audience) has accepted her assertion when he has not. Since the risk of such an outcome is (or should be) anticipated by any competent participant in the conversation, silent rejection is not merely uncooperative, it courts the accusation of acquiescing in a situation in which the anticipated likely outcome constitutes an epistemic harm to others—namely, the harm of false belief. What is at risk is not merely whether others correctly represent whether audience A accepted the assertion. In addition, those who observe A might well regard A's (apparent) acceptance as itself some evidence that the speaker's assertion was accept*able*[53]—and so, insofar as these observers also regard silent A as reliable in determining the truth for herself,[54] these observers are at risk of acquiring an additional false belief regarding the truth of the proposition asserted. With this in mind, it would seem that the (prima facie) injunction against doing something whose anticipated likely outcome would be to harm others is in place: one has a reason not to act like this. This then, too, is part of the source of the normative pressure on audiences not to remain silent in doubt or in rejection.

---

[51] It would also give rise to the possibility of exploitation by unscrupulous parties, of course. But perhaps this is why nature made us sensitive to the presence of defeating evidence. Some (Cosmides and Tooby (2005); Ermer et al. (2006)) go so far as to claim that nature has afforded us a hardwired 'cheater detection' system or module. But we need not go so far as that to appreciate that humans are sensitive to evidence of others' untrustworthiness.

[52] This language, which I quoted at length in Chapter 4, is from Anscombe (1979).

[53] This is a theme to which I will return in Chapters 9–11, under the rubric 'the social epistemology of public uptake'.

[54] With thanks to Jennifer Lackey for reminding me of the need for this qualification.

6

I just argued that insofar as one is entitled to regard one's speech exchange as a conversation, one has an entitlement to expect that, in the absence of relevant reasons for doubt, the audience who remains silent in the face of a public assertion has not rejected (and so has accepted) that assertion. But clearly there are all sorts of situations in which it would be inappropriate to have this expectation. Can these sorts of situations be accommodated in a principled way by the theory above? I think they can. In arguing for this I aim to present an account of the *defeat* of observers' presumptive entitlement to expect no silent rejection. I should add, too, that this account is simultaneously an account of the dissipation of the conversational pressure on an audience to signal rejection.

Happily, the account we want emerges naturally out of the model itself. According to the model, the presumptive status of the entitlement to expect no silent rejection is based on two claims. The first is that the parties are entitled to regard the speech exchange in question as (a conversation, and so as) a cooperative activity. The second is that participants have a conversation-generated practical reason to be cooperative (where silent rejection is uncooperative). Given this, we would predict two fundamental types of reason that can defeat the presumptive status of the expectation of no silent rejection: considerations that constitute reasons for questioning whether the particular speech exchange is (a conversation, and so) a cooperative activity; and considerations that constitute reasons for thinking that the listener's silence is best explained by factors that *outweigh* her conversation-generated practical reasons to be cooperative.

In light of this, I submit that there are two propositions that constitute potential defeaters. The propositions in question are these:

NON-CONVERSATION The particular speech exchange is not a conversation—it is not a cooperative exchange—in the first place;

OUTWEIGHING EXPLANATION The best explanation of the audience's silence appeals to *other* practical reasons[55] that audience has; these practical

---

[55] There is a constraint on the sort of practical reasons that can outweigh one's cooperation-generated reason to speak up in disagreement: not just any practical reason will do. Consider: I might have a strong desire to mislead you whenever I can, which generates a practical reason e.g. to remain quiet when I reject your assertion (in the hope that you are misled into thinking I have accepted it). Clearly this sort of practical reason does not undermine your entitlement to expect me to speak up in disagreement. To a first approximation, the constraint would appear to

reasons outweigh the audience's *pro tanto* conversation-generated practical reason to be cooperative (and so permit the audience to remain silent *whether or not* he has accepted the assertion).

The truth of NON-CONVERSATION entails that one was not entitled to expect cooperation in the first place, whereas the truth of OUTWEIGHING EXPLANATION entails that while one was entitled to expect cooperation, this entitlement (or rather the more specific entitlement to expect no silent rejection) is defeated by the stronger practical reasons that the audience has to remain silent in her rejection. In either case, when there are factors constituting adequate evidence to think that either NON-CONVERSATION or OUTWEIGHING EXPLANATION holds,[56] the result will be that observers do not enjoy the entitlement to expect no silent rejection. What is more, when either NON-CONVERSATION or OUTWEIGHING EXPLANATION holds, there is correspondingly no conversational pressure on an audience to signal rejection publicly.[57]

I believe that this approach can bring order to the wide range of cases in which we don't and shouldn't rely on the expectation in NSR:

NSR In all speech exchanges which are Gricean conversations, all competent language users enjoy a default (albeit defeasible) entitlement to expect that an audience who was manifestly silent in the face of a publicly made assertion has not rejected that assertion.

To fix ideas, let's start with some examples. (This list is not meant to be exhaustive.) I submit that, when it comes to observed assertions made in public settings, we typically *don't*—and in any case we *shouldn't*—expect

---

be this: the practical reasons in question must provide one with a *legitimate justification* for one's silent rejection. How to construe the conditions on legitimacy here is a non-trivial task to which I hope to return on another occasion. Having said this, I will continue to speak of one's practical reasons *simpliciter*.

[56] Here I would also want to include cases where, while the participant does not have sufficient evidence for either of NON-CONVERSATION or OUTWEIGHING EXPLANATION taken singly, she does have sufficient evidence for the disjunction. (With thanks to Tim Williamson for indicating the need for this qualification.)

[57] I would want to say something stronger: in contexts in which a hearer *should have had* evidence (where the evidence in question supports NON-CONVERSATION or OUTWEIGHING EXPLANATION), the entitlement is defeated. In such cases the defeater is what Lackey (1999) calls a 'normative' defeater. For an account of such defeaters, see Goldberg (2018).

that the silent audience has accepted the assertion when there are reasons to think that

- it would be practically difficult for a hearer to indicate her reaction (e.g. she is part of a huge crowd listening to a speaker, or is in a large classroom listening to a lecture);
- it would be socially improper for a hearer to indicate her reaction (e.g. she is in a situation in which there is a mutually known expectation of silence, or considerations of politeness predominate and tell against public rejection);
- there would be serious costs to the hearer for objecting or manifesting her rejection (e.g. she is listening to a vindictive boss's speech, or is observing an assertion under conditions of intimidation or repression; etc.);
- the assertion itself is not reasonably regarded as part of a cooperative endeavour (e.g. the person sitting next to you on the plane simply won't stop talking at you; or without warning and without any prior basis for doing so, a speaker starts telling you intimate details of his private life);
- the matter at hand is trivial, and so does not warrant the effort it would take to object (e.g. a speaker tells you of the number of blades of grass on his front lawn, or of what was on the sale rack at Macy's last year, or who got only minimal playing time in last week's 4th grade game);
- the context is one characterized by general sexism or racism or other forms of oppression, where various people are, or feel, 'silenced'.

In each of these cases (and others besides), I suspect that most observers would not expect that the silent audience has accepted the assertion. In any case, they shouldn't do so. We can get this result in terms of the proposed account of defeaters.

In a good many of these cases, there are adequate reasons supporting NON-CONVERSATION. (I analyse such cases as cases in which *there was no entitlement to expect no silent rejection to begin with*, since there was no conversation entitling participants to expect cooperation.) Thus, it is plausible to think that cases in which it is a salient fact that the speaker's speech contribution is unwelcome are not conversations. In this way we might handle the cases involving the seatmate on the plane who talks at one, or the person whose contribution is trivial and serves no common purpose. Relatedly, there can be cases in which it is manifest that a hearer's silence is grounded in her desire not to be part of the conversation: in effect, she has 'opted out.'[58] Alternatively, there are the cases involving a speaker speaking before a crowd: the forum in question is not the place for debate and dialogue, and in any case there is no expectation that one's audience will do so.[59] Finally, contexts of oppression are contexts of coercion, in which speech exchanges are not properly regarded as cooperative in nature.

In other cases, there are adequate reasons supporting OUTWEIGHING EXPLANATION. (I analyse such cases as cases in which the presumptive entitlement to expect no silent rejection is *defeated* by the epistemic reasons one has. That is, these are cases in which one has epistemic reasons to think that audience A has practical reasons not to indicate her doubts, where these reasons are weightier than, and permit not acting on, the conversation-generated practical reasons A has to publicly signal rejection.) Various of the cases above can be analysed in this way.

In this category I would place the range of cases in which cost–benefit considerations (involving A's practical reasons) support OUTWEIGHING EXPLANATION: the best explanation of A's silence might be that speaking out in rejection is not worth the effort in this context, where (given these costs and this context) silent rejection is both interpersonally permissible[60] and practically rational. Such an explanation is plausible in a variety of cases involving a significant threat to one's self-interest: when one fears the repercussions of speaking out (the speaker is a vindictive boss, or a powerful and influential figure, about whom there would be reasonable concerns were one to speak out in disagreement); or, relatedly, when there are salient political costs to speaking out and one is not (morally or otherwise interpersonally) obliged to take those costs on.[61] A related explanation in cost–benefit terms appears to cover cases in which a hearer remains silent after *others* have raised public objections to a mutually observed assertion.[62] Since others have already done the job of preventing the assertion from having its essential effect, it is not usually worth the effort of raising an additional voice of dissent (and it is morally permissible not to do so). What is more, insofar

---

[58] The idea that silence might constitute an attempt to 'opt out' of a conversation was first suggested to me by various colleagues in China. See also Nielsen (2012: 161) and Tirrell (2012: 209–10).
[59] Of course, dissenting crowds are not always silent: consider the phenomenon of *booing*.
[60] See footnote 55 above.
[61] This sort of example—though not my explanation for it!—was suggested to me by Jennifer Lackey, in conversation. Lackey uses this sort of example to motivate an alternative account of the significance of silence. See Lackey (forthcoming).
[62] I owe this example to Jennifer Lackey.

as it is *common knowledge* that others have objected to the assertion, it is (or should be) common knowledge that without further ado the proposed update has not been made—in effect, the assertion has been rejected (at least by some in the group)—and this defeats the entitlement to expect that the audience who remains silent has accepted the assertion. (On the contrary, continued silence under these circumstances might entitle others to regard you as having accepted *the public rejection* of the original assertion.)

There are additional types of consideration that can support OUTWEIGHING EXPLANATION. Prevailing social norms can do so as well. Consider contexts in which there is a social expectation of silence. This expectation gives the hearer a reason to be silent, which, given the costs of violating that expectation, can be weightier than the reason to make public any objections she has. This will be particularly important in any community in which great weight is placed on politeness norms, where it is considered impolite to disagree publicly with a speaker. In such communities, the hearer will always have some (politeness-based) reason not to indicate doubts or dissent (and this reason will make it morally permissible to be silent even when one rejects the assertion). In such communities, the significance of silence will be very different from what it is in communities in which the prevailing politeness norms do not carry as much weight (or where it is not considered impolite to disagree publicly with a speaker).[63]

An interesting hybrid case, where a variety of different considerations appear to support OUTWEIGHING EXPLANATION, concerns assertions made by teachers in pedagogical contexts.[64] Student silence is often best explained in terms other than acceptance: perhaps they are trying to comprehend what is said (or what they do and don't understand); perhaps they fear being humiliated if they object to or raise doubts about what others regard as obvious; perhaps they regard silence among students as proper classroom protocol; and so forth. In these sort of cases it would seem interpersonally permissible, if inadvisable, to remain silent even if one harbours doubts.

What should be said, though, of cases in which oppressive conditions (e.g. of sexism, racism, and so forth) are present? I will have a good deal to say about this in Chapter 9, so here I will be brief. These, too, can be regarded as

---

[63] Does this mean that NSR is false in communities in which strong politeness norms are in effect? I don't think so; it only means that one's entitlement to the assent interpretation is easily defeated in such communities, at least in contexts in which the participants are not intimates. See section 7 below; and see Chapter 11 for a longer discussion.

[64] I owe this example to Mona Simion and Maria Kronfeldner.

cases in which either or both of the defeaters, NON-CONVERSATION or OUTWEIGHING EXPLANATION, are present. In circumstances in which the oppression is acute, where individuals feel threatened to speak at all (resulting in what various authors such as Langton (1993), Langton and Hornsby (1998), and Tanesini (2016) call 'locutionary silencing'), the speech exchange is not reasonably regarded as cooperative, and so NON-CONVERSATION holds.[65] In cases that are less severe, in which individuals tend not to speak up out of a sense of demoralization induced by the oppressive circumstances, audiences have practical reasons to remain silent—namely, the sense that any attempt to speak up will most certainly have no positive effects but many negative effects—which would explain their silence and which, when well grounded in the facts, would provide moral justification for remaining silent even in disagreement.[66] In such cases, OUTWEIGHING EXPLANATION holds.

Indeed, I suspect that the real worry about these cases is not whether we can find a defeater to ensure that oppressors aren't entitled to regard the silence of their demoralized victims as acceptance, but rather whether we ought to be forced to look for a defeater in the first place. That is, the worry these cases bring out is whether we ought to be postulating a default entitlement to expect no silent rejection in the first place; for it is only on the postulation of such an entitlement that we need to look for a defeater. Perhaps these cases show that the very move to postulate such an entitlement is wrong from the start. (Langton (2007) may be read as sympathetic to this worry.) This strikes me as an important objection requiring an extended treatment. Rather than addressing it here, I will devote the entirety of Chapter 9 to it.

7

In this penultimate section I want to consider three other objections to my treatment of silence. All three raise important points; none of them undermine the proposal on offer.

The first objection is that my proposal is trivial. Given that I have argued that the entitlement to expect no silent rejection is defeated when one has a

---

[65] For an excellent discussion of the way in which members of non-priviliged groups can feel threatened by hostile speech in oppressive circumstances, see McGowan (2012, 2020), Gelber (2012), and West (2012).

[66] For an excellent discussion of this, see Dotson (2011, 2014).

better explanation for a hearer's silence, the charge is that my proposal amounts to the trivial claim that we are entitled to expect no silent rejection *except when we're not*.

This charge does not withstand scrutiny.

To begin, the proponent of NSR who acknowledges OUTWEIGHING EXPLANATION as a defeating condition is indeed committed to the following: one who is entitled to regard a speech exchange as a conversation is *ipso facto* entitled to expect that those who are silent have not rejected the public assertion, *except* when there is a better alternative explanation for that silence (on which silent rejection is interpersonally permissible and practically rational). But such a claim is no triviality. This can be brought out in two ways.

First, whereas trivial proposals are consistent with every (consistent) claim, the proposal on offer is inconsistent with the following:

AGNOSTICISM   Even when one is entitled to regard a speech exchange as a conversation, every hypothesis regarding the significance of another's silence is warranted *only by relevant positive evidence*; prior to acquiring such evidence one ought to remain agnostic towards any particular hypothesis.

If NSR is true, conversational participants enter into the conversation *already enjoying a presumptive entitlement* to expect no silent rejection—in which case AGNOSTICISM is false. So NSR is not a trivial claim.

But there is a second way to bring out NSR's non-trivial status. Whereas trivialities cannot be used to explain or illuminate anything of substance, we can use NSR to explain or illuminate at least two distinct (substantial) phenomena.

For one thing, we can use NSR to explain the striking pattern of facts illustrated in section 5. That is, we can explain why many people, at many different historical times and in different cultures, express their endorsement of (some version of) the assent interpretation. The explanation is straightforward. NSR reflects familiar features of the practice of assertion. Such features are appreciated by anyone who is competent in that practice. This means that anyone competent in that practice is in a position to appreciate that silent rejection is uncooperative, hence marked; and so anyone competent in the practice will be in a position to appreciate that audience silence will be presumed to imply acceptance. So, it is unsurprising that throughout history and in different cultures many human beings have manifested their competence in the practice of assertion by making this explicit, in the form of the assent interpretation itself. (It is worth considering how those who reject NSR would explain this striking pattern of facts.)

For another, we can use NSR to illuminate what would otherwise seem to be a coincidental parallelism in our attitudes. This is the parallel between (i) the common attitude regarding silence in the face of others' actions generally and (ii) the common attitude regarding silence in the face of others' assertions. In section 5 I argued that the parallel is this: silence in the face of another's actions is standardly presumed to be a form of acquiescence, whether the act is an ordinary non-linguistic act or a speech act. In thinking of (i), I take it as relatively uncontroversial that this attitude (of standardly presuming that silence implies acquiescence) is proper. Given the parallelism between (i) and (ii), it would be striking if this were not so in connection with (ii). But if NSR holds, we can explain the attitude in (ii), like the attitude in (i), as proper. (Once again, it would be worth considering how those who reject NSR would explain this parallelism.)

I have just argued that, despite initial appearances, NSR is not trivial. But a second objection to my treatment of silence is more serious. I will call this the 'disaggregation objection.'[67] According to the view I favour, when one is entitled to regard a speech exchange as a conversation, one is entitled to regard silent rejection as uncooperative, and so one is entitled to expect no silent rejection. According to the disaggregation objection, we should reject this universal claim, and instead try to generate the warrant for the expectation of no silent rejection on a case-by-case basis, allowing that there can be different explanations in different cases.[68] For example, it might be that when the speaker is a friend, one has duties to the friend which would warrant the friend in assuming that one's silence implies acceptance; or when one is part of a group, where a good deal hangs on the group members' coordinating with one another, and where the group aims to be efficient in its use of time, it may be that these considerations warrant the members in assuming that other members' silence implies their acceptance; or . . .

To this objection I have three related replies.

First, while it can seem that the sheer variety of considerations that defeat the (alleged) default entitlement constitutes grounds for being sceptical of

---

[67] This objection has been suggested to me (in conversation) by Erin Beeghley, Hanoch Ben-Yami, Kati Farkas, Jennifer Lackey, and others.

[68] Although she does not endorse this explicitly, Langton (2007) might be sympathetic to this approach.

the existence of such an entitlement, there are other familiar examples of default entitlements that exist in domains in which defeating conditions are prevalent. Consider for example the leading view in the epistemology of testimony, according to which hearers enjoy a default (epistemic) entitlement to accept what they are told, with defeat of this entitlement contingent on the presence of reasons to doubt the credibility of the telling itself.[69] Defenders of such an 'anti-reductionist' view have explicitly argued against regarding the fact that defeating conditions are prevalent as a reason to doubt the existence of the default entitlement itself (see e.g. Graham 2004). Their point has been that generic considerations from the domain of epistemology favour postulating the default—with the result that cases which might otherwise appear to tell against the existence of such a default entitlement are better construed as cases in which the default is defeated. So, too, I would suggest, for the sort of entitlement for which I have argued here:[70] generic considerations pertaining to the practice of assertion favour postulating the default, so our attitude towards prevalent would-be counter-evidence should be the same.

Second, the disaggregation objection itself comes at a cost. In particular, it will not do simply to say that we can generate the warrant for the expectation of no silent rejection on a case-by-case basis. For my argument for NSR appeals to considerations—aspects of our practice of assertion itself—that are perfectly general. If this argument is sound, then the conclusion should hold in *any* situation in which assertions are made in the course of a (Gricean) conversation. Consequently, the proponent of the disaggregation objection inherits the burden of explaining away appearances to the contrary. To do so, she must either deny that our practice of assertion has the features I claim it has, or else deny that its having these features grounds the claim that silent rejection is uncooperative—my argument to the contrary notwithstanding. This will involve, for instance, explaining the patterns of facts from section 5 without appeal to anything like NSR.

Third, there is reason to doubt whether the proponent of the disaggregation objection *can* explain what needs to be explained on this score, without appeal to *the very features* that motivate NSR itself. It should be

---

[69] Classic versions of this view are Ross (1986), Coady (1992), Burge (1993), Foley (2001), and Graham (2006). See also Chapter 6, where I discuss this view at length.
[70] It should be kept in mind, however, that the entitlement for which I am arguing here is not an epistemic entitlement, so much as a practice-generated one: it is the sort that emerges from our legitimate practices, through which we hold one another accountable as participants in those practices. See Goldberg (2017) for further discussion of this sort of entitlement.

uncontroversial that there are cases in which (i) the expectation of no silent rejection is proper and (ii) there is some normative pressure on those who doubt or reject an assertion to make their doubts public. The task is to explain this in each and every case in which (i) and (ii) hold. The proponent of NSR does so in terms of generic features of the practice of assertion. The proponent of the 'disaggregation objection' must do so in other terms (on pain of motivating the view she aims to criticize). But it is doubtful that we can explain the existence of such cases without appealing to generic features of the practice of assertion itself. After all, the cases are not rare: they are common enough that people regularly express views about the significance of silence. What is more, our pragmatic competence itself renders the assent interpretation psychologically salient: even when one does not ultimately accept it, the assent interpretation is one that readily comes before one's mind when one encounters conversational silence. And while ad hoc considerations pertaining to the relationship between the speaker and her audience, or to the context of the conversation, might *augment* the reasons one has to expect no silent rejection, it would seem that such ad hoc considerations cannot *generate* these reasons—let alone generate them in such a way as to be familiar to pragmatically competent speakers, and in each and every case in which (i) and (ii) hold. There are cases, of course, in which some explicit provision is made for the assent interpretation, as with the 'silence procedure', or with explicit statements such as 'Speak now or forever hold your peace.' However, in the majority of cases in which the assent interpretation is (and is recognized to be) proper, there is no explicit provision of these sorts. Rather, it seems that the reasons supporting the expectation of no silent rejection are generated by features of the practice of assertion itself—which in effect is to grant that there is a generic (conversation-generated) reason to expect no silent rejection.

The third and final objection I want to consider is the 'bad social consequences' objection. The worry is that endorsing the family of norms including NSR, NSR=, and NSR+ would have bad social consequences. In particular, it would lead people to think that they have others' assent when they do not, under conditions that lead to bad (and sometimes even horrific) consequences. Even if it can be argued that in each of these cases those who rely on the assent interpretation do so illegitimately (as there is a defeater present), even so, the worry remains: the claim that the interpreter was not entitled to rely on the assent interpretation (because it was defeated) will be of little solace when the effects of the participant's having acted on the assent interpretation are very bad indeed. (Not unrelated here are worries about the conditions on consent itself.)

I am deeply sympathetic with the basis of this worry. While it would be unreasonable to expect a theory to be free from any possibility of being misapplied—one thinks here of Mill's comment in *Utilitarianism* that 'There is no difficulty in proving any ethical standard whatever to work ill, if we suppose universal idiocy to be conjoined with it'—at the same time it is reasonable to expect a theory to have plausible things to say about reasonable worries. And this worry is imminently reasonable.

But the worry can be met. While I will have much more to say about this in Chapter 9, here it is worth noting that most law codes require *explicit* assent/consent in contexts in which two parties are engaging one another contractually, or where one party's acting without the assent/consent of the other party would constitute a crime. Although these cases don't (or don't always) involve assertions, and so are not central to my topic here, we might still wonder about the status of the assent interpretation of silence in contexts of contracts or other legal matters. My own view is that the law has it right: when the legal status of one's proposal or action turns on another's assent or consent, one needs the other's explicit word, as *this is the best way to ensure our protection against being harmed by others whose views of whether we have accepted or consented might be false even when reasonable.*[71] Once it becomes common knowledge that this is how the law works, our expectations shift accordingly when we recognize (or ought to recognize[72]) that the context is, or might become, a legal one. The same holds true of silence in the face of assertions made in legal contexts. These cases might then be accommodated within my NSR-based account above in one of two ways: either as cases in which whatever reason there is to regard silence as implying assent is not sufficiently strong to justify action on that basis (or to provide one who makes such an assumption with legal protection); or alternatively, as cases in which the entitlement to assume the assent interpretation is defeated by the legal context, which constitutes a (decisive) reason *not to assume acceptance save in the case where acceptance is made*

---

[71] On the assumption that we all value not having our autonomy trampled, we can account for these cases in terms of the notion employed in Chapter 7, that of value-reflecting practical reasons. In particular, in cases involving others' would-be consent (or where our acting on the false assumption of their assent would be disastrous), we have value-reflecting practical reasons to acquire evidence sufficient to constitute *knowledge* of the other parties' consent.

[72] See Goldberg (2017).

explicit. Either way, given that ignorance of the law is no excuse, there can be no defence of one's entitlement to the assent interpretation in such contexts.

8

In this chapter I have argued for three main conclusions. First, in cases involving conversations, participants have a conversation-generated entitlement to expect no silent rejection. This entitlement derives from the presumption of cooperativity in conversation and from the normative features of the practice of assertion itself. But—and this is my second main conclusion—the entitlement is *defeasible*: in any particular case there can be other considerations that explain or justify an audience's silence in the face of an assertion, that outweigh the audience's conversation-generated reason to be cooperative. Correspondingly, and third, audience members are thus under some normative pressure to indicate when they reject, or have doubts concerning, a mutually observed assertion. This pressure dissipates when the participants' default entitlement to expect no silent rejection is itself defeated.

9
Silence Misinterpreted
The Double-Harm of Silencing

1

Recent work in what we might call applied epistemology and applied pragmatics has begun to attend to the (non-ideal) conditions in which actual speech exchanges take place. Owing to the foundational contributions from feminist philosophy and philosophy of race, theorists have begun to attend to such things as various forms of privilege (white, male, cisgender) that affect our speech exchanges,[1] various types of bias that infect our participation in social life (including but not limited to when it involves speech[2]), the unjust aspects of our institutional arrangements that structure our exchanges,[3] the unfair social practices that lead us to form illegitimate expectations of one another based on gender, race, class, sexual orientation, or other social categories,[4] and the kinds of speech act by which we denigrate or express our contempt for others.[5] This work ought to be celebrated by everyone with a serious interest in the nature and importance of language and speech.

Those who are familiar with the thrust of this work might well have serious worries about the conclusion from Chapter 8. There I argued that the

Adapted from Sanford C. Goldberg (2016) 'II—Arrogance, Silence, and Silencing', *Aristotelian Society Supplementary Volume*, 90 (1): 93–112.

[1] Seminal work here includes Collins (1990), Code (1995), Mills (1997, 2007), Mills and Pateman (2007), Townley (2011), Dotson (2011, 2014), and various papers in Maitra and McGowan (2012).
[2] Seminal recent work here includes Longino and Doell (1983), Alcoff (2001), Jones (2002), Richeson and Trawalter (2005), Kelly and Roedder (2008), Gendler (2011), Holroyd (2012), Saul (2013), Mills (2014, 2015, 2017), Brownstein and Saul (2016a, 2016b), and Levy (2017).
[3] Seminal recent work here includes Jagger (1983), Harding (1991), Anderson (1995), Wylie (2003, 2011), and Haslanger (2014).
[4] Seminal recent work here includes M. Fricker (1998, 2007).
[5] Seminal recent work here includes Hom (2010), Croom (2011, 2013), Anderson and Lepore (2013), Camp (2013), Jeshion (2013), and Bianchi (2014).

expectation of cooperation in conversation grounds an entitlement to expect no silent rejection, and that this in turn grounds an entitlement to regard silence in response to an observed assertion as indicating acceptance or assent. But the hypothesis that we are entitled to regard silence as indicating acceptance is precisely the sort of thing that seems ripe for abuse in a system, like ours, in which various forms of oppression prevail. More specifically, the alleged entitlement I defended seems like precisely the sort of entitlement that the powerful would impose on the weak, thereby ensuring that the powerful have the right to hold the weak to standards that disproportionately benefit the former. It doesn't take a cynic to worry that this is a recipe for the powerful to extend their power over the weak: not only do the former have the power (and not only are they ascribed the authority) to make public statements, they also have the power (and are ascribed the right) to interpret the weak's silence as accepting those statements. This seems like a dystopian vision if ever there was one.

Those who worry about the dystopian nature of the foregoing will not be mollified by my brief comments, toward the end of Chapter 8, where I argued that oppressive conditions *defeat* the entitlement in question. They will rightly note that the only reason I needed to find a defeater in the first place was because I had postulated the entitlement. They will say: better to think that there is no such entitlement, not even a defeasible entitlement, in the first place. And what better argument for this no-entitlement view than to point out how easily it would be manipulated by the powerful, or perhaps merely give rise to a reinforcement of power dynamics that we have good reason to want to abolish.

Suppose that these critics are right that there is no entitlement of the sort I described and argued for in Chapter 8. This need not undermine the point that there remains a kind of 'conversational pressure' on those who observe a public statement. Only this will not be seen as a reflection of the norms of our conversational practices. Rather, this 'conversational pressure' will be seen as a kind of raw power (i.e. when conditions are oppressive), or else as arising out of the prior relationships we have with other conversational participants, or perhaps as reflecting some explicit and commonly known practice of treating silence as assent in certain salient circumstances (such as the 'silence procedure' or situations in which one is explicitly advised to 'speak now or forever hold your peace').

I believe that this sort of worry poses an important challenge to my account of the conversational pressure involved when one remains silent in the face of a public statement. But I also believe that this sort of worry can be met.

2

I begin with a quick review of the landscape.

Let 'silence' designate the state of remaining quiet in the face of a publicly made claim (statement or assertion), wherein the audience gives no explicit indication of whether he has accepted or rejected the claim. In Chapter 8 I argued—and in any case it should be uncontroversial—that an audience's silence in the face of a mutually observed assertion is often a significant part of the speech exchange itself. By saying that silence in this sense is significant, I mean that it is taken as such by some or all of the participants in the speech exchange: they *interpret* other parties' silence as indicative of this-or-that. Suppose that someone asserts something in the mutual presence of a group of people, and that one or more of the audience members remains silent in the face of this assertion. It is easy to imagine scenarios in which other participants interpret this silence as indicating that the relevant party is being polite, or that s/he has no objections to what was said, or that s/he thinks that it would be awkward to respond publicly to the speaker's contribution, etc. Whether and how one's silence is interpreted will depend of course on many factors: what the interpreter knows of one's background beliefs and behavioural dispositions, how others in the audience publicly respond to the assertion, the prevailing social norms in the community, what is (taken as) mutually presupposed in the context, and so forth. Schematically, we might summarize the situation by saying that the fact that a hearer is silent in the face of a mutually observed assertion is itself a piece of evidence that other participants will seek to explain (if only to themselves); and they typically seek to do so by way of making an inference to the best explanation of that silence.

Among the candidate explanations of another's silence in the face of a mutually observed assertion, I argued that one stands out as particularly salient. According to this interpretation, one's silence indicates or implies one's acceptance of what was asserted. When a participant P accepts this as the best explanation of audience A's silence, P can then be said to *interpret* A's silence as indicating or implying her acceptance. I designated this sort of interpretation as the 'assent interpretation' of silence. And I argued that among the various candidate explanations for a hearer's silence, the assent interpretation is 'particularly salient' in at least three respects. First, this interpretation is highly *psychologically* salient to speakers: faced with the task of explaining another's silence in the face of a mutually observed assertion, the assent interpretation is typically one of the first to be considered. Second, the assent interpretation is highly *socially* salient to members of language communities: it is a mutually familiar part of the social practice of many speech communities that silence is standardly interpreted as indicating assent. Third—and what was most important for my argument in Chapter 8—this interpretation of silence is *normatively* salient to speakers: at least in cases of Gricean conversation (where cooperation is properly expected), speakers enjoy a default (albeit defeasible) entitlement to expect no silent rejection, and so enjoy a default (albeit defeasible) entitlement to expect that the silent audience has accepted the assertion.[6]

I suspect that my claims asserting the *psychological* and *social* salience of the assent interpretation will be relatively uncontroversial; my claim asserting the *normative* salience of this interpretation is another story. Indeed, various authors have explicitly rejected such an hypothesis. In Chapter 8 I already mentioned Rae Langton's (2007) doubts. While she is speaking of those who would regard silence in terms of consent and approval rather than acceptance, she notes that '... the patterns for default consent look, on the face of it, rather variable', and goes on to ask, '[W]hat prospect is there for a more general condition under which silence speaks approval—and why, if there is, should we want it?'

> ... the expression of disapproval is often voluntary, and sometimes costly: and this means the expression of disapproval may be masked.... Moreover, disapproval itself is sometimes voluntary, and sometimes costly: and this means disapproval may be stifled ... This is particularly clear when (though not only when) one considers *relationships that are oppressive or dependent*.
> (Langton 2007: 203; italics added)

Nor is Langton alone in her explicit repudiation of the hypothesis of a default entitlement to the assent interpretation. More recently, Alessandra Tanesini explicitly rejects the claim of a normative entitlement to presume a strong connection between conversational silence and assent. She writes,

> An asserter is... not entitled to expect that his audience will believe the content of his assertion if they have not challenged it. So they are not entitled to presume that silence means assent.   (Tanesini 2016: 79)

---

[6] This expectation can be strengthened to replace 'accepted' with 'assented to' when the aim of the conversation is or involves the serious exchange of reliable information; if this assumption of such an aim is reasonable in context, I argued, the entitlement to regard silence as implying (not merely acceptance but) assent holds.

Tanesini's concerns, like Langton's, involve contexts in which oppression has the effect of silencing people.[7]

These worries are both well motivated and serious. In Chapter 8 I tried to respond to half of Langton's concern: I argued that certain very general features of conversation underwrite the default entitlement in question. (These include the propriety of the expectation of cooperation in conversation, and the fact that pragmatic competence equips us to recognize the speaker's manifest preference that her assertion be accepted.) What remains, however, is to answer the second part of her concern: 'why, if there is [a more general condition under which silence speaks approval], should we *want* it?' (italics added). While I think the case for the postulation of a default entitlement to the assent interpretation stands, and is to be made in terms of features of the practice of assertion (presented in Chapter 8), even so I think Langton can be seen as rightly questioning our attitude towards this entitlement: why embrace it, rather than calling for a change in our practices (if this is indeed our practice)?

In what follows I will make two claims in defence of the postulation of a default entitlement to presume that silence implies acceptance. First, appeal to this default is part of the best explanation of the harms of oppression-induced silencing. Second, appeal to this default is part of the best way to *address* the oppressive circumstances themselves. I recognize the irony of saying both of these things, but I hope to convince the reader of their truth.

3

In order to bring out how an appeal to the default entitlement is needed to explain the harms of silencing, it will be helpful to start with an alternative account of those harms. Here I turn to Alessandra Tanesini's recent reflections on the effects of arrogance. Her reflections are particularly worthy of attention for my present purposes, as she aims to identify the mechanisms through which arrogance can silence (and thereby harm) others. (While Tanesini is talking about the effects of arrogance, her points would appear to hold regarding the effects of oppression as well; and my reply to her account will be explicitly framed so as to cover the effects of oppression as well.) By raising difficulties for her proposal, I hope to show that the appeal to the

---

[7] For similar worries, see Tirrell (2012: 203).

default entitlement earns its keep by enabling us to reap the benefits of her explanation while avoiding the objections.

Following the groundbreaking work of Rae Langton (1993, 2009) and others, Tanesini employs the distinction between two types of silencing. A person is *locutionarily* silenced by the arrogant speaker, Tanesini writes, when, as a result of systematic treatment in this arrogant fashion, the person acquires the disposition to keep to herself (out of a desire not to have her would-be contributions utterly disregarded or subject to ridicule, disrespect, etc.).[8] The more deep-seated sort of silencing is *illocutionary* silencing.[9] A person is silenced in this way, on Tanesini's construal, when her 'purported assertion misfires due to lack of uptake' (2016: 88).

There can be no doubt that people who have been silenced in either of these two ways have been harmed.[10] As Tanesini herself notes, the harms include being disrespected, having one's self-confidence eroded, losing the chance for influencing the group (in the case of locutionary silencing), and (in the case of illocutionary silencing) losing one's status as someone who is even able to offer inputs into the deliberative process of the group.[11] In addition to these harms, Tanesini suggests the possibility of further harms that might arise downstream when one is systematically silenced through arrogance:

> the silenced individuals will soon learn that it is less risky to share the views of those who are capable of silencing them. These individuals may bite their tongues, unless what they think coincides with powerful views. Over time, one may expect that because of cognitive dissonance such individuals may stop biting their tongues and simply defer to the opinions of others. When they do so, they have become servile. (2016: 90)

Servility of this sort appears to involve the loss of one's sense of oneself as an epistemic subject in one's own right; one who is rendered servile in this way is the victim of what Fricker (2007) characterizes as an *epistemic injustice*.[12]

---

[8] Compare Kristie Dotson's (2011) notion of *testimonial smothering*.
[9] The notion of illocutionary silencing Tanesini has in mind was first developed in Langton (1993, 2009). See also Hornsby (1995), McGowan (2009a, 2009b, 2012, 2020), McGowan et al. (2011), and Maitra (2012).
[10] See MacKinnon (1989), Young (1989), Langton (1993), Schauer (1993), Dyzenhaus (1992), and Hornsby (1995).
[11] I borrow this language from Wanderer (2012).
[12] An epistemic injustice is an injustice that harms an individual in her role as an epistemic subject.

I believe that Tanesini is broadly correct in her assessment of the various harms associated with being silenced by the arrogant. I worry, however, that something is missing in her account of the harms involved when arrogance silences. What appears to be missing is the way in which the harms Tanesini describes are made far worse by the very manner in which the silenced party defends herself—namely, through her remaining silent in the face of the arrogant party's assertions. For my impression is that, when conditions are ripe for silencing—when members of certain groups are systematically oppressed and subordinated—then *the very silence of those who are the victims of this oppression and subordination is itself standardly interpreted as further evidence for the warrantedness of the way these victims are being treated*. While this interpretation of their silence is both false and terribly unfair, my own view is that it can be traced to aspects of our conversational practices themselves; and it is by revealing this faulty interpretation's source in our various conversational practices that we might best hope to be able to understand the full scope of the harms of silencing.

4

Let us now return to the individual who is locutionarily silenced by oppressive circumstances. I now want to argue that a full account of the harms of oppression-induced silencing will need to appeal to the normative aspects of our conversational practices, including the default entitlement to regard silence as implying acceptance. Two points are relevant. First, when an audience A is silenced, the harms of being silenced potentially include the oppressor S construing A's condition of silence as giving S licence to regard A as having accepted what S asserted. In this way, I will argue, the harm of silencing includes a double harm, wherein A is not only silenced, and so prevented from speaking up, but also *rendered complicit in reinforcing her very oppression* (as it were).[13] But second, we can only understand the nature (and particular awfulness) of the latter (*italicized*) harm, as well as why this sort of harm is so pervasive under conditions of oppression, if we assume that there is a default entitlement to presume that silence implies acceptance. In this section I hope to explain this (perhaps initially surprising) point in detail.

---

[13] Compare Tirrell (2012: 203), who notes that this can arise even in contexts in which the oppression is literally genocidal. See also West (2012: 245).

To begin, consider oppressive circumstances which give rise to the locutionary silencing of an audience member. I submit that the harms suffered by that audience member often, and perhaps even typically, include the harm of having her silence—her condition of remaining silent in response to the assertion—regarded by her oppressor as giving him licence to regard her as accepting what he asserted. This is a particularly stinging aspect of the harm of locutionary silencing, since in effect the point is that people who have been silenced are susceptible to having *the very effects of their oppression regarded as a kind of endorsement on their part*.[14]

To see how this works, suppose that we are in a community in which the assent interpretation is itself psychologically and socially salient. And suppose further that the community is one in which conditions are ripe for silencing: members of certain social groups are systematically oppressed and subordinated. Now it is plausible to think that under such conditions some people (including perhaps some victims themselves) are ignorant of the phenomenon of silencing: they don't acknowledge it, recognize it, discern when conditions for it obtain, etc. Such people will be oblivious to reasons that ought to prompt them, in particular contexts in which circumstances are oppressive for individual audience members, to doubt the propriety of relying on the presumption that audience silence implies acceptance. To these oblivious individuals, the assent interpretation will remain psychologically and socially salient; they will continue to regard this interpretation as a live option as they seek to explain their fellows' silence in the face of a mutually observed assertion. Insofar as they are oblivious to the phenomenon of silencing, we would expect that many of them will end up endorsing this interpretation, and so will end up regarding the silenced subject's silence as indicating her acceptance of what is said. When they do, these oblivious individuals not only participate in the silencing-constituting oppression itself, but also harm the silenced victim a second time over; they do so by interpreting the very effects of that oppression (the victims' demoralized silence) as indicating the victims' acceptance of the assertion.[15] This is a further harm, I submit, not (or not merely) because it falsely represents them as accepting what they (most likely) reject, but also, and more nefariously,

---

[14] This is the basis of the idea that those who are silenced have a positive duty to resist this oppression—and so have a positive duty *not* to remain silent; see Hay (2013). Hay herself comes at these matters from a very different perspective; her approach is Kantian, and her central thesis is that 'people who are oppressed are bound by the duty of self-respect to resist their own oppression'.

[15] This is a point that has been emphasized by Rae Langton; see Langton (2007).

because in so doing it *renders them complicit in reinforcing their own oppression*: in being taken to agree with the arrogant speaker's claim, they are being rendered in a way that will only reinforce the prevailing but unfair attitude which regards members of the relevant social group (of which she herself is a member) as lacking an independent perspective that is worth taking seriously in its own right.

So far, I have been arguing that the best explanation for the harms of oppression-induced silencing makes use of the widespread practice of regarding silence as implying acceptance. But why think that we need to appeal to a *default entitlement* to the assent interpretation? Isn't it enough, to get the explanation we seek, that as a matter of empirical fact there is a tendency of people to rely on that interpretation—their entitlement to do so being utterly irrelevant?

It might be thought that we *don't* need the appeal to the default entitlement to get the explanation we seek. I can imagine this point of view developed as follows. What needs to be explained is why the demoralized silence of the oppressed is often interpreted by others—including but not limited to those who benefit from the oppression—as implying acceptance. But (the thought continues) the explanation we seek need not appeal the existence of an entitlement to presume that silence implies acceptance. To be sure, those who would interpret another's silence as implying acceptance need to be represented as having *some* basis for this interpretation. After all, if there were no basis for doing so, then it would be irrational and unwarranted to do so, in which case we would not expect this phenomenon to be as prevalent as it is. However, in order to represent those who rely on the assent interpretation as having a basis for doing so, we need not appeal to anything as strong as an entitlement to presume that silence implies acceptance. For the purpose of the explanation we seek, it would suffice that people generally *believe* in the existence of such an entitlement.[16] For if in general people believe that we enjoy a default entitlement to presume that silence implies acceptance, then—*whether or not we do in fact enjoy such an entitlement*—in general people will proceed to interpret one another as if such an entitlement were in place. And this suffices to explain why the demoralized silence of the oppressed is often interpreted by others—including but not limited to those who benefit from the oppression—as implying acceptance. Or so it might be thought.

---

[16] With thanks to Erin Beeghly for suggesting this objection, in conversation.

But it seems to me that such an explanation is inadequate. Suppose we ask why people regularly believe that there is such an entitlement. Is this belief *arbitrary*, as it would be if it were based on nothing? Presumably not, since if this belief were arbitrary then we wouldn't expect it to regularly happen that people acquire such a belief, in a variety of different cultures and historical periods.[17] But the explanation needs the belief to be pervasive in a community, on pain of not being able to explain why it is that people regularly interpret the silence of the oppressed as implying their acceptance (again, in a variety of different cultures and historical periods). For this reason, the various participants' belief in the entitlement cannot be seen as *arbitrary*, but rather must be seen as reflecting real features of our very conversational practices themselves.

Perhaps at this point my opponent will simply appeal to the fact that people regularly employ the assent interpretation as part of our de facto interpretative practices in conversation. The thought here is to regard our reliance on the assent interpretation as a kind of de facto regularity of our practice, and to appeal to this regularity to provide the explanation we seek. That explanation would go something like this: so long as everyone recognizes that, *as a matter of fact*, the assent interpretation is a regularity of our conversational practice, people will regard themselves as *epistemically justified* in relying on it themselves in a particular situation (so long as there is no evidence to the contrary). And if that is so, we can explain why under conditions of oppression people tend to regard even the *demoralized* silence of the audience as implying their acceptance.

But this response seems to me to put the cart before the horse. Why is it that the assent interpretation is a regular part of our conversational practice? My opponent will want to treat this as a brute fact of the practice itself. (By saying that this regularity is 'brute', I mean that it is not susceptible of further explanation.) Unfortunately, the 'brute regularity' hypothesis—the hypothesis that the assent interpretation is a brute regularity of our conversational practice—yields some false predictions and fails to predict other things that are relevant part of our conversational practice. I will take these up in reverse order.

The brute regularity hypothesis fails to predict aspects that are a relevant part of our conversational practice. Take a case in which you assert that p, observe your audience's silence in the face of this assertion, and so (lacking

---

[17] See section 5 of Chapter 8 for evidence of this.

evidence to think otherwise) regard them as having accepted that p. Suppose that in fact your total evidence—your evidence for thinking that the assent interpretation is a regularity of our conversational practices, and your evidence in this particular context regarding your audience—supports this interpretation. But suppose you learn that in fact the silent audience had in fact rejected your assertion but hadn't bothered to indicate this. You are likely to experience some sort of reactive attitude, which you might express with an irritated 'Why didn't you let me know?' or 'You should have indicated this to me!' What is more, you are likely to feel *entitled* to this reaction. This is mysterious on the brute regularity hypothesis: the fact that some piece of behaviour is a brute regularity does not entitle you to *hold people responsible* (in the way associated with the reactive attitudes) when they deviate from the behaviour.

It might be thought that the proponent of the brute regularity hypothesis can make sense of this reaction. After all, if the assent interpretation is a regularity of our conversational practice, then we might well be justified—epistemically justified—in expecting everyone to recognize this; and if that is so, then an audience who remains silent in rejection does something he should have anticipated would have the harmful effect of inducing a false belief in those who observed his silent reaction. This might be thought to be the basis of the reactive attitudes above. But these appearances of explanatory adequacy are misleading. To see this, notice that the foregoing account helps itself to the assumption that *everyone recognizes* the status of the assent interpretation (as a regularity of conversational practice). By what right does it make this assumption? The only justification it can offer for this assumption would presumably be an epistemic justification: we have evidence that everyone recognizes this. But this is the wrong sort of justification, as it misconstrues what is to be explained. For it is part of our conversational practices that we regard ourselves as entitled to expect others to appreciate the status of the assent interpretation, *merely in virtue of their status as competent users of the language*.[18] This expectation is *not* something we arrive at only *after* we have acquired sufficient evidence from our previous speech exchanges to justify us in expecting others to appreciate the status of the assent

---

[18] Individuals can be wrong in their particular applications of the assent interpretation; indeed, this is precisely what goes on when one is oblivious to the oppressiveness of one's present conditions. But one is wrong here in application of that interpretation, not in endorsement of its general status.

interpretation. Rather, it is an expectation we bring with us to all of our speech exchanges. The expectation here is a normative one, not a predictive one, and its status reflects the normative standards of our practice, not merely the regularities of that practice.

I have been arguing that it will not do, if we hope to explain the systematic way in which the demoralized silence of the oppressed is (wrongly but regularly) taken to imply acceptance, to regard the assent interpretation as a brute regularity of our conversational practices. Doing so fails to explain salient features of our practice, and insofar as these features go into the explanation for the prevalence of the phenomenon, the proposed explanation (in terms of mere regularities of our practice) will fail. Having seen this, it is easy to appreciate how we can explain why the demoralized silence of the oppressed is (wrongly but regularly) taken to imply acceptance. The explanation we seek is one that treats the assent interpretation itself as reflecting a *normative dimension* of our practice. In that case, we can make sense of why belief in the propriety of the assent interpretation is so widespread: it is because such belief correctly captures a real (normative) dimension of our practice. And we can make sense, too, of why reliance on the assent interpretation persists even in the face of oppressive circumstances: it suffices that there be many who are oblivious as to the oppressiveness of the circumstances. For belief in the propriety of the assent interpretation is belief as to one's *permission* to presume (defeasibly) that silence implies acceptance; and if this belief is present in the mind of someone who is oblivious regarding oppression (or its effects), we would predict that such a person will persist in relying on the assent interpretation even in conditions of oppression. In short, what we require is an explanation which postulates the existence of a (default but defeasible) entitlement to presume that silence implies acceptance.

5

I just argued that the hypothesis of a default entitlement to the assent interpretation will be an essential part of the best explanation of the double-harm of silencing. (We can only understand the pervasiveness of these harms if we regard our reliance on the assent interpretation as reflecting normative features of our conversational practices.) I now want to argue that this hypothesis is also part of our best explanation of another one of the harms of silencing. We might characterize this harm as the 'transition to servility'—the process by which those who are silenced become 'servile' (Tanesini 2016: 89–90).

Recall Tanesini's characterization of the process. In the passage I quoted above, she notes that '[o]ver time' those individuals who are silenced 'may stop biting their tongues and simply defer to the opinions of others' (90). Tanesini explains this transition as owed to the need to relieve 'cognitive dissonance'. The thought appears to be this: at first the silenced individual regards herself as knowledgeable, even on those occasions on which she disagrees with those who are more powerful; however this self-conception is in tension with her observation that those who are more powerful or 'authoritative' (read: arrogant) mock her, and disregard her claims, indicating that they regard her opinion as without merit; and the result is a cognitive dissonance between her intially confident self-regard, on the one hand, and the low regard others have for her, on the other. Tanesini's explanatory hypothesis is that the transition from biting one's tongue to deferring to others is made in order to relieve this dissonance.

Now it is worthwhile bearing in mind that there are two ways to relieve the noted dissonance: *either* by downgrading one's self-assessment, *or else* by downgrading one's assessment of others' assessment of one. So a question remains: why does the silenced subject relieve the dissonance by downgrading her own self-assessment? We can discern Tanesini's proposed answer from what she has to say about the 'risk' a hearer would continue to run were she to continue to hold an independent perspective (as opposed to deferring to those with power and authority). Tanesini notes that

> [w]henever illocutionary silencing is deployed to prevent dissent, the silenced individuals will soon learn that *it is less risky to share the views of those who are capable of silencing them.* (Tanesini 2016: 90; italics added)

The risks Tanesini has in mind are those of '[h]aving one's claims ignored or dismissed', and of 'being made out to be so emotional that one's intentions cannot be even discerned' (2016: 89). Thus, Tanesini's account appears to be that the silenced party makes the transition (from biting her tongue to deferring to others) in order to attain a *practical* benefit (the avoidance of being ignored, dismissed, and/or made out to be overly emotional).

Suppose Tanesini is right that those who are silenced sometimes undergo a transition from biting their tongue to deferring to others (what Tanesini calls the condition of 'servility'). Even so, there are reasons to be uneasy with Tanesini's account of this transition to 'servility'. For one thing, the suggested account appears to assume a kind of doxastic voluntarism. In particular, it appears to assume that one can choose to follow belief-fixing policies (such as the policy of deferring to others) on the basis of practical considerations. Insofar as one can't choose to believe at will—insofar as the thesis of doxastic voluntarism is false—it is hard to see how one could follow a policy based on such considerations. For another (related) thing, the suggested account renders the silenced party, uncharitably, as *epistemically irrational* in making the transition from keeping to herself to deferring to others. The suggested account represents the transition as *practically rational*, of course; but insofar as the silenced party's reasons for the transition are exclusively practical considerations, the transition is (like the beliefs formed on the basis of the adopted policy) *epistemically irrational*.

I say that it is uncharitable to construe the silenced party's transition to servility, as Tanesini has, as epistemically irrational. But it may be thought that Tanesini's interpretation captures something important which will be lost in any (allegedly) more 'charitable' interpretation: namely, the power of arrogant interlocutor to induce in his audience the sort of cognitive dissonance that saps them of their ability to assess evidence properly.[19] In response, I want to allow that this can happen; but I want to suggest that it can also happen that there are cases in which the transition is *not* epistemically irrational. If I am correct about this, we are left with the need to seek an explanation of these sorts of case.

This leaves us with a question: is there another account of the transition from keeping to oneself to deferring to others, which (a) doesn't assume any version of doxastic voluntarism and (b) is more charitable to the silenced party? I think that an alternative explanation becomes apparent once we recognize the role that other parties' silence plays in one's own reactions to observed assertions. Once we appreciate this role, we are in a position to see that those who are silenced often *do* have evidence—albeit of a highly misleading kind—that can seem to justify[20] the move to deference. At the very least, we will see that those who are silenced are responding to epistemic reasons when they make the transition to servility. While the conclusion that they reach—that they ought to defer to others (especially the powerful)

---

[19] I thank an anonymous referee for suggesting that I address this matter explicitly.

[20] I say that it 'can seem to justify' this move. Whether it *does* justify this move—or, better, whether it justifies the beliefs formed on the basis of the doxastic policy—will depend on one's views regarding such things as the nature of epistemic justification and the relationship between (and relative weights of) higher-order evidence and first-order evidence. These are very deep waters on which I remain silent here.

when they disagree with them—is false, they are not epistemically irrational in the manner by which they arrive at it.

To see the details of the sort of alternative explanation I am envisaging, return to the individual who has been silenced by systematically arrogant treatment. As we have been imagining her, she is in a community in which the assent interpretation is psychologically and socially salient. In that case, she herself is likely to interpret the silence of others as indicating that *they* assent to the arrogant speaker's assertions. If she does so, she then has further evidence in support of the acceptability of the arrogant speaker's assertions.[21] The evidence in question is *higher-order* evidence: she regards others' silence in the face of these assertions as implying their acceptance of the assertions, and so regards their silence as evidence of the (by others' lights) acceptability of the assertions. Insofar as she interprets others' silence in this way, this (higher-order) evidence might well prompt her to question her own assessment in those cases in which she regards the assertions themselves as dubious.[22] Indeed, as she gets more and more evidence of this kind, she has (what she has reason to believe is) ever greater epistemic grounds for doing so. In this way we can see the road that eventuates in a loss of self-confidence and a deference to others' opinions can start off through the subject's appreciation of the evidence itself—evidence which, unbeknownst to her, is highly misleading (as the other participants might be silent, as she is, out of motives *other than acceptance*).

I submit that this 'higher-order evidence' ('HOE') account of the transition from keeping to oneself to deferring to others is to be preferred to the 'pragmatic' account Tanesini favours.

For one thing, the HOE account (unlike the pragmatic account) preserves the hypothesis that the silenced party remains epistemically rational throughout the transition from keeping to herself to deferring to others. The transition is epistemically rational because it is based on (what the silenced party has reason to regard as) higher-order evidence of the acceptability of the arrogant speaker's assertion. The silenced party's perspective is this: she is aware of the social practice whereby silence in the face of a

---

[21] On the further assumption that there a default entitlement to the assent interpretation, she will regard herself as entitled to this interpretation as well. As above, my opponents will think that we can do without this wrinkle, using only the brute regularity with which people rely on the assent interpretation. But also as above, I think such an 'explanation' won't succeed in explaining what wants explaining.

[22] A point in this vicinity was made by Karen Jones (2012).

publicly observed assertion is taken to imply assent.[23] So she has reason to regard others' silence as implying their acceptance, and so as indicating the acceptability (from their perspective) of the assertion. The more of this evidence (of others' silence) she acquires, the more evidence she has for thinking that deference is the right policy. Consequently, insofar as conditions of oppression often induce silence in others, we reach the conclusion that—at least insofar as she non-culpably fails to realize that others are silent out of motives other than acceptance and assent—it can be epistemically rational for her to make the transition from keeping to herself to deferring to others. (Once she is apprised of the facts, of course, she ought to take the higher-order evidence for what it is: highly misleading as to the acceptability of the arrogant speaker's assertions.)

For another, the HOE account (unlike the pragmatic account) is charitable. Part of its charity consists in the fact that the HOE account can preserve the hypothesis that the silenced individual remains a thoroughgoing epistemic subject—that although she has a diminished sense of her own epistemic competence, she remains an epistemic subject whose beliefs reflect her best assessment of the evidence. By contrast, the pragmatic account construes her as suffering from a complete loss of epistemic agency: on that account's construal, she simply opts to defer in belief-fixation to others out of a desire to avoid being humiliated, ignored, etc. Even if we waive my concerns about doxastic voluntarism, such an account appears to render her in such a way that it is no longer true of her that her beliefs reflect her best assessment of the evidence.

---

[23] It might be wondered: why, if she is aware of the practice of interpreting silence as indicating assent, does *she herself* remain silent in those periods in which she has doubts? More specifically still: why isn't she aware of the likelihood that others will interpret her silence as indicating her assent—in which case, assuming she does not assent, she is allowing them to misinterpret her silence? The brief answer is this. Even though the assent interpretation is psychologically and socially salient, it is also part of the practice that one should reject this interpretation whenever there are better explanations for an audience's silence. (This is the model of defeat I gave in Chapter 6.) What is more, in remaining quiet despite her misgivings, she might be waiting to see whether others speak up, and when they don't, she might decide that it is practically best not to speak up. She might well acknowledge that her policy of silence runs the risk that others will misinterpret her silence, but she might think that it is still best, all things considered, for her to remain silent. This is a *practical* judgement about what it is best to do (speak up or not), not an *epistemic* judgement about what it is proper to believe (accept the assertion or not). Epistemically speaking, at early points in the process, before she has acquired a good deal of this higher-order evidence, she might persist in her own independent views; and during this time she remains epistemically rational insofar as her first-order evidence isn't swamped by her higher-order evidence.

But there is an additional reason to prefer the HOE account to the pragmatic account of the silenced party's transition (from keeping to herself to deferring to others). The HOE explanation makes use of considerations that we will need independently of the present matter, and so the HOE account is more economical than the pragmatic account. I will return to this point in section 6.

In this section I have been arguing that we need to consider the role of silence itself in the sustainment of the oppression of those who have been silenced. Doing so enables us to supplement Tanesini's account of the harms of conversational arrogance. What is more, if we bracket for the moment our account of the transition to servility, we can see that the resulting picture is very much in the spirit of Tanesini's own account. For my point might be put like this. When the arrogant speaker's assertion meets with pervasive silence, there is a risk that *everyone* will regard this silence as indicating that the others accept this assertion.[24] This is a risk just as much for those who aren't victims of being silenced as for those who are. But those who are victims of silencing suffer more when this risk materializes. The reputations of those who are regularly accorded respect remain intact even as those individuals are silent in the face of an arrogant person's assertion. By contrast, those who already suffer from an unjustly ascribed reputation for lacking an independent perspective are likely to be seen, when *they* remain silent, as further confirming this (unjust) reputation. This is, of course, an unfair double standard. But, I submit, this is precisely the double standard that makes the arrogant speaker's assertions far worse for those who are already victims of systematic oppression and subordination than they are for those who aren't victims of such oppression. This sort of harm is in addition to the harms Tanesini associates with the phenomenon of arrogance-induced silencing.

6

Langton's challenge above concerned our *attitude* towards NSR, the entitlement to expect No Silent Rejection: why should we embrace this aspect of our practice, rather than opting instead to change the practice, or at least to criticize it? To address this, it does not suffice to argue that NSR helps us to explain the extent of the phenomenon or to understand the nature of the

---

[24] The result is a case of *pluralistic ignorance*. For a discussion of how this might be rational, see Bjerring et al. (2014).

harms oppression brings in its wake (sections 3–5). For if—as I have been arguing—the nature of that harm reflects the improper use of NSR itself by the oppressors, then we might think that Langton is exactly right to challenge any view of NSR that stops short of critiquing this aspect of our practice. But I disagree. In this section I argue that NSR itself provides the basis for an effective way to *resist* the morally bad outcomes I have been describing in connection with the phenomenon of silencing.[25]

Two points are relevant here.

First, an appeal to NSR itself forms a part, albeit an important part, of an effective argumentative strategy for addressing the phenomenon of silencing itself. To be sure, the most important case against silencing is that it is unjust and harmful to its victims, period. Nothing that I say here should cast any doubt on that. Still, all else equal, it would be good to have additional arguments with which to address those who (whether knowingly or not) participate in the oppression, and it would be good as well if at least some of those arguments made appeal to what is in the self-interest of *everyone in the community*. Here is where the entitlement might earn part of its keep. For if my analysis above is correct—the entitlement to expect no silent rejection remains in place, albeit as systematically defeated, in contexts of silencing—then in effect contexts of silencing *deprive all conversational participants of a very important conversational and epistemic good*: namely, the good of interacting with others of equal standing *any of whom can signal their acceptance by remaining silent*.[26] Thus by eliminating the phenomenon of silencing we render communication much more reliable and efficient, thereby enhancing our efforts at planning and coordination—something that is a good for everyone.[27] In short, an appeal to NSR makes clear that, in addition to being the morally required thing to do, addressing the phenomenon of silencing also has practical advantages for our entire community: it enables us to *recover the epistemic significance of conversational silence itself.*[28]

---

[25] With thanks to Carry Osborne for urging that I put the point in this fashion.
[26] This is a point on which I agree with Pettit 1994. See also Chapter 11, where I discuss this point at greater length.
[27] Compare Grice (1968/1989: 28), who says, of the norms of conversation, that their purpose is the promotion of 'a maximally effective exchange of information'.
[28] It is important to appreciate that the point here is not merely an epistemic one. All of us, as people who engage in linguistic communication, have an interest in not undermining the linguistic, communicative system, and so we all have reason to preserve the ability to communicate what we mean straightforwardly and efficiently. In effect, what I am suggesting is that we diminish the efficiency of our communicative system if we criticize NSR itself. This point is in the spirit of Pettit's comments about the role of silence under free speech regimes; but as I argued in Chapter 8, he goes too far in ascribing to silence itself a Gricean meaning. (I thank an anonymous referee for highlighting the need to make this point.)

But there is a second reason for thinking that an appeal to NSR itself will be part of an effective way to resist the morally problematic features noted above. In Chapter 8 I gave evidence for thinking that the assent interpretation is both psychologically and socially salient, and I speculated that a deep part of our psychology accounts for this. If this is so, there will be no getting around having to deal with the tendency of humans to rely on this interpretation. From this vantage point, the key question for those of us who aim to resist the harms just described is how best to manage this aspect of our social lives as speakers, so as to ensure fairness and respect for all. But NSR itself has the resources to do just this: the point is to make clear that when conditions are oppressive, what many of us take to be conversations are no such things—so *even by the lights of our own practices*, there is no entitlement to expect that those who are silent have not rejected the publicly observed assertion. In short, it is not the practice itself, but improper participation in the practice that is the problem; and NSR, properly understood, is part of the solution.

10
The Social Epistemology of Public Uptake

1

In Chapters 8 and 9 I have focused on the *non-epistemic* normative dimension of the uptake of uptake. That there is a non-epistemic normative dimension to conversation itself should not be surprising to anyone who has read Grice. As I noted in Chapter 8, his Cooperative Principle, which enjoins us to 'make [our] conversational contribution[s] such as is required, at the stage at which it occurs, by the accepted purpose of direction of the talk exchange in which [we] are engaged' (1968/1989: 26), is explicitly normative in orientation. Grice remarks that

> I would like to be able to think of the standard type of conversational practice not merely as something that all or most do *in fact* follow but as something that it is *reasonable* for us to follow, that we *should not* abandon.... [A]nyone who cares about the goals that are central to conversation/communication (such as giving and receiving information, influencing and being influence by others) must be expected to have an interest, given suitable circumstances, in participation in talk exchanges that will be profitable only on the assumption that they are conducted in general accordance with the Cooperative Principle and the maxims.
> (Grice 1968/1989: 29–30)

The non-epistemic dimension of conversational normativity, then, arises at least in part from the expectation of cooperation—an expectation Grice thinks we are entitled to have given our manifest and abiding common interest in 'giving and receiving information, influencing and being influenced by others' and hence in 'talk exchanges that will be profitable only on the assumption that they are conducted in general accordance with the Cooperative Principle and the maxims'. My argument in Chapter 8 was that this non-epistemic normativity is seen in the uptake of another participant's uptake of a public assertion. My claim was that silent rejection of a public assertion is uncooperative, and so we are (defeasibly) entitled to expect that others not behave in this way.

However, throughout this book I have been insisting upon the distinction between being entitled to have a normative expectation of conversational participants' behaviour—call this an 'N-expectation' (with the 'N' designating that the expectation is a normative one)—and being epistemically justified in believing that the expected behaviour is (or will be) present. Thus, in Chapter 4, I argued that one who tells an audience something entitles her audience to N-expect that she was relevantly responsible in the telling; but we should not confuse this with the claim that she gives her audience an epistemic reason to believe that she is relevantly responsible. So, too, in our present context: we should not confuse our entitlement to N-expect no silent rejection, for our being epistemically justified in believing that the silent audience has not rejected the assertion. Nor should it be particularly surprising that there can be cases in which the two come apart—that is, cases in which (i) one is entitled to N-expect that one's silent audience has not rejected the assertion, and yet at the same time (ii) one is *not* epistemically justified in believing that one's silent audience has behaved as one was entitled to N-expect. This should not be surprising: people don't always behave as they ought to behave, and there are cases in which we have adequate evidence that this is so. So even if normative expectations and justified belief often go hand in hand—even if we often have independent reasons to think that people behave as normatively expected—the two should not be conflated. For this reason, Chapters 8 and 9 constitute only a partial investigation of the conversational pressure involved in the uptake of uptake: we need to move from the former (interpersonal but non-epistemic) normativity to the normativity of epistemology itself.

This is what I propose to do in this chapter, where I focus on *the social epistemology of public uptake*.

I see this topic as an important subfield within social epistemology itself. Here the focus is on others, not as informants, but as *consumers* of testimony, where their public uptake of a mutually observed assertion is regarded as yet further evidence bearing on the acceptability of the assertion itself. Juanita sees the sceptical look on your face as you hear Jones tell you that he got an A in the course; this gives Juanita some reason to be doubtful herself. The point is that we often rely on others' acceptance or rejection as *higher-order* evidence of the acceptability (or not) of a mutually observed assertion: we treat others' acceptance of a particular testimony as an indication of their having taken the testimony to be true, and insofar as we regard them as reliable in their determination, we regard their taking the testimony to be true as evidence that the testimony *is* true. (*Mutatis mutandis* for rejection.) Elsewhere I have described this phenomenon as involving the *social diffusion of the task of assessing testimony for reliability*.[1] To be sure, this use of others' public uptake is fallible along two different dimensions: we can be mistaken about whether they have accepted the assertion (the topic of Chapter 8), and we can be mistaken about whether they are in fact discerning in their consumption of testimony. But when all goes well, others' public uptake of an assertion provides evidence of a distinctly social sort, and this evidence aids us in our attempts at testimonial knowledge.

None of this is particularly newsworthy. What is newsworthy, and in any case what I will focus on here, are two implications of this picture. First, this familiar picture of the social epistemology of public uptake yields a provocative claim asserting the possibility of something that looks like legitimate epistemic bootstrapping—cases where a speaker warrantedly asserts that p, and yet is epistemically justified in *increasing her confidence* in the truth of p after she observes others accept her assertion. Second, many of the materials that underwrite such a possibility appear to be in play in cases of groupthink and belief polarization. The aim of this chapter then is to highlight how the epistemic dimension of the conversational pressure involved in the uptake of uptake gives us mixed news.

2

Before proceeding to these implications, it will be helpful to start with a model of the social epistemology of public uptake. For my purposes it will be easiest to do so in terms of a very simple evidentialist model. I will say that one person, O, is epistemically justified in believing that another person, A, has accepted speaker S's assertion that p when O's total evidence supports

---

[1] See Goldberg (2010, 2011a).

that A has accepted S's assertion. O's belief to this effect is doxastically justified, then, when O forms and sustains this belief on the basis of that evidence.

Simple as it is, this model permits us to address the relation between *having an entitlement to N-expect* that one's audience is not silent in rejection and *being justified in believing* that one's audience is not silent in rejection. How might having the entitlement to N-expect no silent rejection be used to arrive at a justified belief to the effect that an observed audience member A was not silent in rejection of speaker S's assertion?

The first is by way of generic evidence that people behave as they are N-expected to behave. (The evidence might be restricted to certain types of circumstance, as when one has evidence that people *in this or that type of circumstance* typically behave as N-expected.) If O has evidence like this, she is in a position to infer that (it is likely that) A will behave as he is N-expected to behave. Then, assuming that O is aware that she is entitled to N-expect no silent rejection, O is in a position to infer that A will not be silent in rejection. So long, then, as O's evidence that people generally behave as they are normatively expected to behave is sufficient to justify the inference—that is, so long as it is sufficiently weighty and is not defeated by other evidence O has—O is epistemically justified in believing that (it is likely that) S is not silent in rejection.

The second is by way of evidence regarding A in particular. Suppose O knows A well, and knows too that A always speaks up when he has doubts. Alternatively, suppose that O knows that A always does what is N-expected of him (where O is also aware that she, O, is entitled to N-expect no silent rejection). Either way, O is in a position to form the justified belief that A is not silent in rejection. Again, this depends on the adequacy of O's evidence, and its not being defeated by other evidence O has.

We can generalize this account along two different dimensions: the content of O's belief, and the evidence to which we hold O's belief answerable.

We can generalize the account along the content of O's belief by moving from the belief that A is not silent in rejection, to the belief that A has accepted the assertion that p, to the belief that A herself believes that p. The first transition—from the belief that A is not silent in her rejection, to the belief that A has accepted the assertion that p—is warranted on the basis of our construal (following Stalnaker) of non-rejection as acceptance. The second transition—from the belief that A has accepted the assertion that p, to the belief that A herself believes that p—can be warranted on the basis of adequate evidence for thinking that the aim of the conversation is, or includes, the serious exchange of reliable information. (See Chapter 8 for further discussion of these transitions.)

More controversially, we can generalize the account by expanding the evidence to which we hold O's belief answerable—in particular, by endorsing a certain social conception of normative defeat. (Though controversial, this is a conception I have defended at length in Goldberg (2018).) Suppose we think that it can be (morally, socially, professionally, institutionally, or politically) proper to N-expect another to have certain evidence, such that if he doesn't have this evidence then it would be proper to say that he *should have had it*. Evidence one should have had is then a potential (normative) defeater of one's belief.[2] If this is right, then we might revise our model of the social epistemology of public uptake to take into account the possibility of normative defeat. On the revised view, O is epistemically justified in believing that A has accepted speaker S's assertion that p when O's total evidence supports that A has accepted S's assertion and there are no normative defeaters among the evidence O should have had. O's belief to this effect is doxastically justified, then, when O forms and sustains this belief on the basis of some epistemically adequate subset of that evidence. This picture is admittedly controversial. But it might be thought to earn its keep in connection with cases in which people are oblivious to conditions of oppression or of salient power dynamics. For we might want to say that if O is such a person, and if conditions are oppressive or relevant power dynamics are salient, then whether or not O is aware of this, the evidence of oppression and of the play of power dynamics is evidence O should have. If that evidence strongly supports the hypothesis that A has various (morally permissible) motives in remaining silent *whether or not* she accepts, then, whatever evidence O has for thinking that A is not silent in rejection, the epistemic justification of O's belief to that effect is defeated by the evidence O should have had.

Still, whether or not one chooses to generalize the simple account in this latter (more controversial) way, we can use the account as we aim to characterize the epistemic dimension of the uptake of uptake. I will do so in what follows, as I aim to argue that the social epistemology of public uptake has two surprising implications.

---

[2] To see the sorts of questions that arise for such a framework, and how defeat might work, see Goldberg (2016, 2017, 2018).

3

The first of the surprising implications concerns the possibility of something in the neighbourhood of *legitimate epistemic bootstrapping*. I will formulate the claim in question as a claim asserting 'epistemic self-improvement through assertion' (or 'Self-Improvement' for short):

Self-Improvement
There are conditions under which (i) S warrantedly asserts that p and (ii) S observes that her assertion is accepted by another (or others), where the result of (ii) is an enhancement in the strength of S's own epistemic position with respect to p (as compared to S's strength of epistemic position regarding p prior to (ii)).

To some, the doctrine of Self-Improvement will seem obviously false. In particular, the falsity of Self-Improvement would appear to be supported by a variety of related considerations. All of these considerations are variations on the ideas of *non-independence* and *double-counting*. When an audience accepts a speaker's assertion that p, the audience is relying on the speaker to have been relevantly (epistemically) authoritative. As a result, the audience's epistemic perspective regarding whether p is *not independent of* the speaker's epistemic perspective regarding whether p. And for this reason the move to regard the speaker's epistemic perspective as improving, in virtue of her observing the audience accept her (the speaker's) own assertion, involves an illicit sort of *epistemic double-counting*.

As I say, there are various versions of this idea, corresponding to various different ways one might argue against the doctrine of Self-Improvement. Here I offer four. (1) Observing another person accept one's own assertion that p does not provide one with any new relevant evidence bearing on the question whether p. On the further assumption that the strength of one's epistemic condition supervenes on one's relevant evidence, we can conclude that Self-Improvement is false. Relatedly, (2) when one apprehends that another person accepts one's own assertion that p, one's epistemic perspective is not affected any more than it would be in the case where the audience simply *reasserts that p back to one*. On the further assumption that one gets no epistemic improvement from such a minimal epistemic circle, we can conclude that Self-Improvement is false.[3] (3) If there is an additional

---

[3] I owe this version of the argument to Stephen Wright.

epistemic benefit to one when one apprehends that another person has accepted one's own assertion that p, then there should be an additional epistemic benefit to one if one were to accept one's own assertion that p. On the assumption that there is no such epistemic benefit in the latter case, there is no epistemic benefit in the former case—so Self-Improvement is false. Finally, (4) there is something objectionably (viciously) circular about a speaker treating another's acceptance of her own assertion that p as evidence confirming the speaker's own reliability on the question of whether p. After all, the is *relying on* that reliability in her acceptance, and so can hardly be used to *confirm* that reliability. Once again, Self-Improvement begins to look like a non-starter.

The sorts of consideration I have been canvassing, as reasons one might have for rejecting Self-Improvement, have analogues in the debate over the epistemic significance of disagreement. One issue that has arisen in this debate concerns the epistemic significance of greater numbers of people with a particular view: how does an increase in the number of people on the opposing side affect the rationality of one's own view? A first thought is this: the greater the number on the opposing side, the more one ought to reduce confidence in one's own (contrary) view. But many epistemologists have resisted a bald principle of this sort. They have argued that numbers matter only insofar as the beliefs of the individuals in opposition are *epistemically independent* of one another. Thus Adam Elga writes that 'an additional outside opinion should move one *only to the extent that one counts it as independent from opinions one has already taken into account*' (2010: 177; italics added). Tom Kelly writes that

> even in cases in which opinion is sharply divided among a large number of generally reliable individuals, it would be a mistake to be impressed by the sheer number of such individuals on both sides of the issue. For *numbers mean little in the absence of independence.* (Kelly 2010: 148; italics added)

And Alvin Goldman writes, 'If two or more opinion-holders are totally nonindependent of one another, and if the subject knows or is justified in believing this, then *the subject's opinion should not be swayed—even a little— by more than one of these opinion-holders*' (Goldman 2001: 99; italics added).[4]

---

[4] See also McGrath (2008) for a similar view. For a discussion of and argument against views in this vicinity, see Lackey (2013).

It is not entirely clear that these authors would reject Self-Improvement. For while they are appealing to a principle of *independence*, they are talking about the epistemic effects, not of assertion and testimony, but of disagreement. Still, it would seem that what these authors have to say about independence in the context of disagreement is in the spirit of those who would reject Self-Improvement. We can make the connection explicit if we assume that accepting another's testimony is a paradigm case of the sort of *non-independence* of which Elga, Kelly, and Goldman are speaking. Anyone who accepts such an assumption would endorse the idea that, when it comes to assessing the evidence bearing on the hypothesis that p, fact f_2 ought to be ascribed no additional evidentiary weight over and above the epistemic weight ascribed to fact f_1:

f_1 S believes that p
f_2 A believes that p (through having accepted S's testimony that p)

In that case, *S herself* ought not to ascribe any evidentiary weight to f_2, and since the argument for this is general, it would appear to preclude the very possibility described in Self-Improvement. Of course this leaves open the possibility that Elga, Kelly, and Goldman reject the initial assumption (that testimonial belief-formation is a paradigm instance of non-independence), rather than accept this conclusion. My point is merely that if they don't reject the initial assumption, they appear committed to the denial of Self-Improvement.[5]

In short, for a variety of reasons it can seem that *the very possibility* of the sort of legitimate epistemic bootstrapping alleged in Self-Improvement is dubious.

And yet I think that such cases are not only possible, but actual. In what follows I will present several cases that illustrate the possibility of Self-Improvement (section 4), extract and defend the core assumptions that I am making in regarding these cases as instances of Self-Improvement (section 5), revisit and criticize the reasons offered in this section *against* Self-Improvement (section 6), and then go on to suggest that the very mechanisms responsible for Self-Improvement might *also* be responsible

---

[5] As we will see in section 4, there is a way of interpreting 'independent' so that there are cases in which S and H are in fact partially independent of one another; but this only suggests that the notion of 'independent' that Elga, Kelly, and Goldman are working with is likely to be hard to apply in practice, and so likely to be of less significance than they suspect. See Lackey (2013) for additional reasons in support of the view for which I will be arguing.

for such unhappy social effects as groupthink and belief polarization (section 7). If successful, this case for Self-Improvement highlights a distinctly epistemic dimension of conversational pressure that arises in connection with the uptake of uptake. In particular, one's public reaction to another's assertion constitutes a distinctive source of normative pressure on those who observe one's reaction, where the pressure in question derives from the evidentiary role that can be assigned[6] to one's acceptance of the assertion in question.

4

These appearances to the contrary notwithstanding, I believe that the phenomenon described in Self-Improvement is not only possible but actual. The best way to establish this is to describe plausible cases that instantiate the phenomenon. In this section I do just this. Here I offer four:

SCIENCE TEAM
Research Team X specializes in a certain subfield of physical chemistry. The members of X have assembled excellent evidence for their hypothesis H, where (they recognize that) this evidence would be sufficient to convince even the most demanding physical chemist of the acceptability of H. Consequently, they go to a prestigious national physical chemistry conference and announce their findings, concluding that H is acceptable on these grounds. Now the members of X acknowledge that in such a large audience there will be other people who have different background knowledge, different evidence, and different expertise. Given (their knowledge of) the prestige of the conference and the excellence of the audience, as well as the norms of conference behaviour, they reasonably think to themselves that if there had been a flaw in their experimentation or an alternative explanation for their data someone in the audience would most likely have known of this and would have spoken up. So, seeing no one raise any such objection, and observing the audience's favourable reaction to their announced findings, they increase their confidence in the thought that *there are no relevant pieces of counter-evidence, alternative explanations for their data, or flaws in their experimental set-up.* Accordingly, since

---

[6] Here, 'can be assigned' should be read as 'it would be epistemically proper to assign' (under conditions to be made clear in what follows).

hypothesis H is supported by their experiment, they become a bit more confident in H itself.

DETECTIVE WORK
There has been a murder, and Sherlock Holmes and Watson are put on the case. Sherlock has excellent evidence for thinking that it was one of A, B, C, D, or E. After a long and exhaustive inquiry, Sherlock conclusively rules out all of the suspects in his group except D, and so concludes that D was the murderer. But Sherlock is self-aware enough to know that he is fallible, and that on very rare occasions he overlooks or puts improper weight on some piece of evidence or else fails to identify a possible suspect. He also knows that Watson can be of help on those rare occasions: his trusty sidekick can be relied upon to raise questions on 'elementary' matters, so that on those rare occasions when Sherlock *does* miss something, Watson's questions serve to prompt Sherlock to recognize the lacuna. Happily, this is no such occasion, and so when Sherlock observes that Watson enthusiastically endorses his (Sherlock's) conclusion that D was the murderer, he (Sherlock) ever so slightly increases his confidence that there was no such lacuna on this occasion.

PEER COLLEAGUES
Sally and Hermione are colleagues who are epistemic peers with respect to a given domain of inquiry. (They rightly regard each other as such that on matters in this domain they are roughly equally likely to be right: they have roughly the same competences, possess roughly the same evidence, etc.) Neither of them has yet to consider whether p (where [p] is some proposition in the domain in question). Sally sets herself to do so, alone. After a good deal of careful reviewing of the evidence in their mutual possession, Sally comes to conclude that p, and announces this to Hermione. On observing that Hermione endorses her conclusion, Sally's confidence is enhanced, if ever so slightly, that she did not make any untoward mistakes in reviewing and assessing the evidence in their mutual possession.

LOGIC TEACHER
Simone is a professor of logic who is teaching an advanced logic class at her university. The class is a large one, and while many of the students are indifferent, several of them are very good—so good, in fact, that they occasionally catch flaws in the more accessible parts of the 'proofs' she puts up on the board. When one of the good students asks whether some

complicated proposition, p, is a theorem, she addresses it by trying to construct a proof on the spot. The proof is long and complicated, taking her half of class time to construct it, but she ultimately presents the whole thing, and so says to the class, 'So you see, p is a theorem.' When she notes to herself that none of the very good students raises any objections, her confidence is enhanced, if ever so slightly, that there are no flaws in the more accessible parts of the proof.

I submit that in each case we have an illustration of Self-Improvement: there is an epistemic improvement in the speaker's epistemic condition with respect to some proposition she properly (warrantedly) asserts, consequent upon her observing that her audience accepts the assertion. If my characterization of these cases is correct, there are at least two ways in which audience endorsement of a speaker's assertion can improve the speaker's epistemic position. In PEER COLLEAGUES, LOGIC TEACHER, and DETECTIVE WORK, the audience's endorsement serves as some evidence that *the speaker made no relevant error (of reasoning, evidence assessment, memory, etc.) in reaching the verdict in question*. In SCIENCE TEAM and DETECTIVE WORK, the audience's endorsement serves as some evidence that *there is no relevant counter-evidence against the asserted proposition, and no relevant alternative hypothesis that might have accounted for the data equally well or better*. Insofar as (the speaker has reasons to think that) audience acceptance serves as evidence of one or both of these things, a speaker who observes an audience accept her warranted assertion thereby enjoys an enhancement of her epistemic position on the matter. It would seem, then, that Self-Improvement is true.

5

In this section I want to extract and defend some of the core assumptions I am making in representing the four cases above as instances of Self-Improvement. As these assumptions reflect the epistemic dimension of conversational pressure arising in connection with the uptake of uptake, articulating these assumptions enables us to illuminate the source and nature of that pressure.

My first assumption is that an audience's acceptance of S's assertion is itself evidence for S—that it is a kind of higher-order evidence. By itself, this assumption would appear to be innocuous. But I am assuming further that

THE SOCIAL EPISTEMOLOGY OF PUBLIC UPTAKE 217

this (higher-order) evidence is evidence *of* certain things, and this assumption might not seem as innocuous. In particular, I am assuming that there are cases in which an audience's acceptance of S's assertion that p constitutes (higher-order) evidence, for S, of one or both of the following: S herself has not made any relevant error in reaching her determination regarding whether p; and/or there is no relevant counter-evidence bearing against p, and/or no relevant alternatives that ought to have been considered. I am *not* saying how strong this evidence is—in particular, I leave it open whether it is sufficiently strong to *justify belief* in one or both of these hypotheses, or merely strong enough *to warrant a slight increase in S's credence* in these hypotheses. This will depend on the details of each case, I think. The general point I am assuming is only that it is *some* evidence for these conclusions.

Since this construal of the higher-order evidence may not seem entirely innocuous to everyone, I want to do more by way of defence than merely note that I find such a construal plausible. I think that it is easy to see how the details of the cases above support construing the higher-order evidence in this fashion. In each of the cases described, the speaker had reasons to regard the audience as knowledgeable in a certain way, with the result that it was reasonable for the speaker to think that the audience would probably have known if, for example, there had been any relevant counter-evidence, or the speaker failed to consider an alternative hypothesis, or the speaker had made some other error in reasoning. Thus in SCIENCE TEAM the members of the team knew that their audience consisted largely of world-class scientists, including experts in physical chemistry and related fields; in DETECTIVE WORK Sherlock knew that despite his run-of-the-mill intellect, Watson was careful in collecting the evidence and in reasoning from it, and that on rare occasions Watson had brought to Sherlock's attention people Sherlock himself had improperly neglected to consider as a suspect; in PEER COLLEAGUES the very fact that the speaker knows that her interlocutor is an epistemic peer gives the speaker reason to think that her audience is well positioned to have appreciated any improper inferences from the evidence they mutually possess, or any errors of recollection; and in LOGIC TEACHER the teacher has evidence that there are a few excellent students in the class who, on occasion, have pointed out small errors in the more accessible parts of the (would-be) proofs she did in class. What is more, in each of these cases the speaker also had reasons to regard the audience as such that if anyone in the audience *had* had an objection of any of these kinds, he or she would have spoken up. (We can simply read this into each case.) Now, while the degree of support provided by one's evidence for the hypothesis that one will be corrected (when wrong) is greater in some of these cases than in others, in each of these cases the evidence supports such an hypothesis to some degree. Under such conditions, a speaker who observes an audience accept her assertion acquires evidence that there were no relevant objections, since if there had been any someone among her audience would have said so.[7] In short, there are cases in which my proposed construal of the higher-order evidence is warranted, and so my assumption that there can be cases of this sort is established.[8]

A second set of assumptions I am making pertains to the epistemic significance of this higher-order evidence. In particular, I am assuming both of the following things:

EN1 A subject who forms the belief that p on the basis of evidence E enhances her epistemic position further when she acquires additional evidence that she made no relevant errors in arriving at this belief

and

EN 2A subject who forms the belief that p on the basis of evidence E enhances her epistemic position further when she acquires additional evidence that there is no relevant counter-evidence and/or no additional relevant alternative(s) she ought to have considered.

I believe that both of these claims are imminently plausible. But we can employ a variety of different epistemic tests to confirm that what EN1 and EN2 allege to be epistemic enhancements are in fact epistemic enhancements. For example, the additional evidence mentioned in EN1 and EN2 enables the subject to rule out alternatives that she might not have been able to rule out previously. Thus the additional evidence mentioned in EN1 enables her to rule out hypotheses pertaining to errors in e.g. memory or reasoning, whereas the additional evidence mentioned in EN2 enables her to rule out the hypothesis that, for instance, someone among her

---

[7] Compare the sort of reasoning Goldberg (2010, 2011c) calls 'coverage-based' reasoning, where a subject S infers that not-p, on the grounds that if p were true she would have heard about it by now.

[8] A quick parenthetical remark is in order. I am not claiming, nor do I assume, that audience acceptance is *always* higher-order evidence of one of these two things. On the contrary, in section 7 I will argue that insofar as conversational participants themselves make such a strong assumption, this is likely to have grave consequences for our epistemic communities. My point here is only that *there are some cases* in which audience acceptance constitutes higher-order evidence of this sort; and clearly this is compatible with the claim that audience acceptance *does not always* constitute such evidence.

knowledgeable peers has relevant counterevidence, or that, for example, there is an additional relevant alternative she should have ruled out (but did not). Thus it would seem that the higher-order evidence, enabling her to rule out additional alternatives, enhances her epistemic position. So, too, we might think to establish the enhancement by appeal to the greater reliability (or sensitivity; or safety) of the beliefs formed with the additional evidence. In short, the assumptions of EN1 and EN2 seem sound.

Another assumption that I am making is that a speaker S can make a warranted assertion and yet still be such that there is room for further improvement in her epistemic perspective on the matter. Although this assumption appears to go hand in hand with EN1 and EN2, it is worth singling this additional assumption out—if only because one particular view of warranted assertion might seem to jeopardize it. The view in question, which I will call *Williamson's view* (since it is endorsed by Williamson 2000), combines the claim that warranted assertion requires knowledge, with the claim that knowledge requires probability 1 on one's evidence. In short, Williamson's view is that warranted assertion requires probability 1 on one's evidence. If that is so, then no new evidence could increase that probability, from which it follows trivially that no new *higher-order* evidence could increase that probability. This can make it seem that my assumption, that S can make a warranted assertion and yet still be such that there is room for further improvement in her epistemic perspective on the matter, is false.

But to this three responses can be made.

First: contrary to appearances, Williamson's view is compatible with my assumption. Williamson's view entails that if S is warranted in asserting that p, then the proposition that p has probability 1 on S's evidence, and so there is no room for further enhancement of the epistemic probability of p on S's evidence. But leaves open the possibility that S's epistemic perspective on the matter might improve, not on the question whether p, but on the question whether *S knows that p*. For as Williamson himself notes in various places, the probability on one's evidence *that p* can be distinguished from the probability on one's evidence *that one oneself knows that p*.[9] Indeed, Williamson himself even acknowledges that there can be cases of 'improbable knowing', in which the probability on one's evidence that p is 1, but the probability on one's evidence that one oneself knows that p is closer to 0 than to 1. The general point is that the probability on one's evidence

---

[9] See e.g. Williamson (2011, 2014).

associated with one's knowing that p can be lower, and in normal cases will be lower, than the probability on one's evidence associated with the hypothesis that p itself—in which case one's epistemic perspective can improve even when one knows that p, for example, by an enhancement in the probability on one's evidence that one knows that p.[10] In sum, Williamson's view is compatible with the assumption that S can make a warranted assertion and yet still be such that there is still room for further improvement in S's epistemic perspective on the matter.

My second response to the threat posed by Williamson's view is that it is possible to recast the assumption in question so as to bypass this potential objection altogether. To bring this out, I want to make clear how I could modify the formulation of Self-Improvement itself, and with it the assumption under consideration, so as to make the point I wish to make without inviting any Williamson-inspired worries. The point I wish to make in this chapter is this: one can be in an excellent epistemic position on some proposition that p, assert it on that basis to others, and yet come to acquire an enhancement in one's epistemic position on the matter by observing that others accept one's assertion. This could happen even if, for instance, one's evidence was (excellent but) just short of that warranting knowledge. To be sure, in that case a Williamsonian will regard the assertion as unwarranted (for failing to be knowledgeable); but insofar as one's evidence was just short of what is needed for knowledge, it might still be reasonable for one to *think* that one knew, and so reasonable for one to assert as one did. With this in mind, I could modify Self-Improvement to speak of *reasonable* assertions rather than *warranted* ones. And I could modify the present assumption accordingly, so that it amounted to the following: a speaker S can make a *reasonable* assertion and yet still be such that there is room for further improvement in her epistemic perspective on the matter. Nothing in the spirit of Self-Improvement would be lost in this weakening.

A third and final response is less concessive than the first two. Although Williamson's view (combining the knowledge norm of assertion and the doctrine that knowledge requires probability 1 on one's evidence) does have its proponents—one thinks here of Williamson and his followers—even so it amounts to a radical position, one which most people do or would reject. If

---

[10] I stipulate that by 'epistemic improvement on the question whether p' I mean to include (as a positive case) an improvement regarding *one's own epistemic standing* on whether p. (Of course another positive case is the case in which new evidence increases the probability for one that p.)

the cost of resisting my present assumption is a commitment to Williamson's view, many will regard that as too high a cost: better we should accept the assumption and reject Williamson's view.

In addition to the foregoing assumptions, another assumption I am making, when I regard the cases above as positive instances of Self-Improvement, is this: a subject S can be warranted in asserting that p even under conditions in which S recognizes that that there are people in her audience who are in a position to correct her if she is wrong (alternatively: who are in a position to criticize the basis on which she arrived at her determination, if that basis does not properly support her belief that p; who are in a position to cite counter-evidence, if such exists; who are in a position to raise another relevant alternative, if she neglected to rule one out). Once again, I think this assumption is imminently plausible: it appears to reflect the possibility of warranted assertion under conditions in which one recognizes both *one's own fallibility* on the matter at hand and *the possible corrective role* others might play. Of course, it is one thing to assert something when one has reasons to think that if there *were* relevant defeating considerations one's audience would possess them (and would correct one); it is quite another to assert something when one has reasons to think that there *are* relevant defeating considerations (in the expectation that one's audience will correct one). The latter case is plausibly a case of an unwarranted (and even unreasonable) assertion.[11] The former case, however, is not: insofar as one has adequate grounds for what one asserts, one has grounds for thinking that there are no relevant defeaters, and under such conditions one is warranted in making the assertion even as one might think that if there *were* such defeaters one's audience would bring them up. As I say, this seems nothing more than a recognition of one's own fallibility combined with an acknowledgement that others are often in a position to correct one's errors.

Might one criticize the present assumption—that S can be warranted in asserting that p even when S recognizes that her audience would correct her if she were wrong—by arguing that it invites Moorean paradoxicality? To

---

[11] There can be a point to such assertions. Suppose that the police speculate that the murder weapon was a candlestick and want to confirm this. Then, having taken the suspect into custody, they might assert 'The weapon was a candlestick; we know this' in the hope of discerning in his reaction some confirmation of this. Cases like this are familiar; they are like the sorts of case I am describing, only here it is not surprising in the least that one can learn that p, or at least enhance the strength of one's epistemic position on p, by observing others' reactions to one's assertion that p. What is interesting is that this can happen even when one is warranted in asserting that p.

address this, let us recognize there is something absurd about acknowledging one's fallibility regarding whether p in the very act of asserting that that one *knows* that p: 'I know that p, though I might be wrong' seems bizarre (Lewis 1996). And let us recognize as well that it also seems strange to assert 'p, though I might be wrong about this.' But here the strangeness of such an assertion can be accounted for without calling my present assumption into question. For what is strange in an assertion of 'p, but I might be wrong about this' is this: the very act of asserting one's fallibility regarding whether p will inevitably raise doubts in the minds of the audience about one's authoritativeness regarding whether p, thereby undermining the point of an assertion that p (which is to present the proposition as true in a way that is backed by one's authority).[12] This analysis is perfectly compatible with the claim that one can be warranted in asserting that p even as one acknowledges (if only in one's own mind) one's own fallibility on the matter. After all, it is not as if the conditions on warranted assertion require one to be, or to regard oneself as, *infallible*.

With these assumptions in place, I have my argument for construing each of the cases above, or some suitably developed version of them, as positive instances of Self-Improvement. What is more, these assumptions articulate precisely why another's reaction to a publicly observed assertion can exert (epistemic) normative pressure on those who observe that reaction: that reaction constitutes evidence such that, under certain (widely obtaining) conditions, the evidence in question is *higher-order evidence for the acceptability of the assertion itself.*

6

If the foregoing argument is sound, there is something wrong with the four mini-arguments from section 4, which appeared to underwrite scepticism regarding the doctrine of Self-Improvement—and there must be something wrong as well with the line of reasoning, inspired by some comments in the epistemology of disagreement literature, which assumed that testimonial belief is invariably non-independent belief. In this section I try to identify where these arguments go wrong.

---

[12] See Brown (2010) as well as the analysis of assertion in Goldberg (2015a).

Starting with the four mini-arguments from section 4, I think it is possible to diagnose their flaw in one go: they all assume, illicitly, that an audience who accepts a speaker's testimony is akin to a human parrot, someone whose acceptance does not itself reflect any critical sensibility of her own at work. For insofar as we recognize that the audience *does* bring such a sensibility to the acceptance of testimony, we regard her as being in a position to reject the testimony if (employing that sensibility) she regards it as false or otherwise unwarranted. In that case, her acceptance indicates that, having employed such a sensibility, she finds nothing to warrant rejection. And in those cases in which she finds nothing to warrant rejection, but where she was relevantly positioned to have done so had the occasion required, her acceptance of the testimony does make some positive contribution to the speaker's epistemic position on the asserted proposition.

With all of this as background, we can now diagnose what is wrong in each of the four mini-arguments from section 1 above. I take them up in order.

(1) Observing another person accept one's own assertion that p *does* provide one with new relevant evidence—it is a form of higher-order evidence. Sometimes that higher-order evidence bears on the question whether p itself—as when the audience's acceptance constitutes evidence that she has not found any relevant evidence bearing against p. At other times the higher-order evidence bears on the speaker's own assessment of the evidence bearing on p—as when the audience's acceptance constitutes evidence that the speaker did not make any easily detectable errors in assessing her, the speaker's, evidence.

(2) Let it be granted that when one apprehends that another person accepts one's own assertion that p, one's epistemic perspective is not affected any more than it would be in the case where the audience simply reasserts that p back to one. Still, depending on what one knows or reasonably believes of one's audience, such a reaffirmation might enable one to rule out certain kinds of error on one's own part—the sorts of error that one's audience would have been in a position to detect, had one made an error of that sort.

(3) It is not true that if there is an additional epistemic benefit to one when one apprehends that another person has accepted one's own assertion that p, then there should be an additional epistemic benefit to one if one were to accept one's own assertion that p. For the relevant difference is that *another person constitutes a distinct*

epistemic perspective, using which the other person might have corrected mistakes or errors (if one had made them), or brought in evidence one hadn't considered (if there had been any).

(4) It is not objectionably (viciously) circular for a speaker to treat an audience's acceptance of her own assertion that p as evidence providing some confirmation of the speaker's own reliability on the question of whether p. After all, even if the audience is relying on that reliability in her acceptance, even so, she brought her critical faculties to bear, such that if she had detected any unreliability, she would have objected (or would have refrained from accepting the assertion). So while the speaker cannot *establish* her own reliability merely on the basis of having observed that an audience accepted her assertion, still (there are cases in which) she can claim enhanced confidence in her own reliability from this observation, at least when she has grounds for thinking that the audience had the critical dispositions described above.

In short, none of the arguments against Self-Improvement hold up under scrutiny.

It would seem that a very similar diagnosis is in place for those who would assume that testimonial belief is non-independent belief. We can bring this to bear on the literature on the significance of numbers in disagreement cases. Consider a theorist who wonders whether or how numbers matter in disagreements. Such a theorist might be tempted to reason as follows. If H believes that not-p, and then encounters many people who believe that p, only to come to learn that all of these people who believe that p acquired their belief on the say-so of a common source, S, then the fact that so many additional people believe that p *does not add any contrary weight*, beyond the weight that is assigned to S's own belief that p. After all, everyone depended on S for their belief that p, so counting them as adding weight to the opposition involves an illicit double-counting!

We can now see that, while there is much to this reasoning, it can't be quite right.[13] For insofar as each person brings his or her own critical sensibility to the situation in which he or she encounters the original source S's testimony that p, the fact that so many people accept S's testimony, and so believe that p, does give *some* added weight to the opposition, beyond the

---

[13] See also Lackey (2013), who makes a similar point.

weight already assigned to the fact that (common source) S believes that p. How much weight to assign to the numbers will of course depend on the scope and quality of the critical sensibilities others brought to accepting S's assertion that p: how much background evidence they had, how likely it would have been that had S gone wrong they would have detected this, and so forth. If all of S's 'followers' are what Goldman (2001) called 'uncritical reflectors' of S's opinion, then the additional numbers don't matter. But presumably there are few cases in real life where an audience is an 'uncritical reflector' of another's assertion: usually, we are not human parrots. And when S's 'followers' are not uncritical reflectors of S's opinion, the additional numbers do matter. It is true, of course, that numbers matter *less*, and in standard cases *much* less, when everyone's opinion can be traced to a common source than when each person thinks for herself; but they still do matter. Any temptation to the contrary position is unfairly assuming the human parrot model of testimonial acceptance.

7

So far, I have argued for the doctrine of Epistemic Self-Improvement through Assertion: there are cases in which a speaker S's observation of the fact that her assertion that p is accepted by another person enhances the strength of S's own epistemic position with respect to p, as compared to S's strength of epistemic position with respect to p prior to having made the assertion. This would seem like good news. In this final section, however, I want to present some news which, though it too derives from the social epistemology of public uptake, is decidedly less good. In particular, the sort of possibility I just described can be a bad thing, epistemically speaking: the considerations that support the possibility of Self-Improvement appear to be implicated in the phenomena of *groupthink* and *belief polarization*.

Let me begin by characterizing the phenomena themselves. By *groupthink* I have in mind the phenomenon whereby various members of a group each arrive at a particular conclusion in such a way that the desire for group harmony or conformity plays what from an epistemic perspective is an inappropriately significant role.[14] And by *belief polarization* I have in

---

[14] The term 'groupthink' itself was originally coined by William Whyte in a 1952 *Fortune* magazine article entitled 'Groupthink'. For a helpful review of the phenomena grouped under this label, see Janis (1982).

mind the phenomenon whereby individuals discussing some topic gravitate towards more extreme views than they had on entering the discussion, despite the fact that the only new evidence they encounter in the discussion is the evidence concerning what others believe on the matter.[15] In what follows I want to suggest that the mechanisms that underlie the possibility of Self-Improvement may themselves be partly responsible for enabling groupthink and belief polarization as well.

To bring out the relevant point, it is helpful to review how the speaker gets the epistemic benefit advertised in Self-Improvement. According to the simple evidentialist model I presented in section 3, the speaker S must have evidence that the Audience Accepted S's assertion

AA   The audience accepted S's assertion that p;

and that the Audience was relevantly Knowledgeable on the issue

AK   The audience was relevantly positioned so that had there been a flaw in the procedure by which S reached her determination that p—missed evidence, an overlooked relevant alternative, a mistake in the reasoning, an error in her memory, etc.—there is some non-negligible likelihood that she (the audience) would have caught it (and not accepted S's assertion).

For it is only when AA and AK are true that we have the prospect for the epistemic enhancement described in Self-Improvement; and it is only when the speaker *has evidence* that both AA and AK are true that she is epistemically justified in regarding the audience's reaction as evidence which enhances her epistemic perspective with respect to p. If AA is false, then far from providing further support for what S asserted, the audience's reaction potentially provides evidence against that assertion; and if S lacks sufficient *evidence* to believe that AA is true, then S lacks sufficient evidence to think that the audience accepted what she said, and so has no higher-order evidence with which to receive the epistemic enhancement in Self-Improvement. If AK is false, then even if the audience did accept S's assertion, her doing so did not manifest the sort of critical perspective which, in section 6, I argued is required if there is to be any Self-Improvement in S's epistemic position; and if S does not have sufficient

---

[15] The notion of group polarization has been discussed in Lord, Ross, and Nepper (1979). See also Gilovich (1991, chapter 3).

evidence to believe that AK is true, then the audience's reaction does not constitute (higher-order) evidence of the acceptability of S's assertion.

Now the difficulty is that the sorts of evidence a speaker might have for thinking that AA and AK are true in a given case is *far from perfectly reliable*. So, for example, standard evidence for thinking that AA is true will include audience A's silence in the face of the assertion, or perhaps A's acquiescence in going along as if p, or as if A accepted p. But as an indication that A has accepted S's assertion, this evidence is far from perfectly reliable: it is not always so that when A is silent, or when A goes along as if he believed what was asserted, he actually believes what was asserted. Next, consider the standard evidence one might have for thinking that AK is true. In the ordinary case, this will involve evidence regarding such things as A's epistemic character and competence, A's relevant expertise, A's background knowledge, etc. But of course such evidence here is also far from perfectly reliable: we all have a strong motive to come across as competent and knowledgeable, and so what an arbitrary speaker has evidence to believe of an audience may well paint a better picture than is warranted by the actual facts. So the sort of evidence we are likely to have in connection with AK's truth is far from perfectly reliable as well.

Given the highly fallible route from S's evidence regarding AA and AK to the conclusion that AA and AK hold, it can often happen that S has *misleading evidence* for thinking that AA and AK hold. What is more, the same point holds for *anyone* who observed the interaction between S and A. Now suppose that the evidence regarding AA and AK is misleading. And consider the situation of those who have such evidence—whether they are the speaker herself, or merely some other conversational participant. Any such person who has misleading evidence of this sort will be such that on the basis of that evidence she will acquire the false belief that the audience accepted the speaker's assertion, or, alternatively, will acquire the false belief in the audience's knowledgeableness and/or outspokenness. In short, when the evidence on one or both of these matters is misleading, the result will be that the person with the misleading evidence *will most likely misconstrue the epistemic significance of the audience's reaction to the speaker's assertion*.[16] It is here, I submit, that we see the basis for belief polarization; and insofar as the participants are influenced in what they take to be evidence for AA and

---

[16] For particularly awful scenarios in which this can happen, see Maitra (2012: 116) and Tirrell (2012: 203).

AK by their desire to be good members of the group, we will see the basis for groupthink. Let me explain.

Take a case in which S asserts that p to a large group, and every member appears to every other member to silently acquiesce in acceptance. Then insofar as each member of the group has what she regards as evidence to think that AA and AK hold, each member of the group has what each regards as evidence to think that the support for p is greater, and perhaps even much greater, than the support S herself has—in which case they will increase their confidence in the hypothesis that p, despite getting no new first-order evidence regarding whether p. The trouble, of course, is that this sort of reaction would appear to them to be warranted *whether or not* the various members' evidence for believing that AA and AK hold is misleading. And where this evidence *is* misleading, the result would be an increase in the confidence various members of the group have towards p, despite no new first-order evidence—*a classic case of belief polarization*.

Now suppose that among the considerations that prompt members of the group to believe that AK hold are considerations of group solidarity: we want to believe that the members of our group are relevantly knowledgeable, since to deny this is to risk jeopardizing our status in the group. (At least this is so for a good many groups.) Alternatively, suppose that among the considerations that prompt members of the group to believe that AA holds are considerations of group solidarity: when a member of the group observes other members of the group being silent in the face of a group member's assertion, it would jeopardize one's membership in the group to suggest that such silence indicates anything other than acceptance. (Again, this is so for a good many groups.) This sort of 'evidence' for believing that AK or AA hold in these cases is, of course, not real evidence. But when these factors are present, and when the members of the group rely on their belief that AA and AK hold to shape their own reactions to observed assertions by other members of the group, we have a classic case of groupthink: the members of the group allow their desire for continued good standing in the group to guide their reactions to group discussion, resulting in believing what others in the group say so long as there are no explicit objections by other group members.

In short, I am suggesting that the very mechanisms that, in the good case (where the higher-order evidence is not misleading), lead to the phenomenon of Self-Improvement, are also present in the bad case, where the higher-order evidence is misleading, and where the result is (or can be) belief polarization and/or groupthink. Of course, the mechanisms I've cited to explain such unhappy social effects provide at best very partial explanations for the phenomena in question. For all that is said by the explanations just canvassed, we still need to understand the forces that prompt people not to reveal their doubts about a speaker's assertion that p, or to act as if they accept assertions even when they don't, or to assign such great weight to their continued good standing in their groups. No doubt, there are all sorts of social pressures operating here, and a full explanation of the phenomena of belief polarization and groupthink will need to advert to the existence of such pressures.[17] Even so, the foregoing 'partial' explanations should be of interest in their own right. For they raise the intriguing possibility that groupthink and belief polarization are actually *more rational* than they are commonly thought to be. In one sense, I think that this is so: these phenomena are not simply the effects of arational (social) pressures, but instead can be (partially) rationalized by reasons of the sort just described. But in another sense, these phenomena remain as troubling as before. For even if my argument has been successful, it has merely relocated or redescribed the source of the trouble: whereas before we might have described groupthink or polarization as phenomena in which people adjust their credences *in the absence of* new evidence or reasons, we now see that while people do adjust their credences to the evidence or reasons, they do so in a way that fails to appreciate the strength of, or the degree of fallibility in, these reasons.

8

In this chapter I have been focusing on the sort of conversational pressure that is at hand in the uptake of uptake. My core contentions were two: first, that the social epistemology of public uptake makes possible cases akin to epistemic bootstrapping, and second, that the very mechanisms that make this possible may underwrite belief polarization and groupthink. More generally, these mechanisms undergird what we might call the epistemic dimension of conversational pressure, as this arises in the uptake of uptake.

---

[17] For a review of the recent psychological literature, see Kerr and Tindale (2004) and Kugler, Kausel, and Kocher (2004). For three recent philosophical attempts to come to grips with these, see Peter (2013), Bjerring, Hansen, and Pedersen (2014), and Russell, Hawthorne, and Buchak (2015).

11
The Epistemic Costs of Politeness

One is polite when one is courteous and civil towards others, as exhibited in one's speech and behaviour. We might speak of *politeness norms* as norms that mandate the forms of courteousness and civility expected in one's community. We can distinguish at least two different dimensions of such norms: the standards they impose (i.e. what they regard as polite and impolite), and the weight assigned to following the standards. No doubt, politeness norms differ along these dimensions from community to community. The standards clearly differ from community to community: in some communities, belching after a meal is considered impolite, in others it is not; in some communities standing within a foot of another person is considered impolite, in others it is not. So too for the weight that is attached to being polite. Some communities regard politeness as of fundamental social value: in such communities, from the fact that a candidate act violates one of the community's politeness norms, it follows that one has a very weighty reason not to perform the act. We can even imagine communities in which this reason overrides any other reason a subject might have to perform the act in question. Of course, not all communities are like this. Thus, there are communities in which the weight assigned to one's reason not to violate a prevailing politeness norm, while not insignificant, is nevertheless such that it often happens that other reasons (in favour of performing the candidate impolite behaviour) are weightier. (New York City comes to mind here.)

A special case of politeness involves how one responds to another person's claims or assertions. What I will call a norm of extreme conversational politeness will mandate a standard whereby it is regarded as impolite to express *any* public dissent or doubt about another person's claim. If a community places an extremely high importance on matters of politeness,

---

Reproduced from S. Goldberg and G. Yang (2017), 'The Epistemic Costs of Politeness', *Think*, 16 (46): 19–23.

Conversational Pressure: Normativity in Speech Exchanges. Sanford C. Goldberg, Oxford University Press (2020).
© Sanford C. Goldberg.
DOI: 10.1093/oso/9780198856436.001.0001

and if the norm of extreme conversational politeness prevails, people have an extremely weighty reason not to express dissent or doubt publicly.

There is one obvious epistemic cost of politeness in such communities: when a person makes a claim regarding which many in the audience harbour warranted doubts, those who are unaware of the grounds for doubt lose out on the opportunity to become apprised of these grounds. Everyone can acknowledge this 'epistemic cost' of politeness.

In this chapter I am interested in arguing for a more subtle epistemic cost of politeness. In particular, I submit that in such communities the opportunity to use audience silence as a signal of the acceptability of a publicly made assertion is lost. To say that this opportunity is lost is to suggest that the prospect of having that opportunity is one that might reasonably be hoped for. This needs defending.

Let us say that the epistemic value of a signal s regarding the obtaining of a condition c is a function of how reliably s indicates the presence c: the more reliable s is—the more probable c is given s—the higher s's epistemic value as a signal of c, with the result that the higher the degree of warranted confidence an informed subject can have regarding the obtaining of c, given s. Now we want to say that there are communities in which *audience silence has a high epistemic value as a signal of audience assent*. These will be communities in which (i) there is a general expectation that if one has objections to an assertion made in one's mutual presence, one will indicate this, and (ii) people regularly conform to this expectation. In such communities, when the audience is silent in the face of an assertion made in their mutual presence, this is a (high-value) signal that they assent to it. Of course, the fact that people assent to another's assertion might be regarded as a fact of little interest in its own right. However, under two further assumptions this fact becomes very interesting from an epistemic point of view. Suppose that in addition to (i) and (ii) above, it is also true that (iii) people in the community are very well informed on many topics that are discussed, so that were there grounds for doubt (regarding something asserted on one of those topics) they would likely be aware of these grounds, and (iv) people are also very well informed about when a topic is such that others among them are well informed on that topic. Under such conditions, the fact that an audience is silent, when the observer has grounds for thinking that the topic is one on which they can be expected to be well informed, is itself *evidence of the acceptability of the assertion itself*. In such communities, people are well placed to discern when silence in the face of a publicly made assertion indicates (not merely assent, but) *acceptability*.

Now insofar as there are communities in which (i)–(iv) hold, there is the prospect that, for at least a broad (and discriminable) range of topics, members of the language community can regard audience silence as an indication of (audience assent, and so) the acceptability of publicly made assertions on those topics. This is a great epistemic boon; in effect, those who satisfy (iv) are in a position to exploit the knowledgeableness of their fellows in determining the acceptability of what is said in their mutual presence.

It is the opportunity for this sort of epistemic social work—of being in a position to exploit the knowledgeableness of one's fellows in determining the acceptability of what is said in our mutual presence—that is lost in communities in which politeness norms are both demanding in their standards and overriding in the weight that is assigned to following those standards. In such communities, silence does not signal assent, and so even if conditions (iii) and (iv) hold, silence gives no basis for reaching a determination of others' sense of the acceptability of the assertion.

Of course, the community that places such weight on following stringent politeness norms is an extreme example. In saying that it is extreme, I do not mean that such communities do not exist; on the contrary, there are many such communities. I mean only that these communities occupy an extreme along the two dimensions just described: the demandingness of the politeness standards (what is considered polite and what not); and the weight assigned to following them. We can imagine communities that exhibit intermediate values along one or both of these dimensions. For example, we can imagine a community in which the range of conversational behaviours that are considered impolite is more restricted: following these more 'liberal' politeness norms would not rule out publicly expressing disagreement with others, but instead would constrain when and how such expressions ought to be made (e.g. avoid disagreements on deeply contentious matters of politics and religion; when disagreeing do so with respect, and only after a charitable reconstruction of the other side's views, and do not persist more than one or two rounds—after that the matter should be dropped etc.). And we can imagine a community in which the weight assigned to following the prevailing politeness norms, though significant, does not ensure that one's reasons to follow them will always outweigh one's reasons to violate them.

This brings us to the main claim, which is that to whatever extent a given regime of politeness norms mandates silence, to just that extent *it degrades the epistemic value of silence as a signal of assent*. The extreme community described above is only a vivid illustration of this. In cases involving more liberal (permissive) norms, or where the weight assigned to following the prevailing norms is decreased (relative to potential reasons one might have for violating such norms), there will be fewer cases of politeness-induced silence. In such communities, silence may still have epistemic value as a signal of assent. But it should be clear that its epistemic value is degraded relative to the epistemic value silence has as a signal of assent in communities in which (i)–(iv) hold.

I make no claims about how this epistemic cost of politeness should be traded off against the value of living in a polite society. That is a difficult question in value theory that I will leave for others to resolve. I only ask that the accounting be an honest one, when it is done. (Perhaps New York City will not turn out so bad by comparison.)

12
Conclusion

The topic of this book has been the phenomenon of conversational pressure. By this I understand the various forms of normative pressure that obtain in conversations, that bear on the various members of a conversation, and which have as their source a speaker's performance of speech acts of one kind or another. In focusing on this topic, I have highlighted three 'moments' in a conversation during which we can discern such conversational pressures: the moment of address (Part I); the moment of the performance (by the speaker) and uptake (by the audience) of the speech act itself (Part II); and the moment of the uptake of uptake (Part III). Focusing on these 'moments,' I have sought to identify the source, scope, and nature of these pressures.

It is perhaps unsurprising that an interest in the conversational pressures we exert on one another should begin with the act of address itself. While there has been a good deal of attention devoted to the significance of second-personal address, to my mind this work fails to discuss what I regard as the central question: namely, how does the fact of address itself—as opposed to the speech act through which one addresses oneself to one's audience—put pressure on one's audience to attend to one in the first place? How does one's addressing an audience transform the situation into one in which attention is something that the audience now *owes* to one? It is by answering this question—by characterizing how it is that one can rightly claim another's attention—that we can discern how conversational pressures are initiated *ab initio*. On this score, my core contention was that our status as rational social creatures whose need to cooperate with others requires us to have some mechanism whereby to initiate our attempts at cooperation, and that it is by addressing others that we are entitled to expect their attention long enough to manifest these intentions to them. At the same time, though, this expectation of another's attention, consequent upon the speaker's having addressed them, reflects the presumed cooperativity of the exchange: insofar as the speaker is not being cooperative, or is not intending to initiate a cooperative action, she enjoys no entitlement to expect the addressee's attention. Finally, in the absence of evidence one way or the other, we ought to presume each others' cooperativity.

Once we have another's attention, of course, there are all sorts of downstream pressures that are exerted in conversation, and Parts II and III take these up.

The focus of Part II were the conversational pressures associated with the making of assertions and statements. Some of these are pressures generated by the performance of speech acts themselves. That there is an epistemic dimension to the conversational pressure involved in acts of testimony is not newsworthy. That there is an interpersonal dimension to the conversational pressure exerted by such acts is also familiar from the work on trust and testimonial injustice. What is challenging—what has occasioned the need for further theorizing—has been the need to characterize the interaction between these conversational pressures. How can it be that by testifying to another (or making an assertion in her presence), a speaker both puts interpersonal pressure on her audience to treat her properly—in the way befitting one who performed such an act—while at the same time puts epistemic pressure on her audience to respond in ways that conform to the norms of epistemology? Some theorists have thought to try to reduce epistemic pressures to interpersonal pressures; others have seen the interpersonal pressures arising in connection with particular relationships (e.g. of friendship) as potentially pulling apart from the norms of epistemology proper. For my part, however, I have sought to show that, while neither of the normative domains can be reduced to the other, nevertheless their demands can be simultaneously met.

Part III then takes up what I regard as a rather underexplored area of conversational pressure: the uptake of others' uptake. Here I have tried to argue that, given our interests in conversational participants' reactions to observed speech, there are norms concerning our public reactions, and that these norms are the basis of yet another form of conversational pressure. My main focus was on conversational silence: I argued that (under conditions that hold widely) silent rejection of another's public statement is marked, and that insofar as we are entitled to regard others as cooperative we are (defeasibly but presumptively) entitled to expect that they not remain silent in rejection. This was the basis of an argument in defence of our entitlement to presume that silence indicates acceptance. And after defending this argument against objections raised against a similar account offered by Philip Pettit, I went on to discuss the limitations of this entitlement, and the conditions that defeat the presumption itself. But here, too, we can distinguish the interpersonal dimensions of conversational pressure—those that derive from what I called the practice of assertion itself—from the epistemic dimensions of such pressure—what I called the social epistemology of public uptake.

If there are any general lessons to be taken from this discussion, it is the need to distinguish the two types of conversational pressure that arise in our everyday speech exchanges with one another—the epistemic and the interpersonal—and the challenges that arise when we try to account for the interaction between them. A theme that has guided my thinking for the past decade or so has been that the source of these pressures is to be found in the nature of the sort of speech act we are performing when, for example, we make statements or assertions or testify to one another. This was the central theme of my (2015) book, where I sought to show that a proper account of assertion could make sense of the centrality of that speech act for a number of topics at the heart of philosophical theorizing. But it is also a central theme of this book: it is through the performance of acts of this type that speakers exert various forms of conversational pressure on their audiences, and it is by recognizing the nature of the speaker's act that audiences can hold speakers as well as other audience members accountable as we engage with one another in speech.

References

Alcoff, L. 2001: 'On Judging Epistemic Credibility: Is Social Identity Relevant?' In N. Tuana and S. Morgen (eds.), *Engendering Rationalities* (Albany, NY: State University of New York Press): 53–80.
Anderson, E. 1995: 'Feminist Epistemology: An Interpretation and a Defense', *Hypatia: A Journal of Feminist Philosophy*, 10 (3): 50–84.
Anderson, L., and Lepore, E. 2013: 'What did you Call Me? Slurs as Prohibited Words', *Analytic Philosophy*, 54 (3): 350–63.
Anscombe, E. 1979: 'What is it to Believe Someone?' In C. F. Delaney (ed.), *Rationality and Religious Belief* (South Bend: University of Notre Dame Press).
Arendt, H. 1970: 'Civil Disobedience', *The New Yorker*, 12 September 1970.
Audi, R. 1997: 'The Place of Testimony in the Fabric of Knowledge and Justification', *American Philosophical Quarterly*, 34 (4): 405–22.
Austin, J. 1975: *How to Do Things with Words* (Oxford: Oxford University Press).
Bach, K., and Harnish, M. 1979: *Linguistic Communication and Speech Acts* (Cambridge, Mass.: MIT Press).
Bach, K. 1987: 'On Communicative Intentions: A Reply to Recanati', *Mind and Language*, 2 (2): 141–55.
Baier, A. 1986: 'Trust and Antitrust', *Ethics*, 96: 231–60.
Baker, J. 1987: 'Trust and Rationality', *Pacific Philosophical Quarterly*, 68: 1–13.
Ballantyne, N., and Coffman, E. J. 2011: 'Uniqueness, Evidence, and Rationality', *Philosophers' Imprint*, 11 (18): 1–13.
Benatar, D. 2011: 'A First Name Basis?', *Think*, 10 (29): 51–7.
Berridge, G. 2010: *Diplomacy: Theory and Practice*, 4th edn. (New York: Palgrave Macmillan).
Bianchi, C. 2014: 'Slurs and Appropriation: An Echoic Account', *Journal of Pragmatics*, 66: 35–44.
Bird, A. 2002: 'Illocutionary Silencing', *Pacific Philosophical Quarterly*, 83 (1): 1–15.
Bjerring, J., Hansen, J., and Pedersen, N. 2014: 'On the Rationality of Pluralistic Ignorance', *Synthese*, 191: 2445–70.
Brown, J. 2008: 'Subject-Sensitive Invariantism and the Knowledge Norm for Practical Reasoning', *Noûs*, 42 (2): 167–89.
Brown, J. 2010: 'Knowledge and Assertion', *Philosophy and Phenomenological Research*, 81: 549–66.
Brown, J., and Cappelen, H. (eds.) 2010: *Assertion: New Philosophical Essays* (Oxford: Oxford University Press).
Brownstein, M., and Saul, J. (eds.) 2016a: *Implicit Bias and Philosophy, Volume 1: Metaphysics and Epistemology* (Oxford: Oxford University Press).

Brownstein, M., and Saul, J. (eds.) 2016b: *Implicit Bias and Philosophy, Volume 2: Moral Responsibility, Structural Injustice, and Ethics* (Oxford: Oxford University Press).

Brueckner, A., and Bundy, A. 2012: 'On "Epistemic Permissiveness"', *Synthese*, 188 (2): 165–77.

Burge, T. 1993: 'Content Preservation', *Philosophical Review*, 102 (4): 457–88.

Camp, E. 2013: 'Slurring Perspectives', *Analytic Philosophy*, 54 (3): 330–49.

Chang, R. 2013: 'Commitments, Reasons, and the Will', *Oxford Studies in Metaethics*, 8: 74–113.

Clark, H. 1996: *Using Language* (Cambridge: Cambridge University Press).

Clark, H., and Schaefer, E. 1989: 'Contributing to Discourse', *Cognitive Science*, 13: 259–94.

Coady, C. A. J. 1992: *Testimony: A Philosophical Study* (Oxford: Oxford University Press).

Code, L. 1995: *Rhetorical Spaces: Essays on Gendered Locations* (New York: Routledge).

Collins, P. 1990: *Black Feminist Thought: Knowledge, Consciousness, and the Politics of Empowerment* (New York: Routledge).

Cosmides, L., and Tooby, J. 2005: 'Neurocognitive Adaptations Designed for Social Exchange'. In D. M. Buss (ed.), *Handbook of Evolutionary Psychology* (Hoboken, NJ: Wiley): 584–627.

Craig, E. 1999: *Knowledge and the State of Nature: An Essay in Conceptual Synthesis* (Oxford: Oxford University Press).

Croom, A. 2011: 'Slurs', *Language Sciences*, 33 (3): 343–58.

Croom, A. 2013: 'How to do Things with Slurs: Studies in the Way of Derogatory Words', *Language & Communication*, 33 (3): 177–204.

Cuneo, T. 2014: *Speech and Morality: On the Metaethical Implications of Speaking* (Oxford: Oxford University Press).

Darwall, S. 2006: *The Second-Person Standpoint: Respect, Morality, and Accountability* (Cambridge, Mass.: Harvard University Press).

Dickey, E. 1997: 'Forms of Address and Terms of Reference', *Journal of linguistics*, 33 (2): 255–74.

Dogramaci, S., and Horowitz, S. 2016: 'An Argument for Uniqueness about Evidential Support', *Philosophical Issues*, 26 (1): 130–47.

Donnellan, K. S. 1966: 'Reference and Definite Descriptions', *Philosophical Review*, 75 (3): 281–304.

Dotson, K. 2011: 'Tracking Epistemic Violence, Tracking Practices of Silencing' *Hypatia: A Journal of Feminist Philosophy*, 26 (2): 236–57.

Dotson, K. 2014: 'Conceptualizing Epistemic Oppression', *Social Epistemology: A Journal of Knowledge, Culture, and Policy* 28 (2): 115–38.

Douven, I. 2009: 'Uniqueness Revisited', *American Philosophical Quarterly*, 46 (4): 347–61.

Durante, A. 1988: 'Intention, Language, and Social Action in a Samoan Context', *Journal of Pragmatics*, 12: 13–33.

Dyzenhaus, D. 1992: 'John Stuart Mill and the Harm of Pornography', *Ethics*, 102 (3): 534–51.

Elga, E. 2010: 'How to Disagree About How to Disagree'. In R. Feldman and T. Warfield. (eds.), *Disagreement* (Oxford: Oxford University Press).

Ermer, E., Guerin, S., Cosmides, L., Tooby, J., and Miller, M. 2006: 'Theory of Mind Broad and Narrow: Reasoning about Social Exchange Engages TOM Areas, Precautionary Reasoning Does not', *Social Neuroscience*, 1 (3–4): 196–219.

Evans, M., Dillon, K., Goldin, G., and Krueger, J. 2011: 'Trust and Self-Control: The Moderating Role of the Default', *Judgment and Decision Making*, 6 (7): 697–705.

Fantl, J., and McGrath, M. 2009: *Knowledge in an Uncertain World* (Oxford: Oxford University Press).

Farkas, D., and Bruce, K. 2009: 'On Reacting to Assertions and Polar Questions', *Journal of Semantics*, 27: 81–118.

Foley, R. 2001: *Intellectual Trust in Oneself and Others* (Cambridge: Cambridge University Press).

Fricker, E. 1987: 'The Epistemology of Testimony', *Proceedings of the Aristotelian Society*, Supplemental Vol. 61: 57–83.

Fricker, E. 1994: 'Against Gullibility'. In B. K. Matilal and A. Chakrabarti (eds.), *Knowing from Words* (Amsterdam: Kluwer Academic Publishers): 125–61.

Fricker, E. 1995: 'Telling and Trusting: Reductionism and Anti-Reductionism in the Epistemology of Testimony', *Mind*, 104, 393–411.

Fricker, E. 2006: 'Second-Hand Knowledge', *Philosophy and Phenomenological Research*, 73 (3): 592–618.

Fricker, E. 2017: 'Norms, Constitutive and Social, and Assertion', *American Philosophical Quarterly*, 54 (4): 397–418.

Fricker, M. 1998: 'Rational Authority and Social Power: Towards a Truly Social Epistemology', *Proceedings of the Aristotelian Society* 98: 159–77.

Fricker, M. 2007: *Epistemic Injustice: Power and the Ethics of Knowing* (Oxford: Oxford University Press).

Fricker, E. 2012: 'Stating and Insinuating', *Aristotelian Society*, Supplementary Vol. 86 (1): 61–94.

Friedman, J. 2017: 'Why Suspend Judging?' *Noûs*, 51 (2): 302–26.

Garcia-Carpintero, M. 2004: 'Assertion and the Semantics of Force-Markers'. In C. Bianchi (ed.), *The Semantics/Pragmatics Distinction* (Palo Alto, Calif.: CSLI/Stanford University Press): 133–66.

Gelber, K. 2012: '"Speaking Back": The Likely Fate of Hate Speech Policy in the United States and Australia'. In I. Matira and M. K. McGowan (eds.), *Speech and Harm: Controversies over Free Speech* (Oxford: Oxford University Press): 50–71.

Gelfert, A. 2014: *A Critical Introduction to Testimony* (London: Bloomsbury).

Gendler, T. 2011: 'On the Epistemic Costs of Implicit Bias', *Philosophical Studies*, 156 (1): 33.

Gibbard, A. 1990: *Wise Choices, Apt Feelings* (Oxford: Clarendon Press).

Gilbert, D., Tafarodi, R., and Malone, P. 1993: 'You Can't not Believe Everything You Read', *Journal of Personality and Social Psychology*, 65 (2): 221–33.

Gilbert, M. 1989: *On Social Facts* (Princeton: Princeton University Press).
Gilbert, M. 2011: 'Joint Commitment: How We Make the Social World'. In H. Ikaheimo and A. Laitinen (eds.), *Recognition and Social Ontology* (Leiden: Brill).
Gilbert, M., and Priest, M. 2013: 'Conversation and Collective Belief'. In A. Capone, F. Lo Piparo, and M. Carapezza (eds.), *Perspectives on Pragmatics and Philosophy* (Dordrecht: Springer International Publishing): 1–34.
Gilovich, T. 1991: *How We Know What Isn't So* (New York: Free Press).
Ginzburg, J. 1996: 'Dynamics and the Semantics of Dialogue'. In J. Seligman and D. Westerstahl (eds.), *Language, Logic, and Computation*, Vol. 1. (Stanford, Calif.: CSLI Lecture Notes): 221–37.
Goldberg, S. 2007: *Anti-Individualism: Mind and Language, Knowledge and Justification* (Cambridge: Cambridge University Press).
Goldberg, S. 2010: *Relying on Others: An Essay in Epistemology* (Oxford: Oxford University Press).
Goldberg, S. 2011a: 'The Division of Epistemic Labour', *Episteme*, 8 (1): 112–25.
Goldberg, S. 2011b: 'Putting the Norm of Assertion to Work: The Case of Testimony'. In J. Brown and J. Cappelen (eds.), *Assertion* (Oxford: Oxford University Press): 175–95.
Goldberg, S. 2011c: 'If that were True I Would have Heard about it by Now'. In A. I. Goldman and D. Whitcomb (eds.), *Social Epistemology: Essential Readings* (Oxford: Oxford University Press): 92–108.
Goldberg, S. 2014: 'Interpersonal Epistemic Entitlements', *Philosophical Issues*, 24 (1): 159–83.
Goldberg, S. 2015a: 'A Proposed Research Program for Social Epistemology'. In P. Reider (ed.), *Social Epistemology and Epistemic Agency* (Lanham, Md.: Rowman and Littlefield): 3–20.
Goldberg, S. 2015b: *Assertion: On the Philosophical Significance of Assertoric Speech* (Oxford: Oxford University Press).
Goldberg, S. 2016: 'On the Epistemic Significance of Evidence You Should Have Had', *Episteme*, 13 (4), 449–70.
Goldberg, S. 2017: 'Should Have Known', *Synthese*, 194 (8): 2863–94.
Goldberg, S. 2018: *To the Best of our Knowledge: Social Expectations and Epistemic Normativity* (Oxford: Oxford University Press).
Goldberg, S. (ed.) 2020: *The Oxford Handbook of Assertion*. (Oxford: Oxford University Press).
Goldman, A. 2001: 'Experts: Which Ones Should You Trust?', *Philosophy and Phenomenological Research*, 63: 85–110.
Ginzburg, J. 2012: *The Interactive Stance: Meaning for Conversation* (Oxford: Oxford University Press).
Goodwin, C. 1995: 'The Negotiation of Coherence within Conversation'. In G. A. Gernsbacher and T. Givon (eds.), *Coherence in Spontaneous Text* (Amsterdam: Benjamins): 117–37.
Graham, P. 2004: 'Metaphysical Libertarianism and the Epistemology of Testimony', *American Philosophical Quarterly*, 41: 37–50.

Graham, P. 2006: 'Testimonial Justification: Inferential or Non-inferential?', *Philosophical Quarterly*, 56: 84–95.
Greco, D. and Heddon, B. Forthcoming: 'Uniqueness and Metaepistemology', *Journal of Philosophy*.
Grice, P. 1957: 'Meaning', *Philosophical Review*, 66 (3): 377–88.
Grice, P. 1968/1989: 'Logic and Conversation'. In *Studies in the Way of Words* (Cambridge, Mass.: Harvard University Press, 1989): 22–40.
Habibian, S. 1995/2002: *1001 Persian-English Proverbs*, English and Farsi edition (Bethesda, Md: IBEX Publishers).
Harding, S. 1991: *Whose Science? Whose Knowledge? Thinking from Women's Lives* (Ithaca, NY: Cornell University Press).
Hare, R. M. 1952: *The Language of Morals* (Oxford: Oxford University Press).
Haslanger, S. 2014: 'Studying While Black: Trust, Opportunity, and Disrespect', *Du Bois Review*, 11 (1): 109–36.
Hawley, K. 2014a: 'Partiality and Prejudice in Trusting', *Synthese*, 191: 2029–45.
Hawley, K. 2014b: 'Trust, Distrust, and Commitment', *Noûs*, 48 (1): 1–20.
Hawthorne, J. 2004: *Knowledge and Lotteries* (Oxford: Oxford University Press).
Hay, C. 2013: *Kantianism, Liberalism, and Feminism: Resisting Oppression* (Houndmills and New York: Palgrave Macmillan).
Hazlett, A. 2013: *A Luxury of the Understanding: On the Value of True Belief* (Oxford: Oxford University Press).
Hinchman, T. 2005: 'Telling as Inviting to Trust', *Philosophy and Phenomenological Research*, 70 (3): 562–87.
Hinchman, T. 2014: 'Assertion and Warrant', *Philosophers' Imprint*, 14 (17): 1–58.
Holroyd, J. 2012: 'Responsibility for Implicit Bias', *Journal of Social Philosophy*, 43 (3): 274–306.
Holton, R. 1994: 'Deciding to Trust, Coming to Believe', *Australasian Journal of Philosophy*, 72: 63–76.
Hom, C. 2010: 'Pejoratives', *Philosophy Compass*, 5 (2): 164–85.
Hornsby, J. 1995: 'Disempowered Speech', *Philosophical Topics*, 23 (2): 127–47.
Jaggar, A. 1983: *Feminist Politics and Human Nature* (Totowa, NJ: Rowman and Allanheld).
Janis, I. 1982: *Groupthink: Psychological Studies of Policy Decisions and Fiascoes*, 2nd edn. (Boston: Houghton Mifflin).
Jeshion, R. 2013: 'Expressivism and the Offensiveness of Slurs', *Philosophical Perspectives*, 27 (1): 231–59.
Jones, K. 1996: 'Trust as an Affective Attitude', *Ethics*, 107: 4–25.
Jones, K. 2002: 'The Politics of Credibility'. In L. Antony and C. Witt (eds.), *A Mind of one's Own: Feminist Essays on Reason and Objectivity*, 2nd edn. (Boulder, Colo.: Westview): 154–76.
Jones, K. 2004: 'Trust and Terror'. In P. DesAutels and M. Walker (eds.), *Moral Psychology* (Lanham, Md.: Rowman and Littlefield).
Jones, K. 2012: 'The Politics of Intellectual Self-Trust', *Social Epistemology*, 26 (2): 237–51.

Jones, K. 2016: 'But I Was Counting on You!' In P. Faulkner and R. Simpson (eds.), *The Philosophy of Trust* (Oxford: Oxford University Press): 90–109.
Kawall, J. 2013: 'Friendship and Epistemic Norms', *Philosophical Studies*, 165: 349–70.
Keller, S. 2004: 'Friendship and Belief', *Philosophical Papers*, 33 (3): 329–51.
Kelly, D., and Roedder, E. 2008: 'Racial Cognition and the Ethics of Implicit Bias', *Philosophy Compass*, 3 (3): 522–40.
Kelly, T. 2010: 'Peer Disagreement and Higher-Order Evidence'. In R. Feldman and T. Warfield (eds.), *Disagreement* (Oxford: Oxford University Press).
Kelly, T. 2013a: 'Disagreement and the Burdens of Judgment'. In David Christensen and Jennifer Lackey (eds.), *The Epistemology of Disagreement: New Essays* (Oxford: Oxford University Press): 31–53.
Kelly, T. 2013b: 'Evidence can be Permissive'. In Matthias Steup and John Turri (eds.), *Contemporary Debates in Epistemology* (Oxford: Blackwell): 298–312.
Kerr, L., and Tindale, R. 2004: 'Group Performance and Group Decisionmaking', *Annual Review of Psychology*, 55: 623–55.
Kolodny, N. 2003: 'Love as Valuing a Relationship', *The Philosophical Review*, 112 (2): 135–89.
Kopec, M. 2015: 'A Counterexample to the Uniqueness Thesis', *Philosophia*, 43 (2): 403–9.
Kugler, T., Kausel, E., and Kocher, M. 2004: 'Are Groups More Rational than Individuals? Review of Interactive Decision Making in Groups', *Wiley Interdisciplinary Reviews of Cognitive Science*, 3: 471–82.
Kukla, R. 2014: 'Performative Force, Convention, and Discursive Injustice', *Hypatia*, 29 (9): 440–56.
Kukla, R. and Lance, M. 2009: *'Yo!' and 'Lo!' The Pragmatic Topography of the Space of Reasons* (Cambridge, Mass.: Harvard University Press).
Lackey, J. 1999: 'Testimonial Knowledge and Transmission', *The Philosophical Quarterly*, 49 (197): 471–90.
Lackey, J. 2008: *Learning from Words: Testimony as a Source of Knowledge* (Oxford: Oxford University Press).
Lackey, J. 2010: 'Testimonial Knowledge'. In S. Bernecker and D. Pritchard (eds.), *Routledge Companion to Epistemology* (London and New York: Routledge): 316–25.
Lackey, J. 2011: 'Testimony: Acquiring Knowledge from Others'. In A. I. Goldman and D. Whitcomb (eds.), *Social Epistemology: An Anthology* (Oxford: Oxford University Press): 71–91.
Lackey, J. 2013: 'Disagreement and Belief Dependence: Why Numbers Matter'. In D. Christensen and J. Lackey (eds.), *Disagreement* (Oxford: Oxford University Press): 243–68.
Lackey, J. Forthcoming: 'The Duty to Object', *Philosophy and Phenomenological Research*.
Lackey, J., and Sosa, E. (eds.) 2006: *The Epistemology of Testimony* (Oxford: Oxford University Press).

Lance, M., and Kukla, R. 2013: 'Leave the Gun; Take the Canoli! The Pragmatic Topography of Second-Person Calls', *Ethics*, 123 (3): 456-78.
Langton, R. 1993: 'Speech Acts and Unspeakable Acts', *Philosophy & Public Affairs*, 22 (4): 293-330.
Langton, R. 2007: 'Disenfranchised Silence'. In G. Brennan, R. Goodin, F. Jackson, and M. Smith (eds.), *Common Minds: Themes from the Philosophy of Philip Pettit* (Oxford: Oxford University Press): 199-215.
Langton, R. 2009: *Sexual Solipsism: Philosophical Essays on Pornography and Objectification* (Oxford: Oxford University Press).
Langton, R. 2018: "Blocking as Counterspeech." In D. Fogal, D. Harris, and M. Moss (eds.), New Work on Speech Acts (Oxford: Oxford University Press): 144-64.
Langton, R., and Hornsby, J. 1998: 'Free Speech and Illocution', *Legal Theory* 4 (1): 21-37.
Lasonen-Aarnio, M. 2010: 'Unreasonable Knowledge', *Philosophical Perspectives*, 24 (1): 1-21.
Lasonen-Aarnio, M. 2014: 'Higher-Order Evidence and the Limits of Defeat', *Philosophy and Phenomenological Research*, 88 (2): 314-45.
Levy, N. 2017: 'Implicit Bias and Moral Responsibility: Probing the Data', *Philosophy and Phenomenological Research*, 94 (1): 3-26.
Lewis, D. 1979: 'Scorekeeping in a Language Game'. In R. Bäuerle, U. Egli, and A. Stechow, *Semantics from Different Points of View* (Berlin and Heidelberg: Springer): 172-87.
Lewis, D. 1989: 'Dispositional Theories of Value', *Proceedings of the Aristotelian Society*, 63: 89-174.
Lewis, D. 1996: 'Elusive Knowledge', *Australasian Journal of Philosophy*, 74 (4): 549-67.
Longino, H., and Doell, R. 1983: 'Body, Bias, and Behaviour: A Comparative Analysis of Reasoning in Two Areas of Biological Science', *Signs: Journal of Women in Culture and Society*, 9 (2): 206-27.
Lord, C., Ross, L., and Lepper, M. 1979: 'Biased Assimilation and Attitude Polarization: The Effects of Prior Theories on Subsequently Considered Evidence', *Journal of Personality and Social Psychology*, 37 (11): 2098.
Lubensky, S.1995/2013: *Random House Russian-English Dictionary of Idioms* (New York: Random House).
McGowan, M. K. 2009a: 'Oppressive Speech', *Australasian Journal of Philosophy*, 87 (3): 389-407.
McGowan, M. K. 2009b: 'On Silencing and Sexual Refusal', *Journal of Political Philosophy*, 17 (4): 487-94.
McGowan, M. K. 2012: 'On "Whites Only" Signs and Racist Hate Speech: Verbal Acts of Racial Discrimination'. In I. Matira and M. K. McGowan (eds.), *Speech and Harm: Controversies over Free Speech* (Oxford: Oxford University Press): 121-47.
McGowan, M. K. 2019: *Just Words: On Speech and Hidden Harm*. (Oxford: Oxford University Press).

McGowan, M. K., Adelman, A., Helmers, S., and Stolzenberg, J. 2011: 'A Partial Defense of Illocutionary Silencing', *Hypatia*, 26 (1): 132–49.

McGrath, S. 2008: 'Moral Disagreement and Moral Expertise'. In R. Shafer-Landau (ed.), *Oxford Studies in Metaethics*, 3 (Oxford: Oxford University Press): 87–107.

McHugh, C. 2013: 'The Illusion of Exclusivity', *European Journal of Philosophy*, 23 (4): 1117–36.

MacKinnon, C. 1989: *Towards a Feminist Theory of the State* (Cambridge, Mass.: Harvard University Press).

McKinnon, R.2015: *The Norms of Assertion: Truth, Lies, and Warrant* (Basingstoke: Palgrave MacMillan).

McMyler, B. 2011: *Testimony, Trust, and Authority* (Oxford: Oxford University Press).

McMyler, B. 2012. 'Testimony, Address, and the Second Person', *Rethinking Epistemology*, 2: 257–88.

Maitra, I. 2009: 'Silencing Speech', *Canadian Journal of Philosophy*, 39 (2): 309–38.

Maitra, I. 2012: 'Subordinating Speech'. In I. Maitra and M. McGowan(eds.), *Speech and Harm* (Oxford: Oxford University Press): 94–120.

Maitra, I., and McGowan, M. (eds.) 2012: *Speech and Harm* (Oxford: Oxford University Press).

Matheson, J. 2011: 'The Case for Rational Uniqueness', *Logos & Episteme*, 2 (3): 359–73.

Mills, C. 1997: *The Racial Contract* (Ithaca, NY: Cornell University Press).

Mills, C. 2007: 'White Ignorance', In S. Sullivan and N. Tuana (eds.), *Race and Epistemologies of Ignorance* (Albany, NY: State University of New York Press): 11–38.

Mills, C. 2014: 'Unwriting and Unwhitening the World'. In A. Anievas, N. Manchanda, and R. Shilliam (eds.), *Race and Racism in International Relations: Confronting the Global Colour Line* (London: Routledge): 204.

Mills, C. 2015: *Global White Ignorance* (London and New York: Routledge).

Mills, C. 2017: 'Black Radical Kantianism', *Res Philosophica*, 95 (1): 1–33.

Mills, C., and Pateman, C. 2007: *Contract and Domination* (Cambridge: Polity Press).

Moran, R. 2006: 'Getting Told and Being Believed'. In J. Lackey and E. Sosa (eds.), *The Epistemology of Testimony* (Oxford: Oxford University Press): 272–306.

Morand, D. A. 1996: 'What's in a Name? An Exploration of the Social Dynamics of Forms of Address in Organizations', *Management Communication Quarterly*, 9 (4): 422–51.

Nielsen, L. 2012: 'Power in Public: Reactions, Responses and Resistance to Offensive Public Speech', In I. Matira and M. K. McGowan (eds.), *Speech and Harm: Controversies over Free Speech* (Oxford: Oxford University Press): 148–73.

Olson, K. 2011: 'Legitimate Speech and Hegemonic Idiom: The Limits of Deliberative Democracy in the Diversity of its Voices', *Political Studies*, 59 (3): 527–46.

Owens, D. 2006: 'Testimony and Assertion', *Philosophical Studies*, 130 (1): 105–29.

Perrine, Timothy 2014: 'In Defense of Non-reductionism in the Epistemology of Testimony', *Synthese*, 191 (14): 3227–37.

Peter, F. 2013: 'The Procedural Epistemic Value of Deliberation', *Synthese*, 190: 1253–66.

Pettit, P. 1994: 'Enfranchising Silence: An Argument for Freedom of Speech', In T. Campbell and W. Sadurski (eds.), *Freedom of Communication* (Aldershot: Dartmouth): 45–55.
Podgorski, A. 2016: 'Dynamic Permissivism', *Philosophical Studies*, 173 (7): 1923–39.
Powers, R. 2006: *Mark Twain: A Life* (New York: Free Press).
Proust, J. 2012: 'The Norms of Acceptance', *Philosophical Issues*, 22 (1): 316–33.
Raleigh, T. 2017: 'Another Argument against Uniqueness', *The Philosophical Quarterly*, 67 (267): 327–46.
Rawls, J. 1980: 'Kantian Constructivism in Moral Theory', *The Journal of Philosophy*, 77 (9): 515–72.
Recanati, F. 1986: 'On Defining Communicative Intentions', *Mind and Language*, 1: 213–42.
Reed, B. 2010: 'A Defense of Stable Invariantism', *Noûs*, 44 (2): 224–44.
Reed, B. 2012: 'Resisting Encroachment', *Philosophy and Phenomenological Research*, 85 (2): 465–72.
Reeve, C. D. C. 1997: *Plato, Cratylus: Translated with Introduction and Notes* (Indianapolis and Cambridge: Hackett). Reprinted in J. M. Cooper. (ed.), *Plato, Complete Works* (Indianapolis and Cambridge: Hackett).
Richeson, J., and Trawalter, S. 2005: 'Why do Interracial Interactions Impair Executive Function? A Resource Depletion Account', *Journal of Personality and Social Psychology*, 88: 934–47.
Ridge, M. 2013: *Impassioned Belief* (Oxford: Oxford University Press).
Rosen, G. 2001: 'Nominalism, Naturalism, Epistemic Relativism', *Noûs*, 35: 69–91.
Ross, A. 1986: 'Why do we Believe what we are Told?', *Ratio*, 28 (1): 69–88.
Russell, J., Hawthorne, J., and Buchak, L. 2015: 'Groupthink', *Philosophical Studies*, 172 (5): 1287–309.
Saul, J. 2013: 'Scepticism and Implicit Bias', *Disputatio*, 5 (37): 243–63.
Sbisa, M. 2001: 'Illocutionary Force and Degrees of Strength in Language Use', *Journal of Pragmatics*, 33: 1791–813.
Sbisa, M. 2002: 'Speech Acts in Context', *Language & Communication*, 22: 421–36.
Sbisa, M. Forthcoming: 'Assertion Among the Speech Acts'. In S. Goldberg (ed.), *The Oxford Handbook of Assertion* (Oxford: Oxford University Press).
Scanlon, T. 1990: 'Promises and Practices', *Philosophy and Public Affairs*, 19: 199–226.
Schauer, F. 1993: 'The Phenomenology of Speech and Harm', *Ethics*, 103 (4): 635–53.
Schoenfield, M. 2014: 'Permission to Believe: Why Permissivism is True and what it Tells us about Irrelevant Influences on Belief', *Noûs*, 48 (2): 193–218.
Schoenfield, M. 2018: 'Permissivism and the Value of Rationality: A Challenge to the Uniqueness Thesis', *Philosophy and Phenomenological Research*. <https://doi.org/10.1111/phpr.12490>
Schroeder, M. 2007: *Slaves of the Passions* (Oxford: Oxford University Press).
Schultheis, G. 2017: 'Living on the Edge: Against Epistemic Permissivism', *Mind*, 127 (507): 863–79.
Sharadin, N. 2017: 'A Partial Defense of Permissivism', *Ratio*, 30 (1): 57–71.
Shieber, J. 2015: *Testimony: A Philosophical Introduction* (New York: Routledge).
Shiffrin, S. 2014: *Speech Matters: On Lying, Morality, and the Law* (Princeton: Princeton University Press).

Simmons, J. 1976: 'Tacit Consent and Political Obligation', *Philosophy & Public Affairs*, 5 (3): 274–91.
Simpson, R. 2012: 'What is Trust?', *Pacific Philosophical Quarterly*, 93: 550–69.
Simpson, R. 2017: 'Permissivism and the Arbitrariness Objection', *Episteme*, 14 (4): 519–38.
Sobel, D. 2016: *From Valuing to Value: A Defense of Subjectivism* (Oxford: Oxford University Press).
Sosa, E. 1994: 'Testimony and Coherence'. In B. K. Matilal and A. Chakrabarti (eds.), *Knowing from Words* (Amsterdam: Kluwer Academic Publishers): 59–67.
Sperber, D. and Wilson, D. 1996: *Relevance: Communication and Cognition* (London: Blackwell).
Stainton, R. 2016: 'Full-on Stating', *Mind & Language*, 31 (4): 395–413.
Stalnaker, R. 1978: 'Assertion'. In P. Cole (ed.), *Syntax and Semantics*, Vol. 9: *Pragmatics*: 315–22. Reprinted in R. Stalnaker, *Context and Content* (Oxford: Oxford University Press, 1999).
Stalnaker, R. 2014: *Context* (Oxford: Oxford University Press).
Stanley, J. 2005: *Knowledge and Practical Interests* (Oxford: Oxford University Press).
Streek, J. 1980: 'Speech Act in Interaction: A Critique of Searle', *Discourse Processes*, 3: 133–54.
Stroud, S. 2006: 'Epistemic Partiality in Friendship', *Ethics*, 116 (3): 498–524.
Swanson, E. 2017: 'Omissive Implicature', *Philosophical Topics*, 45 (2): 117–38.
Tanesini, A. 2016: '"Calm Down Dear": Intellectual Arrogance, Silencing, and Ignorance', *Proceedings of the Aristotelian Society*, 90 (1): 71–92.
Tirrell, L. 2012: 'Genocidal Language Games'. In I. Matira and M. K. McGowan (eds.), *Speech and Harm: Controversies over Free Speech* (Oxford: Oxford University Press): 174–222.
Titelbaum, M., and Kopec, M. (Unpublished manuscript): 'Plausible Permissivism'.
Townley, C. 2011: *A Defense of Ignorance: Its Value for Knowers and Roles in Feminist and Social Epistemologies* (Lanham, Md.: Rowman & Littlefield Publishers).
Turri, J. 2011: 'The Express Knowledge Account of Assertion', *Australasian Journal of Philosophy*, 89 (1): 37–45.
Wanderer, J. 2012: 'Addressing Testimonial Injustice: Being Ignored and Being Rejected', *The Philosophical Quarterly*, 62 (246): 148–69.
Wanderer, J., and Townsend, L. 2013: 'Is it Rational to Trust?', *Philosophy Compass*, 8 (1): 1–14.
Watson, G. 1996: 'Two Faces of Responsibility', *Philosophical Topics*, 24 (2): 227–48.
West, C. 2012: 'Words that Silence? Freedom of Expression and Racist Hate Speech'. In I. Matira and M. K. McGowan (eds.), *Speech and Harm: Controversies over Free Speech* (Oxford: Oxford University Press): 222–48.
White, R. 2005: 'Epistemic Permissiveness', *Philosophical Perspectives*, 19 (1): 445–59.
Williams, B. 1979: 'Internal and External Reasons'. In R. Harrison (ed.), *Rational Action* (Cambridge: Cambridge University Press): 101–13.
Williamson, T. 1996: 'Knowing and Asserting', *Philosophical Review*, 105: 489–523.

Williamson, T. 2000: *Knowledge and its Limits* (Oxford: Oxford University Press).
Williamson, T. 2011: 'Improbable Knowing'. In T. Dougherty (ed.), *Evidentialism and its Discontents* (Oxford: Oxford University Press): 147–64.
Williamson, T. 2014: 'Very Improbable Knowing', *Erkenntnis*, 79 (5): 971–99.
Wylie, A. 2003: 'Why Standpoint Matters', In R. Figueroa and S. Harding (eds.), *Science and Other Cultures: Issues in Philosophies of Science and Technology* (New York: Routledge): 26–48.
Wylie, A. 2011: 'What Knowers Know Well: Women, Work and the Academy.' In H. E. Grasswick (ed.), *Feminist Epistemology and Philosophy of Science: Power in Knowledge* (Dordrecht: Springer): 157–79.
Young, I. 1989: 'Polity and Group Difference: A Critique of the Ideal of Universal Citizenship', *Ethics*, 99 (2): 250–74.

Index

For the benefit of digital users, indexed terms that span two pages (e.g., 52–53) may, on occasion, appear on only one of those pages.

Acceptance 152–4, 156, 158–65, 167–75, 185–8, 194–5, 198, 202, 204, 207–10, 223
   as a psychological default 173–4
   vs. assent 152, 165–7, 190n.6
Acceptance Principle 166–7
Acknowledgement, Doctrine of 116, 118–19
Acts of speech, *see* Speech Acts
Address 5–6, 9, 13–57, 234–5
   and social hierarchies 52
   and epistemic injustice 65–6, 101
   as attention capture 15–16, 22–3, 30–1
   as calling 5–6, 13, 15–16, 29–34
   as claim on one's attention 49–50, 53, 234–5
   in inappropriate contexts 41–5
   involving testimony/telling 64–6
   of the famous 37–8
   must be acknowledged 32–4, 53
   Abuse of 16–17, 33–6, 40, 43–4, 47
   Appearance properties of 30
   Bad track record of 39–41
   Commercial 45
   Cooperative nature of 16–17, 34–5, 44, 47–9, 234–5
   Cultural relativity of 52
   Electronic forms of 25–6, 46
   Epistemology of 36–7
   Malicious 45
   Misuse of 35–6, 40, 43–4
   Mutuality of 35–6, 40–1, 48
   Nonlinguistic forms of 27
   Public see Announcement
Advising 74–7
AGNOSTICISM, dotrine of 181
Alcoff, Linda 187n.2
Anderson, Elizabeth 187n.3
Anderson, Luvell 187n.5

Announcements 24, 29
Anscombe, Elizabeth 64–5, 105, 109n.15, 135n.12, 174n.52
Anti-Reductionism 63, 91, 97–8, 102–23, 182–3
   [*see also* Epistemology of Testimony]
Apology 42
Approval 153–4, 156–7
Arendt, Hannah 170–1, 171n.47
Arrogance 191–203
Artson, Bradley 170–1, 171n.47
Assent Interpretation of Silence 167–75, 181–6, 189–91, 194–8, 201, 205
Assertion 2–4, 6, 62–4, 98–101, 124, 161–2, 235–6
   and avowals 2–3, 71
   and reports 2–3
   and statements 2–3, 61, 71, 189, 236
   and tellings 2–3, 63, 77–8, 124
   and testimony 2–3, 63, 98–101, 236
   as advising to believe 74–5
   as demanding to be believed 73
   as offering guarantee of truth 83
   Essential effect of 152n.5, 153–4, 162–3, 165, 171–2, 178–9
   Knowledge Rule of 98–101, 219–21
   Norm of 151
   Practice of 151, 157–60, 162–4, 167–8, 181–4, 191, 235–6
   Uptake of 151–2
Assurance 7–8, 96–7 [*see also* Testimony, Assurance view of]
Audi, Robert 93n.6
Austin, JL 2n.2
Authority
   Epistemic 73–4, 76–7, 93–8, 102, 109, 161–2, 221–2
   Practical 73–5, 77
   Social 199

250 INDEX

Bach, Kent 155n.11
Baier, Annette 135n.9
Baker, Judith 125n.1, 135n.9
Ballantyne, Nathan 120n.31
Beg 52
Benatar, David 52n.63
Berridge, G.R. 172
Bianchi, Claudia 187n.5
Bird, Alexander 151n.1
Bjerring, Jens 203n.24, 229n.17
Bootstrapping, epistemic 208, 211, 213, 229
Boy who cried wolf 39–40
Bridge Principle
  Hybrid 110–13
  Modal Strength 94–6, 119–23
  Modal Type 107–15, 119–23
Brown, Jessica 139n.17, 151n.2, 222n.12
Brownstein, Michael 187n.2
Bruce, Kim 162–3, 162n.22
Brueckner, Tony 120n.31
Buber, Martin 27n.27
Buchak, Lara 229n.17
Bundy, John 120n.31
Burge, Tyler 93n.6, 98n.17, 103n.2, 166–7, 183n.69

Calls 34, 55 [see also: Address as calling]
Camp, Elizabeth 187n.5
Cappelen, Herman 151n.2
Catcalls 47–8
Chang, Ruth 130n.4
Cheater Detection 174n.51
Chocolate Offer 79
Clark, Herb 31n.36, 32n.37, 44–5, 163n.24
Coady, Tony 98n.17, 103n.2, 151n.3, 183n.69
Code, Lorraine 187n.1
Coffman, EJ 120n.31
Collins, Patricia Hill 187n.1
Common Ground 162–3, 166
Competence 79–80, 99
Consent 156–8, 184–6, 190
  Implied 157–8
  Sign of vs. expression of 157–8
Context 6n.6
  Epistemically sober 166–7, 209–10
  Legal 185–6
  Pedagogical 179
  Regulated Speech 43–5
Contracts 26–7, 86, 111–12, 118–19

Conversation
  as cooperative activity 4, 14–15, 20–1, 31–2, 44–5, 50–1, 152, 157–8, 160–4, 175, 187–8, 234–5
  as joint action 31, 162–3
  Initiation of 51
  Ongoing 51
  Practices of 152
Cooperation 14–16, 19, 30–1, 33, 35, 47–9, 152, 157–60, 187–8, 234–5
  Norms of 9, 32–3, 152
  The presumption of 36–9, 48, 157–8, 163–4, 175–80, 187, 189–91, 206–7, 234–5
Cooperative Principle 48, 160–1, 163–4, 206–7
Coordination 15–16, 173–4, 204
Content Constraint 69, 71, 73–5, 78–80, 83, 89–94, 96
Content Question 68
Convention 15–16, 27, 31–2
Cosmides, Leda 174n.51
Craig, Edward 87–8
Cratylus 169
Credibility
  Default of 87–8 [see also Anti-Reductionism]
Croom, Adam 187n.3
Cuneo, Terence 151n.1

Darwall, Stephen 18n.10, 27n.28, 73nn.1, 2
Declarative mood 100
Declaratives 56–7
Defeasibility, [see Defeaters]
Defeaters 78–9, 107–8, 152, 157–60, 175–80, 182–3, 188, 221
  NON-CONVERSATION as 175–80
  Normative 176n.57, 210
  OUTWEIGHING EXPLANATION as 175–6, 178–80
Demands 72–4, 77
Descriptive Source Question 68
Dickey, Eleanor 52n.63
Different Conclusions, doctrine of 128–32
Directives 29
Disrespect, see Respect
Dissent 158, 178–9, 199, 230–1
Dogramsci, Sinan 120n.30
Donnellan, Keith 54–6
Dotson, Kristie 27n.29, 180n.66, 187n.1, 192n.8

Double-checking 137–41, 143, 145–7
Douven, Igor 120n.31
Durante, Alessandro 32n.37
Duties
  – of address 23–4
  – of friendship 182 [see also Friendship, norms of]
  – to speak up 9, 158, 164n.27
  – to resist oppression 194n.14
  Epistemic 107–15
  Imperfect 31–2
  Moral 84, 131n.5, 158
Dyzenhaus, David 192n.10

Echo Chambers 8–9
Elga, Adam 212–13, 213n.5
Email 25n.25, 38–9, 46
Entitlement Constraint 69, 71, 73–5, 79–83, 85–9, 91–2, 94
Entitlements
  as permissions 32–3, 107–8, 111–14, 198
  in address 30–3
  to believe 78, 80–1, 96–7
  to be believed 73, 102–23
  to expect epistemic trust (EEET) 102–23
  to presume silence indicates acceptance 151–8, 193–8, 209
  to presume cooperativity 157–60, 175–87, 206–7 [see also Cooperativity, Presumption of]
  Epistemic 61, 78, 105–7, 110–11, 113–14, 157–8, 183n.70
  Practice-based 183n.70
Epistemic Injustice 65–6, 101, 123, 151–2, 192, 235
Epistemic Partiality in Friendship (EPF), doctrine of 126–7, 129–30, 137, 140–3, 145–7
Epistemic Reasons [See also Reasons, Epistemic]
  doctrine of 94–5
Epistemic Subjects 202
  Doctrine of 94–5
Epistemological Question 69
Epistemology 7–8
  Social 8–9, 207–29, 231–2, 235–6
  of disagreement 212–13, 222
  of testimony 6n.6, 8, 62, 69, 91–3, 97–8, 102–23, 151, 182–3
Epistemology Constraint 69, 71, 86–7

Ermer, Elsa 174n.51
Ethical requirements 22, 25, 50, 66–8, 83–5, 87, 103, 110n.17, 111–12, 118–19, 151, 157–8, 164n.27, 204
Evans, Anthony 173n.50
Evidence, Higher-order 200n.20, 201–3, 207–8, 216–19, 222–3, 226–7
Expectations
  as N-expectations [See Expectations, Normative]
  Normative 4n.5, 6–7, 23–4, 67–70, 159, 207, 209, 231
  Predictive 30, 37–8, 207
  Speaker's – of proper treatment 68–9, 71–123

Facebook
  tags 26n.26
Fallibilism 214, 221–2, 227–8
Fantl, Jeremy 138–9
Farkas, Donka 162–3, 162n.22
Feminism 65–6, 187
Foley, Richard 183n.69
Free Speech 153–8
Fricker, Elizabeth 64n.4, 91n.2, 93n.6, 98n.16, 100n.23, 106n.7, 108n.13
Fricker, Miranda 27n.29, 65–6, 87–90, 96n.13, 101–3, 103n.2, 105, 109n.15, 120n.29, 162n.20, 187n.4, 192
Friedman, Jane 139n.16
Friendship
  Mutuality in 132–4
  Partiality in 6, 66–7, 112–13, 124–47
  Reasons of 18–19, 118–19, 127, 129, 132–6, 142–3, 235 [see also Reason, doctrine of]

Garcia-Carpintero, Manuel 93n.9
Gelber, Katherine 180n.65
Gelfert, Axel 151n.3
Gendler, Tamar 187n.2
Gibbard, Alan 1, 72–4, 75n.3, 77–8, 89–90
Gilbert, Daniel 173–4
Gilbert, Margaret 16nn.7, 8, 31n.36, 32n.37
Gilovich, Thomas 226n.15
Ginzburg, Jonathan 163n.24
Goldman, Alvin 212–13, 213n.5, 224–5
Goodwin, Charles 32n.37
Graham, Peter 182–3, 183n.69

Greco, Daniel 120n.30
Grice, Paul 47–8, 88n.9, 154–6, 160, 161n.18, 163–4, 204n.27, 206–7
Groupthink 6–9, 208, 213–14, 225–9
Guarantee 7–8, 83, 85–6 [see also Promise]

Habibian, Simin 168n.30
Harding, Sandra 187n.3
Hare, R.M. 27n.28
Harnisch, Robert 155n.11
Haslanger, Sally 187n.3
Hawley, Katherine 25, 112n.19, 125n.1, 127, 135n.9, 140nn.18, 19, 142–3, 145
Hawthorne, John 138–9, 229n.17
Hay, Carol 164n.27, 170–1, 194n.14
Hazlett, Allan 125n.1
Heddon, Brian 120n.30
Hinchman, Ted 27n.29, 62n.3, 65, 77–85, 87–90, 96–7, 97n.15, 102–3, 105, 108n.13, 109n.15, 120n.29, 133n.8
Holroyd, Jules 187n.2
Holton, Richard 80–1, 133n.8, 138n.15
Hom, Chris 187n.5
Hornsby, Jennifer 151n.1, 179–80, 192n.9, 10
Horowitz, Sophie 120n.30

Ignoring 24, 36–7, 53
 – vs. Rejecting 21, 28
Insult 65–6, 105, 174
Interpretative Charity, doctrine of 128–32
Imperatives 26–7
Implicatures 153n.6, 154n.10
Informant 65–6, 87–90
Informing 63, 91
Inquiry 137–9
Instant Messaging 25–6
Intention, Communicative 155–6, ,
 Perlocutionary – 162
Interpersonal Demand Constraint 69, 71, 74, 87, 89–92, 100
Interpersonal Pressure
 Doctrine of 94–6
Interruption 42, 44–5
Invitations 81, 118–19 [see also: Trust, Invitation to –]

Janis, Arthur 225n.14
Jeshion, Robin 187n.5
Jefferson, Thomas 170, 171n.47
Joint action 31–2, 49

Jones, Karen 34n.40, 135n.9, 187n.2, 201n.22
Justification
 – of action 138–9
 Epistemic 61–2, 67, 104, 112, 126–7, 129–30, 132, 137–9, 144–6, 196–8, 200–1, 207–10, 216–17
Justice 66–8, 87, 158, 171–2, 187, 204
 [see also Epistemic Injustice]

Kawall, Jason 112n.19, 125n.1, 136n.13, 140.19, 142–6
Keller, Simon 125n.1, 126–7
Kelly, Dan 187n.2
Kelly, Tom 120n.31, 212–13, 213n.5
Kerr 229n.17
King, Dr. Martin Luther 170–1, 171n.47
Knowledge
 – and assertion 98–101
 – and testimonial injustice 65–6
 – as part of the standard for successful testifying 92–3
 – that one knows 219–20
 Common 16, 30, 43–4, 92–4, 98–101, 178–9, 185–6
 Giver of 65–6, 87–94, 105
 Improbable 219–20
 Mutual 31
 Standards of 144–5
 Testimonial 207–8
Knowledge Rule of Assertion (KRA), [See Assertion, Knowledge Rule of –] 98–101
Kolodny, Niko 130n.4
Kopec, Matt 120n.31
Kugler, Tamar 229n.17
Kukla, Quill (previously Rebecca) 2n.2, 16nn.6, 9, 18n.10, 27n.28, 29n.33, 34, 45n.50, 46n.53, 48n.55, 52, 54, 55n.65, 56n.66, 73n.1, 151n.1

Lackey, Jennifer 93n.8, 100n.23, 151n.3, 176n.57, 178n.61, 212n.4, 213n.5, 224.13
Lance, Mark 2n.2, 16nn.6, 9, 18n.10, 27n.28, 29n.33, 34, 45n.50, 46n.53, 48n.55, 52, 54, 55n.65, 56n.66, 73n.1, 151n.1
Langton, Rae 151n.1, 154n.9, 156, 179–80, 182n.68, 190–2, 192n.10, 194n.15, 203–4
Lasonen-Aarnio, Maria 141n.20

INDEX 253

Lepore, Ernie 187n.5
Levinas, Emmanuel 27n.27
Levy, Neal 187n.2
Lewis, David 130n.4, 164n.28, 221–2
Lies 63, 133, 173–4
Longino, Helen 187n.2
Lord, Charles 226n.15
Lubensky, Sophia 168n.31

MacKinnon, Catherine 192n.10
Maitra, Ishani 151n.1, 158n.14, 164n.27, 171n.46, 187n.1, 192n.9, 228
Matheson, Jonathan 120n.30
McGowan, Mary-Kate 180n.65, 187n.1, 192n.9
McGrath, Sarah 212n.4
McHugh, Colin 136n.13, 140n.19, 143
McKinnon, Rachel 151n.2
Metaethics 23–4
McGrath, Matt 138–9
McMyler, Ben 27n.29, 108n.13, 109n.15, 120n.29
Mill, John Stuart 185
Mills, Charles 187nn.1-2
Moorean paradoxicality 221–2
Morality, see Ethical Requirement
Moran, Richard 27n.29, 62n.3, 65, 83–90, 96–7, 97n.15, 102–3, 105, 108n.13, 109n.15, 120n.29
Morand, David 52n.63
Mutuality 30, 35–6, 40–1, 48, 132

Nature of the Interpersonal Demand Question 68
Negligence 153
Nielsen, Laura 37n.43, 46n.52, 55n.65
No Silent Reject (NSR), doctrine of 159–60, 163–8, 174, 176, 181–6, 203–5, 209
Normative Source Question 68
Norms 103–4
 – of conversation 160–1, 193, 196–9, 202n.23, 204n.27, 206–7 [see also: Cooperative Principle]
 – of friendship 124–9, 133, 142–3, 159n.15, 235 [see also: Friendship, reasons of]
 – of politeness 179, 230, 232–3
 – of trust 9, 102–23, 166–7
 – of silence in conversation See No Silent Rejection, doctrine of]

 – of uptake 151, 166–7, 188, 235 [see also No Silent Rejection, doctrine of]
 Epistemic 62–4, 66–7, 103–4, 108–9, 111–13, 121–6, 129–30, 137–8, 161–2, 207, 235
 Ethical [See Ethical Requirements]
 Interpersonal 64–7, 94, 103–6, 108–9, 124–6, 207
 Legal 111–12, 118–19, 185–6
 Permissive 111–12, 118–19, 121–3, 232–3 [see also Permissivism]
 Social 9, 32–3, 52, 66, 103–4, 111–12, 151, 179–80, 189
 Speech act See Speech Act Norms

Olson, Kevin 52n.63
Oppression 158, 164n.27, 177–80, 187, 205, 210
'Ought' implies 'Can' 37
Overhearer 64, 66, 135n.10
Owens, David 86n.7

Pateman, Carol 187n.1
Permissive Norms, [See Norms, Permissive]
Permissivism 113, 121–3, 140–1, 145–6 [see also Norms, Permissive]
Perrine, Timothy 103n.2
Peter, Fabienne 229n.17
Pettit, Philip 153–8, 169–70, 172n.48, 204n.26
Plato 169
Pluralistic ignorance 203n.24
Podgorski, Abelard 120n.31
Polarization 6–9, 208, 213–14, 225–9
Politeness 9, 177, 179, 189, 230 [whole chapter]
Pragmatic Encroachment 138–9, 143–5
Pressure, Conversational
 and normative expectations 4–5, 153, 235
 Epistemic 3, 62–4, 66–70, 102, 124 [whole chapter], 158–63, 206 [whole chapter], 235–6
 Rational [See Pressure, Epistemic]
 Sources of 61–4, 74, 142–7
 Types of 3–5, 61–70, 235–6
 Interpersonal 94, 102–3, 106–7, 124–47, 158–9, 235, 235–6
Presupposition 36–7, 98, 165
Priest, Maura 32n.37

Prinz, Joachim 170, 171n.47
Promises 4n.5, 7–8, 83–7, 91, 138, 144–5
Proust, Joëlle 151n.3

Query 29

Race Theory 65–6, 187
Racism 179–80, 187
Raleigh, Thomas 120n.31
Rationality 33–4, 67, 114–15, 160, 166–7, 178–9, 199–203, 212, 234–5
Rawls, John 53
Reactive Attitudes 23–4, 45–6, 196–8
Reason, doctrine of 128–32
Reasons
 – of friendship, *see* Friendship, Reasons of
 – to speak up when one disagrees 151–86
 Epistemic 7–8, 84–5, 94, 131–2, 134–6, 139, 199–201
 External 19–20
 Having a 23–4
 Kinds of 34
 Practical 131–40, 142–7, 153, 159–60, 175, 178–80, 199–200
 Value-reflecting 129–47
Reciprocity 18–19
Reductionism 63, 91, 97–8, 105–6 [*see also*: Epistemology of Testimony]
Reed, Baron 139n.17
Reeve, C.D.C. 169n.37
Reference 54
Reid, Thomas 173–4
Relevance 17–19, 21–2, 44–5
Relevance Theory 17–22
Relevant Alternatives 218–19
Reliability 81, 86, 92–3, 173–4, 207–8, 211–12, 224, 227
Request 21, 26–7, 29, 52
Respect 16, 21, 33–4, 40–1, 61, 93–7, 106–7, 115–23, 161–2, 192, 194n.14
Responsibility, *see* Responsible
Responsible 81, 84–6, 91, 106–7, 116, 118–19, 126–7, 129–30, 132, 140–1, 196–7
 Holding vs. believing – 81–3, 85–6, 196–8, 207
Richeson, Jennifer 187n.2
Ridge, Michael 3n.4, 74–8, 89–90
Roedder, Erica 187n.2
Rosen, Gideon 120n.31

Ross, Angus 93n.10, 99n.22, 103n.2, 183n.69
Rules 3, 99
Russell, Jeff 229n.17

Saul, Jennifer 187n.2
Sbisa, Marina 2–3, 14n.2, 38n.44
Scanlon, Tim 7–8, 83–4
Schoenfield, Miriam 120n.31
Schroeder, Mark 130n.4
Scope Constraint 69, 71, 73–4, 89, 91–2, 100
Scope question 68
Sexism 48, 179–80, 187
Shiffrin, Seana 33, 33n.39, 34n.40, 123n.33, 151n.1, 166–7
Schauer, Frederick 192n.10
Schulthies, Ginger 120n.30
Self-improvement, doctrine of 211–14, 216, 220, 222–5, 228–9
Serious Scrutiny, docrine of 128–32
Shaefer, Edward 163n.24
Sharadin, Nathaniel 120n.31
Shieber, Joseph 151n.3
Signal 31–2, 81, 175, 204, 231–3
Silence 189, 231
 and 'speak now or forever hold your peace' 171, 183–4, 188
 Proverbs regarding 168–9
 Significance of 6–7, 151 [whole chapter]
Silence Procedure 172, 183–4, 188
Silencing 187–205
 Harms of 6–7
 How to address 204–5
 Illocutionary 192
 Locutionary 179–80, 192–3
Simmons, John 156–7, 168n.29
Simpson, Robert 65, 105, 120n.31
Sincerity 9, 63, 79–80, 95
Slighting 78, 105
Slurs 187
Snubbing 21, 53
Sobel, David 130n.4
Sociality 15–17, 23–4, 32–4, 234–5
Sosa, Ernie 100n.23, 151n.3
Speech Acts 2, 17–18, 23–4, 26–8, 31, 72–8, 123, 154–5, 171–2, 234–5
 Norms of – 9
 Theory of – 9, 72–87
Sperber, Dan 18n.12
Stainton, Rob 98n.19
Stakes 117, 138–9, 146

Stalnaker, Robert 152–8, 160, 162–3, 165, 209–10
Stanley, Jason 138–9
Statement [See Assertion and –]
Streek, Jürgen 32n.37
Stroud, Sarah 125, 125n.1, 127–9, 147
Subordination 193–5 [see also Oppression]
Swanson, Eric 3n.4, 153n.6, 154

Tanesini, Alessandra 179–80, 190–3, 198–203
Telling 6n.6, 8, 28, 61–71, 73–6, 83–8, 96–8, 124, 133n.8, 147, 182–3
  Authority in 73–4, 89–101, 187–8, 211, 221–2
  and evidence 62 [see also: Assertion and telling]
Testifying 8, 26–7, 61, 63–4, 67–70, 87–8, 90–4, 96–8, 103, 106–9, 112–13, 119, 236
  Epistemic conditions on proper 91–3
  Job description of 89, 91–4, 98–101
  Responsibilities in 84–6, 91, 103–7, 115–19, 207 [see also: Testimony]
Testimonial Injustice 65–6, 87–8, 101, 105, 162n.20, 235
Testimony 26–7, 61, 63–6, 89–90, 104–5, 121–3, 223
  Assurance view of 7–8, 89–90, 96–7, 100, 112–13
  Smothering of 192n.8
  – and double-counting 211
  – and epistemic authority 73, 93–4, 96–8, 109
  – and Non-Independence 211–13, 213n.5, 222, 224–5
  – from friends 125–8, 132, 134–6, 142–5, 147
Tirrell, Lynne 193n.13, 228
Titelbaum, Mike 120n.31
Tooby, John 174n.51
Townley, Cynthia 187n.1

Townsend, Leo 141
Trawalter, Sophie 187n.2
Trust 9, 25, 77–87, 102–23, 235
  in friendship 126–36, 142–3, 146–7
  Deciding to 138n.15
  Invitation to 65–6, 77–83, 133 [see also Norms of Trust]
Trustworthiness 78–9, 127, 174n.51
  Conveying 99
  Presumption of 78–80, 82–3, 85–6, 89–90, 102–23
  Purport vs. presumption of 96–8
Turri, John 93n.7
Twain, Mark 169

Uniqueness 114–23, 136n.13, 140–1, 145
Uptake
  of a speech act 6, 192
  of address 23–6
  of not-at-issue content 164n.28
  of uptake 6–7, 151–2, 155–6, 158–9, 206–29, 235

Values [See Reasons, Value-reflecting]
Vocative 54
Voluntarism
  Doxastic 113n.20, 137, 199–202

Wanderer, Jeremy 22n.18, 29n.32, 65–6, 141, 192n.11
Warrant
  Epistemic 61, 67, 84–5, 94, 151, 166
Watson, Gary 85n.6
West, Caroline 33n.38, 180n.65, 193n.13
White, Roger 120n.30
Williams, Bernard 21n.16
Williamson, Tim 99n.20, 141n.20, 219–21
Wilson, Diedre 18n.12
Wylie, Allison 187n.3

Young, Iris 192n.10